STATES OF MIND

States of mind is a series of dialogues conducted by Richard Kearney with twenty-two leading political, philosophical and literary thinkers. Each has helped to shape some of the most influential debates of our century: the legacy of the European mind, national and international identity, ethics, art, language, psychology and religion.

Through a searching exchange of ideas, the reader is presented with a multitude of provocative visions, which also act as introductions to the work of each thinker. This is a book of considerable range, in which the politics of Václav Havel find a place alongside the literary reflections of Umberto Eco and the philosophy of Jacques Derrida. The discussions open many of the critical questions of our time to a general readership.

RICHARD KEARNEY is a Professor of Philosophy at University College Dublin and Visiting European Professor at Boston College, Massachusetts.

FOR PATRICK MASTERSON
AND WILLIAM RICHARDSON,
dialogical mentors

That dialogue may happen,
ask first,
then listen.

Antonio Machado

STATES OF MIND

Dialogues with contemporary thinkers

RICHARD KEARNEY

NEW YORK UNIVERSITY PRESS
Washington Square, New York

First published in the U.S.A. in 1995 by
NEW YORK UNIVERSITY PRESS
Washington Square
New York, N.Y. 10003

Library of Congress Cataloging-in-Publication Data
Kearney, Richard.
States of mind : dialogues with contemporary thinkers / Richard Kearney.
p. cm.
ISBN 0-8147-4672-1. – ISBN 0-8147-4673-X (pbk.)
1. Europe–Intellectual life–20th century. 2. Intellectuals–
–Europe–Interviews. I. Title.
CB203.K43 1995
001.1'094–dc20 95–18413
CIP

Printed in Great Britain

CONTENTS

GENERAL PREFACE

This book features dialogues conducted with a variety of authors over two decades. They range from my 1976 interview with Herbert Marcuse to the 1994 exchanges with Lyotard and Gadamer. Most of those interviewed could be described as intellectuals, in the broad understanding of that term: contemporary minds who reflect, and reflect upon, their world, interrogating some of the central ideas, images and ideologies which shape us.

The dialogues are divided into three sections, reflecting a difference of emphasis rather than essence. Those included in the first section, 'Political Thinkers', are not professional politicians (with the possible exception of Havel, who, despite his presidential role, has never abandoned his authorly vocation); they are critical minds whose 'disestablished' stance *vis-à-vis* society is precisely what affords them the free insight to say unusual, unprecedented, and often unpopular things. Not that they subscribe to the presumptuous view of the philosopher-king. Far from it. These political thinkers aim to open paths, not to finalise solutions.

Those included under the heading of 'Literary Thinkers' range from creative writers (Warner, Holub, Heaney, Borges, Eco) to theorists of literature (Nussbaum, Darras and Steiner). What defines them all as 'thinkers' is their common readiness to debate mindfully the larger cultural and social issues raised by the practice of writing itself, especially in the European context. Here the *Dichter* and the *Denker* rub shoulders.

Finally, those included under our third heading of 'Philosophical Thinkers' are original speculative minds who have, each in their own way, made a significant contribution to contemporary European thought. All seven have taught as university professors, but this professional affiliation has not confined the range or reference of their work. In the case of most of them it is remarkable how their writings have migrated beyond the specialised universe of academic discourse to exert a wide impact on such diverse disciplines as sociology, history, political theory, art criticism, linguistics, theology, law, psychology and architecture. It is hard to cite a single human science that has not been influenced by one or more of these thinkers.

Our collection draws together dialogues from a number of sources. The conversations with Chomsky, Nussbaum, Gadamer and Lyotard were conducted in 1993–94 and appear here in print for the first time. The others have been collected from a variety of publications including *The Crane Bag* journal (Marcuse, Ricoeur, Borges), *Visions of Europe* (Eco, Warner, Darras, Havel, Ascherson, Steiner, Kristeva, Holub) and *Dialogues with Contemporary Continental Thinkers*, which comprises the third section of our book and reappears here in the integral version first published in 1984, with the addition of the two recent dialogues with Lyotard (1994) and Gadamer (1994) prepared specially for the present volume. As this third section constitutes the main body of this publication, the biographical prefaces and bibliographies for these seven philosophers are more extensive than those provided in the first two sections. This is no reflection of priority or preference, simply a token of the more in-depth and comprehensive character of these exchanges.

By contrast, most of the interviews published in the first two sections were originally conducted for broadcast on the Irish and European media, and bear the style of accessibility, spontaneity and discursiveness appropriate to their initial form of communication. Indeed, I open rather than close the book with these interviews in view of their more immediate appeal to a non-specialised readership.

The volume as a whole aims to disseminate certain contemporary intellectual debates – in philosophy, politics and culture – to academics and non-academics alike. Dialogue is our guiding ideal, not just as interlocutors conversing among ourselves, but as writers committed to communicating ideas to our readers. The following verse of Hölderlin serves as motto for our enterprise – '*Since we are a dialogue/and can listen to one another*'.

The titles of all foreign-language works cited below are given in English where available. The dialogues with Ricoeur, Derrida, Breton, Lévinas, Lyotard and Kristeva were translated from the French by the author. The dialogue with Gadamer was translated from the German by Mara Rainwater, and the dialogue with Havel from the Czech by Vera Taslova. All the other dialogues were conducted in English.

My appreciation goes to my colleagues in University College Dublin and Boston College who have assisted me in my work for this volume, in particular Dermot Moran, Mark Dooley and Mara Rainwater. My thanks also to RTE, Wolfhound Press and The European Cultural Foundation for permission to reprint conversations from the *Visions of Europe* series (1992–93).

INTRODUCTION I

One of the recurring themes in the dialogues that follow is the complex legacy of the European mind. Most talk about the new Europe has been about economics. But there is another question often ignored in this debate – one that goes to the very heart and mind of the continent. I refer to the critical question of Europe's vision of itself and of its formative relationship to the wider world beyond its historic frontiers. What ideas does Europe have of itself and of others? In several of the dialogues in the first two sections of this volume, I endeavour to explore such ideas with a variety of authors, both European and non-European (Chomsky, Said, Nussbaum, Borges).

Many of us think of Europe as a geographical continent of old frontiers and flags. In recent times, we have been obliged to think again. Western Europe has experienced the emergence of an economic space resounding with talk of common trade and tariffs, while to the East we have witnessed an unfolding drama of rapidly shifting borders. Berlin, Budapest, Bucharest, Belgrade – the very mention of these names recalls how decisive the changes have been. The multi-coloured map we gazed upon at school no longer tells the full story. Traditional borders have become both too large and too small to respond to the movement towards integration. We are speaking of a continent in metamorphosis.

The whole debate raises fundamental questions about the very nature of sovereignty, about the meaning of words like nationalism and federalism, about the need to balance the moves towards unity with a greater recognition of cultural and linguistic diversity. A battle of ideas is being waged over the very soul of Europe; and the outcome of this battle will determine the future contours of this continent.

The various contributors to these dialogues come from very different countries and cultures. Some still remember the last war and the crimes of Hitler, Mussolini and Stalin, committed in the name of Empire. Others stress the positive achievements of art, science and law which have made European modernity a password throughout the globe. But however various their verdicts, all speak as independent minds. They are public figures unbound by partisan policy. They are, all of them, people who participate in the cultural realm of ideas and images, of education, academia and media, without constraints of party or propaganda. The purpose of these dialogues is to allow each to speak of our contemporary world in alternative ways, in a manner more personal or unpredictable than in normal current affairs commentary.

Many of my interlocutors (European and non-European) share a desire to tell the story of Europe. This means retelling its history in their own particular way and responding to others' views. Above all, as Paul Ricoeur puts it, it means an 'exchange of memories'. For it is only by remembering each other's past, by sharing each other's sufferings and aspirations, that we begin to reinvent a future of mutual respect and atonement.

But can Europe reinvent itself? Can it discriminate between its different legacies – good, bad and ugly? Can it contribute to a new concept of universality freed from the legacy of world domination – a universality which respects diversity and difference? Is it possible to initiate new models of international community in the wake of the collapse of transnational states like Yugoslavia and the Soviet Union? And how might a future Europe obviate the pitfalls of a Eurocentrism by keeping itself open to its 'others' – not only to the other nations outside the member states of the EU but also its non-European neighbours to the East and South?

More pressingly, is Europe capable of surviving the current crisis of collective identity epitomised by the erosion of the old ideologies, and resulting in a general turning inwards – at times, indeed, in the excesses of compulsive nationalism and racism?

These are some of the questions which recur throughout these exchanges. Several of the contributors recall Europe's debts and responsibilities to the other continents. Indeed, we are reminded that the very name of Europe is itself derived from a tradition lying somewhere between Africa and the Middle East! As legend has it, *Europa* was carried by her father across the Mediterranean to Greece, but never abandoned her non-European origins. Such reminders open a Pandora's box of further questions. Would the universalist culture of Athens ever have emerged without its crucial borrowings from Babylonia and Egypt? Can we ignore the fact that the European tradition of Judaeo-Christianity first arose in the lands of the Middle East? Would the teachings of Aristotle and Greek philosophy ever have returned to the heart of Europe after the Dark Ages if it wasn't for the work of great Arab thinkers like Avicenna and Averroes? And is it not the case that seminal cultures like Byzantium and Andalusia were themselves melting-pots of hybrid cultures and creeds? Finally, we ask if Europe's self-recollection today should not include both a repossession of its rich cultural heritage *and* a recognition of the sins committed in its name – from colonial domination to economic exploitation and ecological waste?

The interviews which follow in the first two sections seek to inaugurate a dialectic between different and sometimes conflicting views. No attempt by the European family to define itself can succeed unless it also remains answerable to its 'others' – those non-European communities which have historically contributed, and continue to contribute, to its identity and development. The concept of the 'One' – a founding principle of European civilisation inherited from the Greek and Judaeo-Christian traditions – already includes the 'stranger' as part of its self-understanding. The European gift of universality must accommodate cultural polyphony if it is to be true to its promises. The alternative is uniformity and intolerance.

What are the implications of such thinking for a new Europe? Whichever form political and economic integration takes in the years to come, it is certain to go beyond the old model of centralised nation states. The newly emerging Europe, as various contributors below suggest, has a unique opportunity to be truly democratic by fostering notions of sovereignty that are inclusive rather than absolute, shared rather than insular, disseminated rather than closed in upon some bureaucratic centre. This will involve not only a greater devolution of powers to smaller regions within the European nation states, but also a greater awareness of Europe's debts and duties to the planet as a whole, as thinkers like Said and Chomsky never cease to remind us.

Europe is like Janus. It has a good face and a bad face. The bad grows from its sometimes arrogant attempt to shape the world in its own image. The good comes from its readiness, once again on probation at this decisive period of history, to shape itself in the image of a wider world.

Section A

POLITICAL THINKERS

JULIA KRISTEVA

Strangers to ourselves: the hope of the singular

JULIA KRISTEVA is Professor of Linguistics at the University of Paris VII. Born in Bulgaria, she came to study in France where she quickly became a celebrity of the avant-garde 'Tel Quel' group. Her publications include *Revolution in Poetic Language*; *Desire in Language: A Semiotic Approach to Literature and Art*; *Powers of Horror*; *In the Beginning was Love: Psychoanalysis and Faith*; *The Black Sun*; *Strangers to Ourselves*; *Nations and Nationalism*, and a novel, *The Samurai*.

RK *How would you describe your identity as a European?*

JK I consider myself a cosmopolitan. I was lucky in my childhood to learn French at an early stage. My parents sent me to a French pre-school in Sofia run by Dominican nuns: it was an offshoot of the Jesuit college in Constantinople. So I started French before my Bulgarian studies. Then those ladies were accused of spying and expelled from Bulgaria. Their work was taken over by the French Alliance. So I learnt French at the same time as Bulgarian and my entry into French culture was somehow a natural one. When I arrived in France to pursue my third level education, I felt that I somehow belonged to the French culture – which is not the case seen from the French side for they still perceive me as a foreigner, although I was very warmly welcomed.

It is easier to consider onself cosmopolitan – as I do – if one comes from a small country like Bulgaria, just as it is probably easier to be European when one is born, say, Dutch, than it would be if one is English. I insist on this point for I believe that the future of Europe lies in this idea of respect between nations, but also of conciliation between nations. I care very much for this cosmopolitan idea which is a heritage of the European culture of the ancient Stoics, later developed by French thinkers of the eighteenth century.

I take this cosmopolitan idea of the Enlightenment very much to heart, and if there is hope for Europe, beyond the recent ethnic divisions that have broken out in Yugoslavia, Czechoslovakia, and the Soviet Union etc.... it is in this spirit of universalism. We must move beyond nations, or archaisms, while also recognising genuine particularities.

RK *To return to your own experience of so-called 'Eastern Europe'. How do you now relate to this lost or amputated part of the continent?*

JK I don't experience this dichotomy of the two Europes in such a painful manner, for two reasons. First, for biographical reasons which I already mentioned, that is my early entry into French culture; but also because I have made an intellectual choice which consists in thinking that the *origin* is not essential, that the origin is a reaction to pain and can become a condensed brew of hate. People who turn back to origins are people who don't know how to metabolise or sublimate their hate, they are wounded people, depressed people; and because they no longer have ideals – religion does not satisfy them, nor does Marxism, and no other providential ideology can come to their rescue – they turn towards the archaism of the origin. My entire intellectual education goes against this idea of origin.

RK *Is it feasible, or even fair, to dismiss the complex reality of nationalism in this way?*

JK I do recognise that we are going to live for a very long time in the frame of nations and nationalities. I am against that tendency of the Left to dismiss the idea of nation. I believe the idea of nation is going to have a long life. But it should be a *choice*, and not a reflex or return to the origin. When one lives it as a choice – that is to say with clarity of vision, knowing the political, ideological, cultural reasons that make us adhere to France, Ireland, Great Britain etc., and not because we are genetically linked to it – it can be a good choice.

So to come to the other aspect of your question: what can my experience of the East give me today? I believe two things: firstly, an ability to winter out, to acknowledge the importance of effort. We were children who suffered quite a lot of economic deprivations (although they weren't disastrous, especially at the age I was). So we were pushed into giving the maximum of ourselves; and those who weren't able to step over this threshold of discipline and endurance were swept away. This gave us a hard-learnt power to concentrate and be disciplined. Secondly, I learned from Bulgaria the importance of *culture*. Bulgaria is the country in which the Slavonic alphabet was created. It was two Bulgarian brothers, Cyril and Methodius, who gave the Slavonic alphabet to the world – it is now the alphabet that the Russians use. There is in Bulgaria a Feast of the Alphabet, probably the only one in the world. Every year on May 24th, children parade through the streets of Sofia each displaying a letter on their fronts, so we are identified with the alphabet.

RK *The Cyrillic script was originally Bulgarian?*

JK Yes, Saint Cyril gave his name to the alphabet. There are discussions still going on about whether he was Greek or Bulgarian; his mother was of Slavonic origin, he knew the Slavonic languages, and when the Pope asked for the Gospels to be translated into Slavonic to evangelise the Eastern nations it was the two brothers, Cyril and Methodius, who were sent on the mission.

So in Bulgaria there is this pull to identify oneself with culture which I experienced very vividly in my childhood as a positive element, and I believe that many people in the former 'Eastern' Europe, especially students, have a cultural avidity and curiosity that Western youth has lost because it has a surfeit of culture (you can buy anything anywhere for your bookshelf), and because the mass media have destroyed the taste for classical culture and great modern culture. Europe is going to suffer the dissolution of culture for a long time to come.

I have just finished writing a novel called *The Old Man and the Wolves*, in which I tell the story of the brutality of the modern world, which one can find as much in Ireland, Great Britain and France as in 'Eastern Europe'. There is a crazed fashion: violence against people, lack of culture, lack of respect, and it is getting worse today with the collapse of the pseudo-classical culture, nothing is left. It is something we will find very hard to get through. There will be two big problems – the market economy, and the need to climb up the slope of fifty years of cultural and moral emptiness. We also have a lot of work to do as intellectuals, for example, in helping with cultural exchanges between the two parts of the continent at the level of the humanities.

RK *How do you combine your comospolitanism as a French citizen with the fidelity to your place of origin? Do you not think that some recognition of national or regional origins is necessary? You suggest that nationalism is a pathological phenomenon, but does it not only become that if we deny the basic human need for a certain national identity?*

JK Baltic, Serbian, Slovak, Croatian nationalism is, in my eyes, a regressive and a depressive attitude. If you'll allow me this little psychoanalytic excursion, these separatist nationalists are people who have long been humiliated in their identity. Soviet Marxism did not recognise this identity, so they have now an anti-depressive reaction which takes manic forms, if I may put it like that. The exaltation of origins and of archaic folk values can take violent forms because one wants an enemy; and as the enemy is not Communism any more – because it doesn't exist – the enemy will be the *other*: the other ethnic group, the other nation, the scapegoat and so on. This pathology can last for a long time and such archaic settling of accounts can prevent, or certainly handicap, the economic and cultural development which those countries need. One can try to accelerate the process, one can try to avoid sinking into stagnancy, to help it go a bit faster; and at that level, there is a huge amount of work that can be done, on one side, by the churches and, on the other, by the intellectuals. It seems to me that in 'Eastern Europe', the Catholic Church played a major role in the rebellion against Communism. It has a great role to play today in helping to transcend nationalism and to give to those people ideals which would not be strictly ethnic or archaically national. Recently the Church wrote an encyclical which shows it to be extremely interested in the moral struggle against totalitarianism but also against a certain 'Americanism'. I am quite struck by this cosmopolitan and universalist idea of the Christian church as a remedy for those nationalisms that one shouldn't dispose of too promptly, but should try to transcend.

RK *If the crisis is not only political, but moral and spiritual as you suggest, does that mean that the solution must also be of a moral and spiritual order?*

JK Even economic problems cannot be solved without this moral renewal. Imagine people who must face a market economy based on the idea of individual competition while their sense of individuality is still extremely weak, wounded, frail. In order to consolidate this sense of one's individuality, of one's autonomy, of one's freedom, one needs a great moral support. That is why I think that those two aspects, the economic and the moral, are linked together. I would give priority to the moral revolution.

RK *Are you advocating therefore a return to nineteenth-century liberal humanism and individualism – I am thinking of the legacy of Locke, Hume and Mill in particular, who advanced the idea of individual rights outside of a communal or social context? Or is what you're talking about something that goes beyond traditional individualism towards some new right to singularity compatible with social solidarity?*

JK In my view, it is a right to singularity. But it is not obvious that the ex-Communist countries will be able to achieve this singularity, coming from an ideology of collectivism, unless they go through some form of individualism.

RK *Are you suggesting a necessary passage through liberalism?*

JK Not rampant or uncritical liberalism. This is why I insist on those better forms of individual identity that one can find in religion and in the Enlightenment. Here I quote a phrase that appears to me to express the aim of Christianity even if it goes far beyond it. It is from Montesquieu's *Pensées*, and goes something like this: 'If I knew something that would be useful to myself, but detrimental to my family, I would cast it from my mind. If I knew something that was useful to my family but detrimental to my country I would consider it criminal. If I knew something useful to Europe, but detrimental to humankind, I would also consider it a crime.' It is a very interesting idea because it recognises the individual, the person, the family, the nation – but it also considers that the individual person can only find its development in a wider frame.

RK *Is this what you would call the cosmopolitan model?*

JK Yes, because the nation, the individual, the family are recognised as transitional objects, to speak like Winnicott, as moments of consolidation which are necessary but not sufficient. It is this transitional logic that Montesquieu develops in this saying. And I consider that it should be studied in all French schools, for example, because it is not clear that all French people apply this logic, far from it. There is difficulty in living as a foreigner in France. Above all it is something we should try to share with our friends from the East, so that both their ethnic belonging and nationhood are recognised, while encouraging them to avoid fixations and limitations at that level, to move forward towards wider horizons.

RK *Are you suggesting that religion could play a positive role by going beyond particular denominations or sects and projecting some common universal vision?*

JK There is a homogeneity in particular religions which makes you into a stranger if you don't share their presuppositions. That said, our monotheistic religions have tried to develop a notion of the Other, and it is this legacy of Western thinking that we should enrich and cultivate, that the Enlightenment tried to extrapolate, and that we need to redevelop today. What does that mean? When a stranger knocks at my door, for instance, I should, as the Bible says, consider that it might be God – a sign of the sacredness and singularity of others. It also means that, as the pilgrimages from the first centuries of Christianity until Saint Augustine taught us, the journey, the idea of carrying the message of Christ towards others and of receiving strangers coming as pilgrims, leads to a kind of osmosis between ethnic groups. The idea of *caritas*, Christian love, of which we know the degenerative form in the terrible history of Western colonialism, gives a strength today to the Christian churches. We can see it being developed, for instance, in '*le secours catholique*', or other forms of action which Christians in France organise for foreigners: teaching migrant workers and their families how to read, providing material aid, etc. I believe it is important to focus on this aspect of religious culture in so far as it enjoys a popular audience and can respond to the dangers of narrow nationalism.

RK *Once religions have done that work is there another kind of work that remains to be done?*

JK Yes. Alongside this work, there is much to be done at the level of the individual, developing the dimension of singularity. Our ideas don't fall from heaven, we have a heritage, and we must bank on it; otherwise we become abstract. There is a radical change which occurred in the eighteenth century in our understanding of human singularity; and there is also much to be done through psychoanalysis – something I am committed to in my daily work.

RK *Are you suggesting that this work on the private realm of the psyche cannot be properly exercised by politics or religion but only by psychoanalysis, a work of the soul?*

JK I am not going to preach psychoanalysis. For the analyst, the person who comes to analysis is a person who must express his or her own desire for it. So I am not going to suggest to your readers to start analysis. But I believe that psychoanalysis is a modern form which takes into account the Jewish and Christian monotheist heritage and the Enlightenment knowledge of the self and of our singularities.

But it is possible to find other forms of learning more about this singularity, which range from personal meditation to art, reading, music, painting.

RK *Is it possible to achieve this through the relationship with another person?*

JK For me the relationship with another person is essential. As forms of sublimation, the arts are extremely important, but insufficient. Sometimes, indeed, they can lead someone to become complacent with singularity, they can induce closure rather than an overcoming of malaise. So, yes, relating to others is indispensable to the development of singularity.

RK *Finally I would like to ask what you feel is the role today of the European project of the Enlightenment? I am thinking of Voltaire's and Montesquieu's dream of a great European cosmopolitan republic. Since they first expressed their vision, we have witnessed not only the breakup of Europe into rival nationalisms, but also two world wars in our century which were a direct result of such antagonisms. After those two world wars, and after Auschwitz in particular, what can we advocate today as a viable and legitimate project for a united Europe?*

JK We have to take seriously the violence of identity desires. For instance, when somebody recognises him or herself in an X or Y origin, it can appear very laudable, a very appealing need for identity. But one mustn't forget the violence behind this desire, a violence that can be turned against oneself and others, giving rise to fratricidal wars. So we need to recognise not only the relativeness of human fraternity but the need, both pedagogical and therapeutic, to take account of the death wish, of the violence *within* us.

RK *How fraternity can become fratricide?*

JK Exactly. Therefore, along with the attention we should pay to the death wish, there is a need for finesse in the way we deal with individuals, and with their relationship to nations. After the Enlightenment, the idea of the nation was for long considered a backward and redundant idea that one could brush aside, do without. I believe that, at least on an economic level, the nation is here to stay; we will have it with us for at least another century. But it is not enough to realise its economic dimension; we have to measure the psychic violence of the adherence to this idea. This is a violence that can also be carried by certain religions, for religions can be another form of originary adhesion. The shapes of fundamentalism that spring up nowadays on all sides cannot be dissipated simply by fraternal good will. One is going to encounter a lot of difficulties. We are faced with a death wish. I believe the closest we've got to it was after the fall of the Berlin Wall. When that happened, whatever screen hid us from this death wish fell. The screens of new Promethean ideologies, like Marxism, don't exist any more. The old religions, even if they are still solid and endure for a long while, are being put in question. Nothing can wipe out or hide this death wish. We are left face to face with it and the most adequate response to be found is, in my view, the sublimatory and clairvoyant forms that art and psychoanalysis offer.

The media propagate this death wish. Look at the films people like to watch after a long tiring day: a thriller or a horror film, anything less is considered boring. We are attracted to this violence. So the great moral work which grapples with the problem of identity also grapples with this contemporary experience of death, violence and hate. Nationalisms, like fundamentalisms, are screens in front of this violence, fragile screens, see-through screens, because they only displace that hatred, sending it to the other, to the neighbour, to the rival ethnic group. The big work of our civilisation is to try to fight this hatred – without God.

(Paris, 1991)

NEAL ASCHERSON

Nations and regions

NEAL ASCHERSON is a British author and journalist. He has written as political correspondent for the *Scotsman* and as European correspondent for the *Independent on Sunday*. His most recent book is *Games with Shadows*.

RK *Do you believe the European Englightenment made a positive contribution to modernity?*

NA I think what it gained above all was the sense of citizenship and a sense of universality. The Enlightenment said two things. First, it said that people have rights. Second, it said all solutions, all ideas, apply equally to everybody. Liberty, equality, fraternity – these are the birth rights of human beings all over the earth, not just in Europe, and all are equally entitled to them. So there is universalism of value. Now, from there you could go in two different ways. On the one hand, you got in Europe the view that certain ideologies were totally true and that since their values were universal, they should be imposed on everybody; this led straight to totalitarian systems, to dictatorship. The other stream from the Enlightenment was a continuous series of empowerings or disseminations of power, of constantly discovering ways in which people at the bottom of the social heap, or undiscovered populations in remote places, could be brought into the light of culture, education and of making their innate rights – as they were known in those good old days – a reality by showing them how to use them and creating conditions in which they could use them.

RK *Isn't there a third path leading from the declaration of those rights of liberty, fraternity and equality? I'm thinking of the way in which Napoleon interpreted that universalism of citizen rights to be the rights of Frenchmen – and turned the universalism of the French Revolution into imperialism by invading other countries and 'liberating' them into a new French empire . . .*

NA Yes, there has been that, and I think it was rather characteristic of the results of the Enlightenment. But then again, Germany is very similar. Germany eventually got into a strange position in which it said that the expansion of Germany is actually a great move forward because Germany is so advanced that it is no longer just a nation state, it actually *is* universality itself. We are the first bits of the future that exists, and if we roll over other bits of Europe they will have the immense privilege of living under the boots of our grenadiers and the tracks of our tanks, of joining the future and leaving behind their petty, divisive particularity. This was a kind of justification for monstrous imperialism.

RK *But you would, presumably see both the Napoleonic and Hitlerite projects as a perversion of universalism.*

NA Yes, it is a perversion. But it goes back further. There is a difficulty here in that the Enlightenment is a creed for intellectuals. Intellectuals build systems: systems on the whole do not allow for exceptions. They lay down laws, which are supposed to apply to everybody because they correspond to the universal laws of what goes on inside all human beings, who are in many ways exactly the same. So, there is this mechanistic element which leads back to the equivalent of the mad professor in the white coat, who in this century in Europe has been the intellectual with his moustache and cup of thick black coffee and his endless newspaper, sitting at some Central European café table, scribbling manifestos and going in and out of concentration camps.

RK *There is a lot said and written today about Middle Europe – Mittel Europa – as the cradle of modern civilisation; and we have what is now almost a cult of the Central European intellectual. Are you convinced by that?*

NA Well, there is no question but that Central Europe, Hapsburg Europe, developed an incredible concentration of talent, most but not all of it Jewish. After the fall of the Hapsburg Empire, of course, most of that talent was annihilated or fled abroad. There is a great sentimentalism about Central Europe which says that if only we could have the old Hapsburg Empire back, we could all rejoin each other, we could sink these nation states back into a regional association. It sounds nice and is a pretty picture; but one should never forget the other side. Central Europe wasn't just a place of progressive cultural and scientific ideas. It was also the place where the most terrible distortions of the Enlightenment arose. Central European intellectuals first of all invented romantic nationalism (which has a good side and a bad side); but then they invented totalitarianism. These ideas first came from that part of the world. This is where Marxism, but particularly the perversions of Marxism, originated. This is where fascism essentially arose – Middle Europe, with its hatreds, its confusions, its whirling melting-pot of populations, in social change, national change, hating each other, looking for ways out, dreaming of somebody else to punish.

RK *To return to the question of 'regional association', I think few people would quarrel with the cultural advantages of regional expression, but many would say it lacks any kind of real political clout. The European Community in Brussels and Strasbourg has recently introduced the notion of 'subsidiarity' to counter that particular accusation. Do you think that this is a persuasive move?*

NA I think we have to consider what exactly subsidiarity means. It is an appalling word, describing something very attractive and quite simple. What it means is that nothing should be done at a higher level which can be done at a lower level. The basic unit of human beings is the local community. If they want to establish another body, let's say a district council, above themselves, to take on some of the things which they can't do, they have the right to do that. And if the district councils want to associate and establish regional councils, and these, in turn, a national government, they can do that. But where it all starts is *at the bottom*, with what many people in Europe call the commune or *communa* – there are many different words for it; this is the basic unit and this is where sovereignty really starts.

RK *The res publica?*

NA That's right. You could put it like that. The basic unit is communal self-government.

RK *Local participatory democracy?*

NA Yes. Of course, it can be more democratic or less democratic in this or that particular cell of democracy. But the point is, the power goes upwards from below.

RK *Again, it sounds fine, but is that principle practicable, and is it at work in Europe as we speak?*

NA It is at work in many countries, most spectacularly in Germany.

RK *In the Länder system, you mean?*

NA Yes. In Germany it works extremely well. People are very relaxed with it, they're happy with it, and it forms a sort of background to people's approach to politics, and morality, and social life.

RK *And how does it work? How much power does each Land or region have within the new united Germany?*

NA Well, in a way, you're already begging the question. The point is, how much power does the basic cell have? And the answer is, quite a lot. And they delegate upwards.

RK *In what ways? Can they levy their own regional taxes?*

NA They often do. The *Gemeinde*, which is a kind of small market town, and the area around it can levy something. And then, a *Land*, which is a state of the federation, can have several million people as a population . . .

RK *Bavaria would be such a Land, North Rhine Westphalia another.*

NA That's an interesting point, because that shows you different sorts of region. You have some regions which are essentially the remains of what was once a self-governing kingdom, like Bavaria. And you have others which were set up for political reasons like North Rhine Westphalia, created by the Allies after the war.

RK *And yet it has been a considerable success.*

NA It was the part of Germany which contained the Ruhr, the main industrial basin of western Germany, which was reconstructed and then decayed, as all those industries decayed in the sixties and seventies. But it has this great North Rhine Westphalian loyalty, a sort of patriotism. It works extremely well.

RK *There are some who would say, including Margaret Thatcher in her day, that we are heading towards a Euro-empire, where the old and cherished notions of national independence, sovereignty and identity, are going to be subverted. Do you subscribe to that view?*

NA I subscribe only to half of it. I think that if one argues that national sovereignty is being transmuted by the new Europe, and changed into something else and eaten away, then I would agree. But national identity is not being eroded. It depends on what you mean by 'national', after all. What is going to come about is not, I think, a super-empire. There are obviously certain trends in the community, pointing towards an enormous irresponsible bureaucracy. But it's not going to happen, because the other institutions of the community, and the nature of the countries themselves, won't allow it.

RK *And how do you see it developing?*

NA I see this united Europe as a place which, like a sort of organism, is going to form an outer skin around itself. And within that outer skin, the present kind of skins which separate one nation state from another will suddenly become porous and they'll cease to matter. They are already becoming porous. National boundaries, nation state frontiers are already fading away. The existing nation state is losing power, but power drains away in two directions – upwards to Brussels, or Strasbourg, or wherever it may be, but downwards also. And that downward movement is what interests me, because it's going downwards to sub-nations and smaller units.

RK *But how do we know that is not just a utopian wish, mere rhetoric emanating from Brussels as a sop to the poorer underdeveloped regions by way of saying, 'if you go for a united Europe, we'll give you some kind of power as compensation'?*

NA I think the answer to that is connected with the way in which the concept of region has changed so much.

RK *Because it was traditionally associated with something backward, and reactionary, and rural?*

NA Yes, it had two kinds of negative connotation. It had, first of all, the connotation of province – it's a province, it's dark, it's superstitious, it's backward, no doubt it's terribly poor as well, and it has a kind of primitive grievance which somebody will have to deal with. And then came the economic definition of regionalism as something negative. This was especially so in British thinking. The region was the place of economic disaster, the rust-belt, the distant north where everything fell to bits and there was mass unemployment and you had to have regional assistance. A region was a disaster area.

RK *When did this change?*

NA It began to change around the 1970s. For about the first twenty years of the Community's existence there was only one member state which was based on the regional structure, and that was West Germany which was a federation. But then things started to change, and one state after another began to break up its old centralised character, in different degrees. Italy has now got fifteen regions. France has twenty-two regions since the early eighties. It was a very surprising change. But this was not only happening in France, traditionally a centralised nation state. Spain is another obvious example. After the fall of Franco, the 1978 Constitution decentralised Spain and allowed regions to take an immense amount of autonomy to themselves – the Basque region is one case, Catalonia another, and there are many others – Galicia and Andalusia, and so on.

RK *And what about Belgium? Could you argue that Belgium is quasi-federal?*

NA Yes, you could. The present solution to the eternal Belgian problems, if it is a solution, is really federal. Belgium now effectively consists of three parts – Flanders, the Walloon section, and Brussels itself.

RK *Why then are Britain and Ireland the two most centralised nation states in the European Community today? What might we gain from looking at our neighbours on the continent?*

NA I'd be cautious about saying why the plague of centralism affects Ireland, but I suspect it is something inherited unconsciously from the old British state. Britain is something I can talk about, it is a very, very archaic state form. There is nothing else like it in Europe. Indeed, there is very little like it in the developed world at all, because the system is one of *absolute sovereignty*. What happened in the seventeenth century was that the English parliament just took absolutism away from the kings, from the divine right of kings, and gave it to parliament, where it still is. So there is no concept of *popular sovereignty*. Instead, you have an elected parliament, but it is completely sovereign – it is not subject to the people as a concept, it is not subject to a constitution. Now, what this means, for our purposes, is that the British parliament cannot give away power. It *can* give it away forever, completely, but what it cannot do is federate, regionalise or devolve, because at any moment it retains the right to take it back – thereby making federation impossible.

RK *And are not the inhabitants of Great Britain, at least in principle, 'subjects' rather than 'citizens'? Does that terminological difference actually mean something?*

NA I think it does. A *citizen* is somebody who has a status in constitutional law: he is a member of the people and sovereignty starts at the bottom with the people, leading up towards the apex of the pyramid. Power does not flow down. In the British state to this day, power flows from the apex of the pyramid, symbolised by the monarch, downward, like a sort of shower of gold, or trickle of influence, into the population. In constitutional law, the flow of power is the other way around. Somebody who lives in a state where power comes down from the top is a *subject*. Somebody who lives in a country with popular sovereignty, where power goes up from the people towards its representatives at the top, is a citizen.

And a citizen has rights, prescriptive rights, which can be found in the constitution.

RK *Isn't there something almost contradictory then in the notion of a British nation state being centralised, with absolute sovereignty, and yet being in effect a nation state made up of different nations – Northern Ireland, Scotland, Wales and England itself?*

NA I think this is why the real challenge to the nature of the British state, which is going on at the moment, is a spreading idea even in England. The British state is a multinational state which in a way refuses to admit it. At the moment it consists of England, Northern Ireland, Scotland and Wales, and yet the sovereignty of parliament, an English-dominated parliament, over those parts, is almost total. There is very little room for manoeuvre. In order to approach regionalism of some kind, which would fit into the currently growing European concept of a *Europe of the regions*, the way forward has got to be a change in the basic constitutional doctrine of the British state. They've got to admit, first of all, that this is a multinational state; secondly, that power which is devolved or federated to the component nations of this state cannot simply be taken back; and thirdly, they've got to break this age-old tradition of increasingly centralising authority. One of the awful things about the Thatcher period was that you had this rhetoric about smaller and smaller government, government withdrawing from economic management and leaving society to manage itself. But the practice was a *continuous* draining of state power to the centre, bleeding local authority power white, extraordinary events like the removal of the elected authority for London itself, which for many years now has no elected authority at all.

RK *And the Scots have been very active too in saying no to that process. You're a Scotsman and, as you know, the Scottish Nationalist Party and the Scottish Labour Party have been very active in arguing for a solution to the Scottish national problem in terms of a Europe of regions. What is the thinking behind that?*

NA The situation in Scotland is very interesting, because essentially this is a national question. Approximately 85 per cent of Scots want some form of Scottish parliament, either within the United Kingdom or in conditions of complete independence. I think there are several reasons why Europe has entered the Scottish debate. One is that a country like Scotland is much more directly involved with the European Community than England is through things like fisheries and agriculture. It's much more a daily matter of concern in the newspapers. But the other reason is that Europe is somehow a way of Scotland getting into the world – because, I suppose, the real urge behind the Scottish Home Rule movement, or movements, is a wish to join the world, not to leave it. Not to have everything mediated through London, but to go directly to the source of power and be represented there. The difficulty about the British system means that if the Scots wish to be at Brussels, and to be represented there, and to have their identity established at Brussels and speak directly, the rules, both of the British state and unfortunately those of the European Community to date, mean that they have to be a nation state. So, in a curious way, Scottish nationalism, in a narrow sense of wanting to be completely independent and sovereign, has been greatly strengthened by the structure both of the Community and of Britain itself.

RK *And yet the catch-cry of the Scottish Nationalist Party is 'Independence Within Europe'. Therefore it's not an absolute independence. It is an independence that is interdependent, as it were, with other regions or regional nations.*

NA Well, you're looking at the Scottish Nationalists, the SNP specifically, at a very tricky moment in their evolution. There *are* some people who see the road to Europe as leading to Scottish independence. That is all they care about. There are others who say, we want to be part of Europe and we want our society to grow up and meet the world again and we think that within Europe we can perhaps be a sort of region, but we must enter it as a nation state and then surrender, or pool, a great deal of our power and newly-won sovereignty. This is very interesting, because it is one of several different kinds of track towards a *Europe of the regions*. And there are a few nations, submerged nations, who feel that in order to become a region of this new united Europe, they have to pass through the phase of being a nation state *first* so that they can then enter Europe and pool their sovereignty on their own terms.

RK *You have written about the notion of 'home', and the importance of regional and national identity in relation to home, requiring a redefinition of home as something hospitable and open and inclusive. Could you explain that?*

NA That comes back to the point about nationalism, regionalism and xenophobia. The greatest luxury of making your own home in the way that you want is the ability to offer hospitality. Everybody knows that. Nothing is more delightful than feeling that you have entered the world, and you can open your doors so that people can come in. I have watched this in a lot of countries which have achieved some form of home rule, self-government or independence. I have seen the unalloyed delight of being able to welcome strangers, even people whom you hated the day before yesterday, those you despised, knew little about, your traditional enemies. I hope for that. I liked intensely what President Mary Robinson said about the Fifth Province in her Inaurgural Address, and about the ideal of hospitality and opening doors to strangers. This is very much part of the new hope for Europe. I once went looking for somewhere to live in Bad Gotensburg, in Germany, many years ago. I came to this sinister, exaggerated villa which was called Haus Stachenburg, and I went in and there was this formidable landlady advancing towards me with a grey bun, and a sinister expression. And behind her was an inscription in poker-work which read – '*Mein Haus ist meine Welt, immer 'raus wem's nicht gefällt*' – which means, 'My house is my world: if you don't like it, be off with you!' That strikes me as exactly the old narrow, exclusivist, hate-defined nationalism from which we are now, hopefully, moving away.

(Dublin, 1991)

CHARLES TAYLOR

Federations and nations: living among others

CHARLES TAYLOR is Professor of Philosophy at McGill University, Montreal. His books on the European history of ideas include *Sources of the Self*; *Hegel, the Pattern of Politics* and *Philosophical Papers*. Born of French and English-speaking parents, he lived and taught for several years in Paris and Oxford, where he was a founder of the *New Left Review*. He has been a key figure in recent debates on nationalism, federalism and bilingualism in Quebec, where he now lives.

RK *Do you think the transition to a new Europe involves a fundamental shift of identity?*

CT People don't have simple identities any more, they aren't just a member of their own nation. They have a complex identity where they relate to their *nation*, and their *region*, and they also have a sense of being *European*. They can exist on three levels. I think that is a fuller way of being, because it means more of your ties and connections are meaningful to you as against shutting some out in favour of simply one. And I don't think the old way of being, where everyone was locked into a nation state with a sense of hostility to others is as good a way. Now, unfortunately, in Canada we may be going in the other direction.

RK *You've had a federalist system in Canada.*

CT We may be losing it now. Because some people can't adjust to that and the strains may pull us apart. But while this is a tragic development taking place at home, I'm really excited to see what's happening in Europe.

RK *Could I tease out the parallels a bit? Some people in Europe at the moment, looking to the history of Canada and America, would say that the federal system in Canada simply didn't work, and that the United States of*

America, as a melting-pot, is now in a situation where people feel they have no real identity, where there are high crime rates and drug problems, and indeed racial problems; and that if people don't have a sense of local attachment – or indeed national attachment to some sort of territory – this leads to a lowest-common-denominator spiritless culture that ultimately issues in violence or war.

CT That's right. There are two kinds of federalism. We have to look at this. The United States is not the model for Europe, because the United States after the Civil War became a homogenising federalist state. Culturally it's becoming more and more of a unitary state, even though it is constitutionally a federal state. The power is flowing more and more to the central government. Canada, by contrast, has a real federal state, with real cultural heterogeneity. Power wasn't flowing to the centre. The regional governments, the provinces, really had an important role in people's lives. People identified with them. You can see this in the vote. The level of voting in democratic elections is high in Canadian provinces. It's very low in American states. It's even low in the American federal system. Now, Europe is plainly heading towards the Canadian kind of federalism. It's not going to try to homogenise cultures. It's going to bring together these different cultures, these different national identities. People are still going to be French, Irish, Italian and so on.

RK *Well, you're optimistic about Europe, and I share your optimism, yet the evidence in your own country at the moment, particularly your own province, Quebec, would seem to suggest that that very federalism which you are invoking as a positive model for Europe is breaking apart at the seams, and that Quebec may well be, in the near rather than far future, a separate nation state.*

CT There are conditions for pulling this off, and we in Canada don't seem to have them, but you in Europe do. One condition is that people sense themselves happy with their identities, that they don't feel that their national identity is in some way put in the shade or looked down upon by others. You know, national identity is a very fascinating thing. In some ways, it's an inward-turning thing but in fact, deep down, it's an outward-turning thing. People want to be recognised by others. And when they feel not recognised, that creates the strains and tensions. We've never got over that, in French and English culture, in Canada.

RK *You yourself are, as it were, a hybrid creature.*

CT My mother was French, and my father was English, and I felt this all my life. Now, what's good about Europe is those strains existed within countries and not between them. Recently, one finds Corsican nationalism, or Breton nationalism, or Irish nationalism, a sense of pulling away within countries. The creation of Europe will allow those to find their own level without necessarily having to break up the units. Because as Europe is formed, paradoxically, the nation state becomes less important and the region can become more important. And the national hatreds *between* European states, because of the bloodbath that ended in 1945, are so discredited that Europe can enter a phase where it's willing to put some of that behind it. So, because of this constellation of circumstances – the memory of Hitler and the hope of more space for regional societies – I think Europe has a real chance of not breaking up the way Canada is. In Eastern Europe, you see something very different, and in the old Soviet Union of course. They never experienced an aftermath of the Second World War in a free society where they could work out their reaction to it. The Communist governments were in a sense in a cultural deep freeze where nothing was worked out.

RK *So the implication is that, if in the post-war era, the Eastern European and indeed Soviet Republics had been given the sort of autonomy and independence that the nation states had in Western Europe, they too would be now ready to pool sovereignty and move towards a supranational federation?*

CT Yes, we can hope so anyway. But we haven't had that. In some cases, there are very deep national hatreds, with recent massacres, you think of Yugoslavia – the Croats and Serbs; but in other cases, like Czechs and Slovaks, there's no reason why those two peoples can't fit together. They haven't massacred each other in recent history. And yet, it looks as though they too are under strain. And that simply is because they didn't have a chance, post-1948, to work this out in the way people in the West did in a free society.

RK *It's been argued that a Europe of regions is all very well culturally or linguistically, where everybody can express themselves with their local colour, vernacular, rituals and festivals, but that when it comes to the hard crunch of economics, it is the centralised nation state that still packs the punch. Of course, that is belied by the performance of Germany, Spain, Italy, France, and Denmark, who actually increased their GNP when they decentralised; whereas Britain, who under Thatcher centralised power to an extreme degree, actually regressed in terms of economic performance.*

CT The argument for central power is sometimes put in terms of controlling the economy, rather than just letting it go, and letting it prosper. But, you see, that tells also against the nation state now, because the economic forces go way beyond the boundaries of the nation state. That's why there's a case to be made for something at the level of Europe, and something at the level of the regions as well.

RK *So economically speaking, there is not really any such thing as absolute national sovereignty any more.*

CT No, it's less and less the case. And nations that clung to it, like Albania, ended very badly.

RK *Perhaps we could pursue the British model a little. You lived there for several years, and taught in Oxford when Margaret Thatcher was the ruler of the land. As you well know, she issued, Cassandra-like, many warnings about the future developments of Europe. She dragged her heels and in the Bruges speech delivered a nightmare scenario about a Fortress Europe that would steamroll national identities and subject us all to a mushrooming bureaucracy in Brussels. Do you think there is anything in that nightmare scenario?*

CT Absolutely not. It's the reaction of a government that itself, paradoxically and strangely, wanted to control everything very firmly, and sensed that in a real federal system nobody controls anything very firmly, because control is split. I say 'paradoxically' because Margaret Thatcher, in some ways, passed for a political leader that wanted to get government out of society. And in one sense that was true – out of the economy. But the attempt to control things, the attempt, for instance, to take over local government, when it got in her way, to remake the whole local tax system from the centre in the poll tax, and so on, these were ways to get control over that society and remake it in the image of a certain ideology. People like that, ideologues like that, don't like federalism. It's the same thing with some of our separatists in Canada. They don't like federalism, because there isn't one place where there are all the levers that you can pull. I think that's really what it's about. Federation is quite the opposite of a large threatening bureaucracy in Brussels. It's the undermining of it.

RK *What would you say to those who suspect that the model of a federal Europe of regions is nothing but camouflage for a new Euro-empire to compete with the other great global economies and geopolitical blocks – Japan on the one hand, America on the other?*

CT I think that's not a danger. We're in a multi-centred world now where nobody is going to have the absolute advantage. However, I see one point in that criticism, Europe could become very inward-turned. And then we are in danger economically of trade blocs, like the North American trade bloc and the Japanese organising a rival trade bloc.

RK *So there is the possibility of a certain European protectionism emerging.*

CT There is a possibility. But I don't think the lesson to be drawn from that is, let's not have Europe, because I don't think that the nation states of Europe have any better record of being outward-turned, if I can put it mildly, than Europe as a whole.

RK *And maybe we do need a certain legitimate protectionism from Japanese cars and American pulp television.*

CT Yes. And if there is going to be a war of the blocs, which I'd regret, Europe must be equipped to deal with it. But there is definitely a danger, the danger of a Europe that can't yet see itself as one great civilisation *among* others. The whole question of how to be *one among others* in the world today is a tremendous problem that nobody has solved, and everybody has to solve it in order to exist. It's the site of all sorts of neurotic hatreds and resentments. You look at it from the standpoint of Tehran, that is full of a sense of resentment at being put upon and despised by the West.

RK *Europe too has its sins!*

CT Oh, definitely. Europe has its complacency too, its sense of being still the definitive civilisation that everybody has to imitate, that doesn't need to learn about what's happening out there. That, of course, feeds into the attitude towards the large number of non-Europeans who are coming to live in Europe – the North Africans, people from Turkey, South Asians, and so on. That is a very big problem. We have that in North America too. I'm not pointing the finger. All of us have to live in more and more multi-cultural societies, because the world is moving that way. And that raises the problem of being one among others, in an acute way, even in domestic politics, let alone in international politics.

RK *There is an attendant fear that a federal Europe, based on a modern tradition of rights going back to the French Revolution and the Enlightenment, might in fact become a melting-pot of atomised individuals, rather like America. This is another scenario often quoted, where the sense of social duties and commitments, fidelity to the common good of the community, is actually traduced and travestied. Do you think it's a grounded fear?*

CT It is. That's not because of Europe though. I think this is a grounded fear because the whole European tradition of rights is heading in the twentieth century in a certain direction which is potentially perilous. You're quite right there. On the one hand the European tradition of rights is one of the great realisations of European civilisation. I think the idea that a human being enjoys a certain indemnity where some things can't be touched and certain freedoms have to be accorded, is obviously a good thing . . .

RK *So the danger is what?*

CT The danger is that if that's the only way you conceive of political right it ends up drawing a fence around the individual and eroding the sense of individuals relating to larger groups, eroding, I would also say, the political process. What worries me about the American scene now is that the best and the brightest minds in America are concerned exclusively with fighting out the major battles in Supreme Court decisions. And the idea of fighting these battles by going out there and creating a majority and convincing fellow citizens to vote for Congress or the legislature, becomes less and less important, less and less vital. It gets to the point where a lot of people I know look at their presidential candidate as a kind of three-quarters dead vehicle for the nomination of Supreme Court Justices when the next vacancy comes up. That's why a lot of conservatives rally behind Reagan or Bush. They don't admire these people – indeed, they knew, in Reagan's case, he was almost brain dead – but they wanted him there because they trusted that when a Supreme Court Justice died off, he'd put one of their guys in and they'd turn around some of the decisions. It is very unhealthy in a democracy that the balance should go exclusively in that direction, and if I thought that the European Court would go in that direction too I'd be worried.

RK *You are worried about too much power being given to a non-representative judiciary?*

CT I'm worried about the political battles being fought out before the judiciary. That's not only bad because it disempowers the political process of majority voting, it's also bad because that way of putting these issues makes them into zero sum games. When you go before a judge, you are not asking for an intelligent accommodation, you're asking for what the law says. The law can say either A or B is right. It's really a zero sum game. And you get issues which could be intelligently accommodated if they were fought out between legislative majority and minority. When they are put before judges, it becomes all or nothing. Tremendous rigidities are introduced. People become shrill because they know they'll either get their whole point or they won't. The abortion debate is a good example of this. When people fight it out in terms either of the right of choice of the mother, which means no restrictions at all, or the right to life of the foetus, which means no abortion under any circumstances whatsoever, it's going to be *total* victory for one side or the other. Nobody can sit down and make an accommodation. On the other hand, if it's a legislative matter, then we're in the domain of a human political judgement which I think we ought to keep alive.

RK *So it is a question of balancing rights with duties.*

CT Yes, a balancing of rights with duties with all sorts of other demands on us – not just duties, but the demands of decency, of harmony, of some kind of coexistence with our fellow-citizens. All these demands, as well as particular rights, can be put into an all-in judgement and worked out in real dialogue with real opponents, where you have to make a compromise, recognise the other. That is the human process of politics, democratic politics.

RK *But,* grosso modo, *you would say that the European legacy of human rights, which has given rise to the UN Charter of Human Rights, is a positive heritage.*

CT It is, in itself, a wonderful heritage.

RK *But it must be continually debated, interpreted, reinterpreted, to accommodate differing points of view?*

CT Yes. It also has to be one element in a constellation. I would say the other essential part of the European constellation is democratic participatory politics. These two have to go together in a constellation. If ever one of them, like a cuckoo, takes over the whole nest and throws out all the other eggs, then you get a very unhealthy political culture, which I think the Americans are in danger of generating now.

RK *Do you feel, at the moment, that there is an idea of Europe, a story of Europe, that is universal and that we can all tell ourselves, a guiding vision, a sense of direction enabling us to say we've come from there, we're here now and we're going there – or do you feel that such a Grand Narrative is no longer feasible and that we've got to treat Europe more as a patchwork, as a medley of diverse voices and identities?*

CT Well, in a way, neither of the above. The really healthy situation in Europe would be that everybody thinks there ought to be some kind of Grand Narrative, but there will be an intellectual contest over what it's going to be, and people are going to make *different* arguments for and against . . .

RK *So Europe should be cultivating a healthy conflict of interpretations which aim towards some kind of dialogue or accommodation?*

CT Exactly. That's what you could hope for as the best realisable situation for Europe. If people came up with a Grand Narrative, and it fell apart into these unsuperimposable perspectives, without any relation with each other, then, you wouldn't have Europe any more.

RK *You'd have a war between obscurantists.*

CT Yes, people falling back into their own particularism – a little world where they don't care about the whole. Then you get the kind of politics that emerges from an exclusive emphasis on rights where people say, 'I've got my demands and who cares how the whole picture ends up as long as I get my demands satisfied'. That's the mentality of people exclusively into rights, and organisations founded to get their rights. And that could be the outcome of the postmodern Europe, where everybody wants their particular perspective realised and no one cares about the whole. That's not a healthy political society.

RK *It's a recipe for fragmentation and fracture without any sense of responsibility.*

CT Yes. A deep sense of alienation from the whole. A sense of cynicism about the political process. In the end, if you like, an abandonment of solidarity. And I wouldn't wish that on Europe.

RK *Is there a sense in which the genius, or positive heritage, of Europe has been a spiritual one which has been somewhat compromised by the contemporary movement towards secularisation?*

CT I think that's true. I tried to discuss this in my book, *Sources of the Self.* I think a lot of the most important streams of thinking of the European Enlightenment, or European secular humanism, have very deep roots in Christianity, Judaism, Islam, the things that are common to them. Deep roots which are not entirely overcome.

RK *You argue that the sense of self is one of those, the sense of self-identity. Another is the sort of affirmation of everyday life.*

CT Yes, the sense that ordinary life, the life of work, of production, of marriage and the family, is something of ultimate significance. The ancients, Aristotle, for instance, had a view that what really matters in life was a range of *higher* activities, contemplation, or the citizen life, to which your life in the home and family or your economic life was simply an infrastructure which you had to have so that you'd carry on the really important things. And the revolution in thinking, sensibility and morality that's part of our modern age is an anti-hierarchical conviction that a very meaningful part of human life consists of how you live your ordinary life, your life as a family person, your life as a worker in the economy. That's something which has very clear roots in Judaism and Christianity.

RK *So the modern invention of self-identity – of an inward, interior sense – is in continuity with a spiritual heritage?*

CT Yes. I take St Augustine as my example. He's perhaps the best instance of a certain Christian line of thinking at the origin of much European thinking about the self. There interiority was not for its own sake, but in order to come to God. And something of that has remained in all the successor forms, even the secular ones. It's something profoundly ambivalent – it can go in two directions. It can go in a direction which is totally focused on the subject, a kind of subjectivism – its most obvious modern variant being the post-Romantic idea that everybody has their own original way of existing, their own thing to do, and that they have to find it themselves: they can't simply take it from someone else. Now, that's something which is a continuation of the idea of interiority. You find in *yourself* what your talents are, what you need to be. And that can take a very subjectivist form, totally focused on 'me', on self-expression. But it can also be the way that people discover their vocation to the universal, for instance, their sense that they ought to militate for ecological sanity, a sense of connection to the larger world, the larger nature that they have to struggle for. It can take you in two directions, and instead of looking at it in a one-eyed way and seeing it simply as the royal road to subjectivism, you can come to understand how it can be inflected in either way.

RK *So the quest of self is not a* fait accompli *but a task?*

CT In our contemporary culture, we can never get away from this modern insight that everybody has their own original way of being. It's very deep in our culture. But we can do different things with it. We aren't locked into one particular form, and that's important.

RK *Finally, what would your hope be as an English-French-Canadian looking at Europe and concerned about Europe?*

CT Well, in the immediate future, that the movement towards a balanced federation would continue.

(Dublin, 1991)

PAUL RICOEUR

Universality and the power of difference

PAUL RICOEUR is a French philosopher who has held Chairs at the Universities of Paris and Chicago. His books include *History and Truth*; *The Rule of Metaphor*; *Time and Narrative*; *Hermeneutics and the Human Sciences*; *The Conflict of Interpretations* and *Oneself as Another.*

RK *Do you believe in the idea of a European identity?*

PR Europe has produced a series of cultural identities, which brought with themselves their own self-criticism, and I think that this is unique. Even Christianity encompassed its own critique.

RK *And how would you see this ability to criticise ourselves operating? In terms of Reformations and Renaissances?*

PR Yes. Plurality is within Europe itself. Europe has had different kinds of Renaissance, Carolingian, twelfth-century, Italian and French, fifteenth century, and so on. The Enlightenment was another expression of this; and it is important that in the dialogue with other cultures we keep this element of self-criticism, which I think is the only specificity of Europe (along with, of course, the enhancement of science). Europe is unique in that it had to interweave several heritages – Jewish-Christian, Greek-Roman, then the Barbarian cultures which were encompassed within the Roman Empire, the heritage within Christianity of the Reformation, Renaissance Enlightenment, and also the three nineteenth-century components of this heritage, *nationalism*, *socialism*, and *romanticism* . . .

RK *How does this pluralist legacy fit with the European claim to universality?*

PR The kind of universality that Europe represents contains within itself a plurality of cultures, which have been merged and intertwined, and which provide a certain fragility, an ability to disclaim and interrogate itself.

RK *This of course opens the question, doesn't it, of how we in Europe relate not just to the differences within our borders, but also how we relate to the differences of other non-European continents and countries; and how the universalist project of Europe can engage in dialogue with their differences, their nationalisms, their fundamentalisms? I mean, can we preach to others if we haven't sorted out our own problems of national identity?*

PR I think we must be very cautious here in Europe when we speak of fundamentalism, because it is immediately a pejorative word, and this prevents good analysis. We have to look at the phenomenon because there are several kinds of fundamentalism. We put one word above a multiplicity of events. But there is, for instance, a difference between a return to a culture close to the practice of the people and a fundamentalism imposed from above.

RK *Well, if we take the example of the Baltic states, do you have a sympathy with what their nationalist claims for sovereignty and autonomy are trying to achieve?*

PR I must say that I am surprised by the extent of the phenomenon, but also the extremist dimension, because in all my own philosophical culture, I had underestimated the capacity of language to reorganise a culture and to unify it. And secondly, I had also underestimated the fragility of each identity which feels threatened by another. People must be very unsure to feel threatened by the otherness of the other. I did not realise that people are so unsure when they claim so emphatically to be what they are.

RK *Wouldn't you agree that there are very good historical reasons for this insecurity, not only in the Baltic states, but also in Yugoslavia, in Czechoslovakia, or in Northern Ireland – hence the need to attach themselves to a separatist national identity?*

PR But there is also the fact that there is no political distribution of borders which is adequate to the distribution of languages and cultures, so there is no political solution at the level of the nation state. This is the real irritator of the nineteenth century, this dream of a perfect equation between state and nation.

RK *That clearly has failed.*

PR Yes, that has failed. So, we have to look for something else.

RK *There is much talk now in Europe about the necessity to go beyond the limitations of the nation state (while preserving it as an intermediary model) to a transnational federation of states on the one hand, and a devolution of power from the nation state to regions on the other hand – to regions that would be more self-governing, that would encourage the practice of local democracy, of participatory democracy. Do you think that might work?*

PR Yes, but there is a political problem here. Is the project of European federalism to be a confederation of regions, or of nations? I don't know the solution because it is something without a precedent. Modern history has been made by nation states. But there are problems of size. We have five or six nation states in Europe of major size, but we have micro-nations which cannot become micro-states in the same way as nation states have done.

RK *One could argue that it's not unprecedented in what some call the 'other Europe' of Canada and the United States, where they did develop a model of federation, and indeed a certain amount of local autonomy in government at the level of the town halls, particularly at the beginning of the American Revolution.*

PR In a sense, the United States is a different case because it is a melting-pot of immigrants.

RK *But surely we've also got an opportunity here in Europe to accommodate the immigrants from those countries we colonised for two or three centuries.*

PR The United States has solved the problem due to its unit of language, English, to a certain extent. We have an opposite problem, with our multiplicity of languages and national dialects.

RK *I'd like to bring in the question of sovereignty here. At the moment we're pooling sovereignty in Europe. The notion of sovereignty, if I'm not mistaken, actually goes back to the idea, first of all, that God is the universal sovereign, later replaced by the King as sovereign, as the centre of one indivisible power. Then, with the replacement of monarchy by republics, with the French Revolution, for example, the nation state becomes sovereign.*

PR In modern republics, the origin of sovereignty is in the people, but now we recognise that we have *many* peoples. And many peoples means many centres of sovereignty – we have to deal with that.

RK *Wasn't one of the problems of the French Revolution the definition of sovereignty as one and indivisible? That creates problems when you export the Revolution to other countries or continents.*

PR Take the Corsican people who are also a member of the French people. Here we have two meanings of the word *people*. On the one hand, 'people' means to be a citizen in a state, so it's not an ethnic concept. But, on the other hand, Corsica *is* a people in an ethnic sense – within the French people which is not an ethnic concept. So, we are struggling with two concepts of people, and I think it's an example of what is happening throughout Europe now.

RK *Does this mean two different kinds of membership – ethnic membership and civic membership?*

PR Yes, because the notion of 'people' according to the French Constitution is not ethnic. Its citizenship is defined by the fact that somebody is born on the territory of France. For example, the son or daughter of an immigrant is French because he or she was born on this territory. So, the rule of membership has nothing to do with ethnic origin. This is why it was impossible to define Corsican people, because we had to rely on criteria other than citizenship, on ethnic criteria, and to whom are we to apply these criteria?

RK *Does this not raise the problem of ethnic nationalism and racism?*

PR The criterion of citizenship is there to moderate the excess of the ethnic criterion.

RK *To enlarge the discussion somewhat, could one not say that there are in fact several Europes?*

PR The German thinker Karl Jaspers used to say that Europe extends from San Francisco to Vladivostok. This raises the issue of the cultural expansion of Europe.

RK *Perhaps the solution, if there is one, is not to be found within the limits of Europe. Maybe we need to extend those limits and go further to what some people have called a world republic, a cosmopolitan society which can harbour differences yet bind all peoples and continents together?*

PR Even in political terms, it may be impossible to solve the problem of the unification of Europe without solving the problem of some international institution which would provide the proper framework.

RK *This utopian vision of a cosmopolitan republic is one that goes back to the Enlightenment, to Kant and Montesquieu . . .*

PR We need now a plurality of utopias, utopias of different kinds. Surely, a basic utopia is a world economy which is not ruled by efficiency, by productivity, but based on needs. Maybe this will be the problem for the next century – how to move from an economy ruled by the laws of the market to a universal economy based on the real needs of people. We are now at the stage where the market is winning and provides the only source of productivity, but this productivity is not shared, because the success of productivity increases inequality. We'll have to address that. And then there's the political problem of resolving the hierarchy of sovereignties – global, Continental (European, American, African etc.), national and regional.

RK *Maybe we can take a step back from the immediate political implications of this problem and say a little about the cultural and philosophical presuppositions of this discussion.*

PR I would like to focus on the role of *memory* in this context. On the one hand, memory is a burden; if we keep repeating the story of wars won or lost, we keep reinforcing the old hostilities. Take the different states of Europe. In fact, we cannot find a pair who weren't at war at one time or another. The French and the British, the Poles and Germans, and so on. So, there is memory which is a prison, which is regressive. But, on the other hand, we cannot do without the cultivation of the memory of our cultural achievements, and also of our sufferings. This brings me to the second element. We need a memory of the second order which is based on forgiving. And we cannot forgive if we have forgotten. So, in fact we have to *cross* our memories, to *exchange* our memories with each other to the point that, for example, the crimes of the Germans become part of our own memory. Sharing the memory of cruelty of my neighbour is a part of this political dimension of forgiving. We have some examples. When the German chancellor went to Warsaw and knelt down and asked for pardon, I think that was very important for Europe. Because, while we have to get rid of the memory of wars, of victory, and so on, we must keep the memory of the scars. Then we can proceed to this exchange of memories, to this mutual forgiveness.

RK *It's an unusual idea.*

PR I don't see how we can solve Europe's problems only in terms of a Common Market or a political institution. We need these, of course. We need the extension of a market which would be the basis of the unification for Europe and also a relationship between Europe and the rest of the world, the invention of new institutions to solve the problem of the multiplicity of nation states. But there is a *spiritual* problem underlying both the economic problem of a Common Market and the political problem of new institutions.

RK *What would be the role of narrative – one of the key concepts in your philosophy – in relation to this cultural crisis we are facing in Europe today? I mean narrative as story-telling, as remembrance or as projection.*

PR I would say three things concerning the role of narrative. First you have the narration of founding events, because most cultures have some original happening or act which gives some basis of unity to the diversity within the culture. Hence the need to commemorate founding events.

RK *Such as the French Revolution, the Soviet Revolution, 1916 in Ireland?*

PR Yes. We have to keep that because we have to retain some claims, some convictions that are rooted in these founding events. Secondly, I would say that one of the resources of the theory of narrativity is that now we may tell *different* stories about ourselves. So, we have to learn how to vary the stories that we are telling about ourselves. And thirdly, we have to enter this process of exchange, which the German philosophers called *Auseinandersetzung*. We are caught in the stories of others, so we are protagonists in the stories we are told by others, and we have to assume for ourselves the stories that the others tell about us, which have their own founding events, their own strategies, their own plots.

RK *So the crossing of memories involves the crossing of stories. But is there any sense in which in Europe today we can tell each other the same story, a common universal story? Is there anything to bind us together?*

PR I would say that this concept of universality may be used in different contexts. On the one hand, you may speak of universal rules of discourse – what Habermas says about rules of discussion, let us say the logic and ethics of argumentation. This is one level of universality, but it is too formal to be operative. Secondly, you have a universalist claim within our own culture. For example, we may claim that some rights to free speech are universal, in spite of the fact that for the time being they cannot be included within other cultures. But it's a claim, and remains only a claim as long as it is not recognised by the others. So we bring to the discussion not only procedures of universality but *claims* of universality. The project of universality is central to the whole debate about human rights. Take the example of the mutilation of women. I am sure that we are right to say that there is something universal in our assertion that women have a right to pleasure, to physical integrity and so on, even if it is not recognised. But we have to bring that into the discussion. It's only discussion with the other which may finally convince the other that it's universal. And thirdly, I would say that you have a kind of eschatological universalism – the universal as an ultimate project or goal as in Kant's *Essay on Perpetual Peace*.

RK *The project of some kind of universal republic.*

(Paris, 1991)

EDWARD SAID

Europe and its others: an Arab perspective

EDWARD SAID is a Palestinian critic and author who has lived and taught most of his life in Europe and America. He is currently Professor of Literature at Columbia University, New York, and his books include *Orientalism*; *Covering Islam*; *The Question of Palestine* and *The World, the Text and the Critic.*

RK *As an outsider, do you think there is such a thing as a distinctively European tradition?*

ES I think there is no question but one can talk about a European tradition in the sense of an identifiable set of experiences, of states, of nations, of legacies, which have the stamp of Europe upon them. But, at the same time, this must not be divorced from the world beyond Europe. In the Algerian context there is a good phrase for this – 'complementary enemies'. There is a complementarity between Europe and its others. And that's the interesting challenge for Europe, not to purge itself of all its outer affiliations and connections in order to try to turn into some 'pure' thing.

RK *What is becoming of the 'European intellectual' today?*

ES The idea that the intellectual is a professional who is rewarded for his or her services has meant in the United States and in Europe that you have this extraordinary gravitation towards centres of power, that the intellectual thinks that the reward or the goal for what he or she does is a policy playing, a policy forming role, to be an opinion maker, a policy maker. Whereas my view is that the intellectual role is essentially that of, let's say, heightening consciousness, becoming aware of tensions, complexities, and taking on oneself responsibility for one's community. This is a non-specialist role, it has to do with issues that cut across professional disciplines. Because we know about professional discourse. I mean, it becomes a jargon, speaking only to the informed, keeping them essentially in a state of acquiescence, and promoting one's own position in the end. That's something I find deeply abhorrent, because it seems to me that society is made up of two kinds of people. There are the maintainers, the ones who keep things going as they are, and there are the ones who are the intellectuals, who provoke difference and change.

RK *You would introduce here an ethical scruple of responsibility for one's fellow-citizens.*

ES Yes, I think that's the essential thing.

RK *And if that means a contamination or confusion of realms, then so be it?*

ES So be it, exactly. For me, what has been terribly important is that I have a sense, maybe it's an accident of birth, that I'm affiliated with a national community – Palestine. Partly because of the universality of the cause, Palestine is not just a simple nationalist struggle, it involves the cultural problem of anti-Semitism. We have become the inheritors of European anti-Semitisim: we are the victims of the victims, if you like. It's a complicated role. Nevertheless, having some connection with a national community – or community, never mind national – keeps one honest.

RK *But is this where you would see a social and moral role for the intellectual, where in inventing or reinventing our traditions, we can actually take apart and analyse the myths and the symbols? There is a lot of talk at the moment about the creation of a new Europe. Do you think there is a danger we could witness the emergence of a new cultural imperialism?*

ES I think the likelihood of an imperialism that one associates with nineteenth-century European imperalism is not very great. And I think the overshadowing power and influence of the United States is also a kind of impediment to it. One would like to think that Europe – at least that's the way I think from the point of view of the Arab world – is a kind of counter to the United States; that it provides, partly because of the Mediterranean links between some of the southern European countries and North Africa, a kind of exchange of cultures that is not imperial, and that there is more give and take than before.

RK *But has Europe succeeded in acknowledging the other in its midst: the traditional other, in this instance, being the Arab or Islamic world?*

ES No, I don't think so. I think there's a problem. Take Italy. Italy now sees itself as saddled with about a million Muslims, all of them from North Africa, largely from Libya and Tunis, some from Egypt. This is unacknowledged, as opposed to France, which has also two or three million Muslims, which is a political issue. But I think discussion and debate, even the kind of rancorous debate that you get between Le Pen and some of his more liberal opponents, is better than the silence you find in Italy. Nevertheless, there is a presence there which is going to provoke more discussion and more awareness. And, interestingly enough, there is now in the Arab world a set of writers, thinkers and intellectuals who are very serious about a Euro-Arab dialogue, exchange between the two that will break down the old hostility, 'Arabs versus the West'. It's very different from the United States where there's none of that. The United States still regards itself as at war with the Arab world, or Islam, or fundamentalism, or something of that sort. So the cultural issue is never even tapped.

RK *But when it comes to concrete political decisions, it would seem that Mediterranean Europe, which has been connected, both in terms of migrations and culturally, to the Arab world, was not able to stop war taking place in that part of the world, for example, the Gulf region.*

ES Not only that, but in the case of Britain, participated rather more avidly than one would have liked. On the other hand, in the post-war period, the Italians and the French did try to broker a political, as opposed to a military, settlement. The Italians have been very active since the war on a negotiated political settlement, obviously not of the Gulf situation, but of the crux, which is the Palestinian issue. Now, they haven't been able to stand up to the Americans for a number of reasons. Partly because their efforts are individual. They're not done in the name of Europe. I mean, the Council of Europe has taken very good positions, but they haven't acted together as a Community. Individually, they are caught. On the one hand, they're pressured by the USA. On the other hand, they need oil from what are essentially conservative, reactionary Arab regimes who are very opposed to a change in the status quo. So their position is difficult. More positive interaction takes place at the *cultural* level, where I think there is greater movement.

RK *You've spoken a lot about the phenomenon of 'orientalism', a cultural phenomenon which basically represents a stereotypical attitude in Europe, and in the West generally, towards the Arab world.*

ES It's very powerful. You don't have to look in the jingoistic press. One thinks of the commentaries that one reads in *The Times* by, to mention names, Conor Cruise O'Brien, who still talks about the Muslims as a depraved family full of incest, and the Arabs as violent people, or books like *The Closed Circle* by David Pryce Jones, which could not be written about any other ethnic cultural group in the world today.

RK *This is a sort of racism?*

ES It's racism, xenophobia; it's a kind of paranoid, delusional fantasy.

RK *And why has Europe needed this?*

ES I'll tell you why. With regard to the Arabs Europe has always had Islam at its doorstep, so to speak. Islam, don't forget, is the only non-European culture that has never been completely vanquished. It is adjacent to and shares the monotheistic heritage with Judaism and Christianity. So, there is this constant friction. And unlike, say, the British in India, the problem has not been settled. The idea of the West, I would argue, comes largely from opposition to the Islamic and Arab world. I think it probably goes back in its root to theological issues. The prophet Mohammed, who saw himself as a continuer of the line of prophecy that begins with Abraham, Moses, Jesus, is seen initially in the first polemics against Islam in the seventh and eighth century as an upstart, a terrifying emanation from exactly the same world that produced Christianity and Judaism. So I think it's a unique case, and the sense of cultural contest is further enhanced by military, and you might say economic and political, contests where a tremendous amount of ignorance pervades, and people are not entitled to look at the concrete experience between Muslims and Europeans which is in reality much more complicated than sheer animosity. I mean, there is a tremendous dependence, for instance, in European history on Islamic science, on the transmission of philosophy from the Greeks to the Muslims and back to the West.

RK *I am struck as a philosopher by the crucial role played by Arab thinkers like Avicenna and Averroes, the Cordoba school, the Andalusian school, and so on, in this transmission of thought.*

ES Absolutely. And the idea of the university flourishes in the Arab world. The idea of a college, you know, *the collegium*, is, in fact, an Islamic idea.

RK *We've had some rather dramatic examples of the confrontation between the European and Arab worlds in recent times. I'm not just thinking of the Gulf War, but also of controversies within Europe itself. We've had the Salman*

Rushdie affair, which raised all kinds of issues around universal rights versus the right to differ; and, in France, the famous controversy over the wearing of the veil by Muslim girls in secular schools. It's been a common argument that if Arab immigrants come to Europe, and have every right to do so having been colonised by Europeans for hundreds of years, they should leave behind them their cultural, religious differences and conform to this secular, universal space which is modern Europe.

ES I think there are universal principles of free speech to which Muslims as well as everyone else must conform; and I think it's important that there is in the Arab world – I can't speak about *all* the Islamic world, Pakistan, Bangladesh, and so on – a very important struggle taking place today between the forces, broadly speaking, of what one would want to call *secularism*, to which I attach myself, and the forces that could be broadly described as *religious*. Now, fundamentalism is a frequent topic on the television, but I think it would be wrong to associate fundamentalism with everything that takes place in the Arab and Islamic world. There are different brands. There is a debate going on, and I think we are now at a point in the Arab world where the religious alternative has been shown to be a failure. You can be Muslim, but what does it mean to have Muslim economics, Muslim chemistry? In other words, there's a universal norm when it comes to running a modern science or state. But the question is, what of those people who represent another side of Islam, which is Islamic resistance to the West? On the West Bank in Gaza, people consider themselves Islamic militants fighting Israeli occupation, because that's the last area of their lives that the Israelis have not been able to penetrate, as was the case in Algeria during the French occupation. So there are different kinds of Islam, there are different kinds of secularism. To come back to the Rushdie question, there were many Arab writers and intellectuals, including myself, who publicly supported Rushdie's right to write whatever he chose. That has to be underlined. But what we also drew attention to is the fact that there are many Muslim writers in the Arab world, in the Occupied Territories for example, who were put in jail by the Israelis as journalists and novelists for reasons of political expediency. For instance, speaking of banning books, on the West Bank today, because of Israeli law, you cannot buy and read Plato's *Republic*. Nor can you read Shakespeare's *Hamlet*! There is a proscribed list of many hundreds of books, prohibited by the Israelis for reasons nobody can understand. Now, where were the Western writers who stood up for Salman Rushdie – I'm glad they did, and I stood with them – when it came to advocation of Palestinian freedom of expression on the West Bank and Gaza today? I don't know whether you know this, but the use of the word Palestine is a punishable offence. If you use the word Palestine you can be put in jail for six months. So what about a single standard for all these things? Why hypocritically use this? We're in the same fight with you. We want also to fight against that kind of thing, but let us fight on *all* fronts.

RK *There's been much talk in recent times about creating a new European order, a federal Europe of regions or nations, and there's been talk about creating a new world information order – I'm thinking especially of the UNESCO Report sponsored by the late Sean MacBride. Are you suggesting we should interpret this as a struggle to create a secular universal order?*

ES I'm not sure I know. I'm not in favour of abstract universalism, because it's usually the universalism of whoever happens to be most powerful. If you look around today, the language of universalism is proclaimed by the United States, which is the superpower – one would like to think it's the last superpower. Without wishing to preach to the converted, it does seem to me that Ireland could play an important role in all of this, because Ireland has a colonial past. Although European, it is different from Europe, noticeably from Continental Europe, and it would seem to me that instead of the submergence of various European countries like Ireland into the general European personality, highlighting the differences would be very important for dealing precisely with other parts of the colonial world. For instance, it seems to me that Ireland has a very special role to play, not only in Palestine, by virtue of the divisions in this country, but also in South Africa. Highlighting differences and allowing that to engage Europe's others in a kind of exchange could be very important in breaking the world into great cultural camps, which in the end become armed camps. I am very suspicious of the kind of universalism that is sometimes talked about.

RK *But would you retain some hope that we can in the Western world, and in Europe in particular, overcome the traditional antagonism between 'them' and 'us'? Do you see the possibility of some kind of solidarity being created between those in Europe struggling for basic liberties and rights, and those within the Arab world who are doing exactly the same thing?*

ES Yes, I think that is the hope, precisely that. It *is* a common struggle. But even more important than that, what struck me the most about the Gulf War and about the behaviour of the Iraqis and even the response of Palestinians, was that this was a war of decrepit or diseased nationalism. I think the great problem is the whole issue of national identity, or what I would call the *politics of identity* – the feeling that everything you do has to be legitimated by, or to pass through the filter of, your national identity, which in most instances is a complete fiction, as we all know. I mean, an identity that says all Arabs are homogeneously the same and against all Westerners who are all the same. There are many Westerners; there are many Arabs. I think the principal role of the intellectual at this point is to break up these large, national, cultural, trans-cultural identities.

RK *Arab nationalism and Euro-nationalism?*

ES Yes. There is an Arab people, there is an Arab nation. It doesn't need defence, we know that. But what we need is to reclaim it from the rhetoric of nationalism which has been hijacked by regimes in the Arab world. You tell me what the Saudi Arabian regime, or the Syrian government, or the Egyptian government has to do with Arab nationalism. I tell you, zero, nothing. They are in the business of *using* Arab nationalism. Or take their defence of Palestine. They betrayed the Intifada, they did nothing for it. And they used the notion, not only of a national identity but of a beleaguered national identity which produces the national security state, the repressive apparatus, the secret police, the army, as instruments of repression. The same in Israel. The same in the United States. Can anyone persuade me that what the United States was fighting in the Gulf was an aggression that threatened the United States? Does security enter into it? That's total nonsense. But the resurgent American identity needed and used the security issue. What about the real struggle for freedoms? Human freedoms which are central – freedom of expression, freedom of assembly, of opinion, and so on. And political freedoms. Europe and the United States underwrite the denial of democratic freedoms for an entire nation, the Palestinians. That's a scandal. But you have to get beyond the politics of identity to be able to talk about these things.

RK *Are you then advocating a movement beyond the rival nationalisms of the Arab world on the one hand, and of Europe on the other hand? And do you see a danger of a relapse into nationalism in Europe that would be a mirror-image for a similar occurrence in the Arab world?*

ES I think that's obviously the great trap. What I would prefer to see is a Europe that is more aware, for example, of its colonial history. In other words, not to simply say we've superseded that, we're something else now. Your history as Europeans is also a colonial history; and North Africa, for example, has to be dealt with as a fact that informs your present behaviour and informs your relationship with these former colonised cultures.

RK *Do you mean acknowledging also the immigrants who are a part of us?*

ES There has to be an understanding, finally, that there is no political or national grouping that is homogeneous. Everything we are talking about is mixed, we deal in a world of interdependent, mongrelised societies. They are hybrids, they are impure.

RK *Which is a strength and a virtue.*

ES To me it's a virtue. What you're beginning to see now is a rhetoric of purification. I'm talking about the Far Right, let's say, in France, Le Pen. The idea that Europe is for the Europeans, you're beginning to hear it now. On one level, of course, it's fighting off the United States, and also Japan. Look at the rhetoric of Japan-bashing. The fundamental question is education. Most systems of education today, I believe, are still nationalist, that is to say, they promote the authority of the national identity in an idealised way and suggest that it is incapable of any criticism, that it is virtue incarnate. There is nothing that lays the seed of conflict in the future more than what we educate our children and students in the universities to believe about themselves.

RK *Would you advocate multi-culturalism, that we should read the texts of other traditions as well as the great Western texts?*

ES I think so. Take America, for example. There has been a tremendous debate recently about the figure of Columbus. The figure of Columbus itself is a highly controversial one, but he has been domesticated, sanitised into this wonderful hero who discovered America, whereas, in fact, he was a slave trader, he was a colonial conqueror, he was very much in the tradition of the *conquistador.* Now, which is better, to prettify and sanitise or to admit the truth? And there is this ridiculous idea that if you don't do this inventing of tradition, which will produce a hero figure, who is basically a conqueror – you threaten the fabric of society. I say just the opposite – the fabric of society, particularly American society, but it's also true of Europe, contains many different elements, and one has to recognise them. I think children are perfectly capable of understanding that. It's the adults who don't want to understand that for base reasons.

(Dublin, 1991)

NOAM CHOMSKY

The politics of language

NOAM CHOMSKY holds the Chair of Linguistics and Philosophy at the Massachusetts Institute of Technology. His work as both a linguist and political theorist ranks as one of the most remarkable intellectual achievements of the present era. Chomsky's books include *Cartesian Linguistics: A Chapter in the History of Rationalist Thought*; *Aspects of the Theory of Syntax*; *Language and Responsibility*; *On Power and Ideology*; *the Managua Lectures*; *Pirates and Emperors: International Terrorism in the Real World*; *Necessary Illusions: Thought Control in Democratic Societies*; *Deterring Democracy*; *Rethinking Camelot*.

Part one

RK *There is a lot of debate in Europe at present about where we should go from here. We seem to be moving towards a more federal arrangement, either of nation states or, as some people would argue, of regions. There is an argument that we have reached the end of the modern period of sovereign nation states with firm borders and boundaries, and that a model of shared sovereignty or post-sovereignty is really what we require, perhaps along libertarian lines of communities in association. Can you see any wisdom in this line of argument?*

NY The nation state is a highly artificial and destructive system. It's enough to look at the history of Europe. Europe has an extraordinarily bloody past, and a large part of it is the effect of the effort to institute such irrational and anti-human configurations as nation states. When Europe tried to export and expand them over the world, it led to a similarly bloody and destructive history, and it's still going on. What's happening in Europe seems to me to be an evolution of the nation state, but in two different and opposed directions – which one wins out will be of great consequence.

RK *One direction is up towards a centralised bureaucracy, the other is down towards regional devolution . . .*

NC Exactly. One movement is towards centralisation of power in a transnational executive authority which is essentially immune from popular influence, because nobody knows what's going on there. These quasi-governmental institutions, like the World Bank, the IMF, the G-7 executive, GATT, and so on, reflect the interests of transnational capital. If they have executive authority, free from the influence of parliamentary institutions, that is extremely dangerous in my opinion. On the other hand, you have the opposite development towards some kind of devolution, and regional autonomy. Now that is double-edged; it could be a healthy development. If regional autonomy is based on hatred of the guy across the river, then it is ugly and unpleasant. If it is based on developing your own authentic culture and individuality and working towards federal arrangements *with* the guy across the river, that would be very healthy.

RK *You have always promoted a libertarian vision of local connection, of participatory democracy, of people joining together on particular issues and struggles, and working from the grassroots up rather than trying to find some global vision which would work from the top down. Do you think this model has implications for the current project to reconstruct a new Europe?*

NC This is a global vision. Take environmental issues, they're not local. They extend generations ahead. Ordinary people would be greatly concerned if they learned that because the West insists on debt-service from sub-Saharan Africa, half a million children are dying every year. People in Europe and the US don't want to think globally about such things. If they knew that they're killing 500,000 children a year, they wouldn't like it and they would do something about it. That's one of the reasons they're usually not told about it. But if they *are* told about it, that becomes a concern, and it's not local. It's just human. Also, when you talk about 'participatory democracy', I would drop the word 'participatory' – that's what democracy is. If democracy, in Europe or anywhere else, isn't meaningful participation in the management of one's affairs, it's nothing.

RK *But it has been replaced by so-called 'representative' democracy . . .*

NC It has been replaced by elite control democracy, not even representative democracy. There is a system *called* democracy, but the real idea behind it is that the population should be spectators. The population are already spectators and it's 'the men of best quality', in the old terms, who are chosen to run things.

RK *I still have a problem with this. If a vision is something global, as you point out, you can't separate out the global from the local, certainly not in the twentieth century. One can argue that* control *is global. And I think of one of your statements in the* Managua Lectures, *where you say the reason why political elites exist is not because bad people run government but because institutions run government. That seems to suggest that it's not good or bad presidents, or district justices, or whatever, who make decisions; it's a* system, *it's an* institution. *And that description of things, if it's true, seems to leave us, as individuals or groups, powerless before this faceless conspiracy of the system. Do you see the problem?*

NC It doesn't seem to me to be a logical problem. There is an institutional structure and as people try to introduce changes, that means first we will try to press the institutions to their limits, and there's a lot that can be done within the framework of existing institutions to democratise them, to make them more just, less oppressive, and so on. Take, for instance, debt-service in Africa, that could be stopped instantly within the framework of present Western institutions, and that would have enormous human value. The same with a lot of other things. On the other hand, it is perfectly true that if you go too far you are going to run up against the structure of institutional power and authority, and then the next move is to dissolve the institutions. They are human creations, they're not granted by nature. Feudalism could go and capitalist autocracy could go. And it must.

RK *And what would you like to see it being replaced by – anarchist socialism?*

NC Freedom and democracy, which means libertarian socialism. It means the adaptation of the old European Enlightenment vision to the current world. In fact, if you take even what's called 'classical liberalism', I think it's grossly misread. If you take the classical liberalism of Smith and von Humbolt, and other eighteenth-century libertarians, including Thomas Jefferson, and you translate it into a late industrial society, those very same principles lead to, in my view, libertarian socialism. In fact, just think: what were they talking about in the eighteenth century? Well, what they're saying is unresponsive power, unaccountable power is illegitimate; power has to be accountable. Now the power that they saw was the absolutist state and the feudal system, slavery, the church – these systems had to be dissolved. They didn't see other systems of power because they didn't exist. But in the nineteenth and twentieth centuries other systems of concentrated power developed which are basically fascist in their nature; that is, power is completely from the top and flows downward, nobody has anything to say about it, you can adapt to it, but you can't do anything about it – that's corporate capitalism. That's a system of absolutist, unaccountable power which has no moral justification, has all sorts of negative effects on all aspects of life, from the cultural to the social. Thomas Jefferson lived long enough to warn that the rise of 'banking institutions and moneyed incorporations' would lead to new forms of tyranny, on a scale he could not imagine 170 years ago. And the very doctrines that led to the overthrow of feudalism apply in this case: to call for the elimination of this tremendous centre of, by now, transnational power, and to place it under public control. Well, public control does not mean state ownership. It means the participation of communities and workers and others in controlling investment decisions, what happens in the workplace, and so on, as well as political decisions.

RK *Most people would think of the liberal European tradition, and its libertarian strand that you invoke, as one that protects individual liberties, and, for example, an unconditional right of the individual to free speech. On the other hand, people who invoke a more socialist or communitarian, collectivist notion of the good might say: well, individual rights to free speech, or to movement, have to be limited for the sake of the social good. How would you reconcile those two claims?*

NC Well, first of all, the classical liberals didn't really believe in freedom of speech. They had a very limited conception of freedom of speech. Take, for example, Thomas Jefferson – he didn't even believe in freedom of thought. During the American Revolution he called for punishment of what he called 'traitors in thought or deed', deed being speech, thought being what is in your mind. That is an extremely narrow conception of freedom of speech, and I think they were wrong about that. But their principles led to it. Freedom of thought ought to be unlimited; to control what people think is such an intrusion into their nature that it makes slavery look limited. Now, if you have freedom of thought, the question is, do you have freedom to articulate to others your thought?

RK *Or to* act *on it?*

NC Well, to act on it is a different question. Because when you act you do begin to infringe on other people's rights. But to think ought to be unlimited. Now, it's very hard to see how you can justify allowing people to think, but not allow them to express to others what they think – that's a tremendous infringement on rights.

RK *What about incitement to violence and hatred?*

NC Incitement is another story. There is a course that takes place from thought to articulation of thought, to participation in criminal acts. So, for example, there are some kinds of speech that nobody would say are protected; suppose you and I go into a store, and you have a gun and we're planning to rob it, and I tell you to shoot, and you shoot the owner. Well, that is speech, but nobody thinks that is protected. That happens to be an action which involves my voice, but it is participation in a criminal act. In my view, a plausible position is articulated by the English thinker Jeremy Bentham, namely speech should be free, articulation of thought should be free, up to participation in imminent criminal action. Now, that is not a precise standard, it is a sort of a principle; like any principle you try to work it out. But that seems to me to be a plausible standard. It means that many things will be articulated that people will feel insulted by and harmed by. But that is just part of allowing freedom. Any kind of freedom at all is going to involve actions that other people wouldn't like to see happen. Now, if we try to restrict that, we're going to really turn people into machines. If we want people to be human we have to permit freedom of speech which others may find injurious. At least up to the point of imminent criminal action. Now, you are right when you say that what was called 'socialism' as it evolved expressed different values, but that's because it just wasn't socialism in my view, just as what has been called 'democracy' is not democracy. Soviet tyranny called itself 'democratic' and 'socialist', one term as ludicrous as the other. Socialism has meant a lot of different things, and there has always been a libertarian strain to it – what's called the 'anarchist' tradition, which did call itself 'libertarian socialist', and which would never have accepted that the right of some community to be free from injury by speech is a right that can be preserved. It can't. You can't properly and justly prevent people from thinking, and hence from articulating what they think, as long as it is not part of something like criminal action. The Rushdie case I think is open and shut.

RK *Well, you're unequivocal on that. Let's take, therefore, a more complicated case. As you know, in Britain and Ireland we had for many years limitations on freedom of speech and access to the media for members of Sinn Fein and the IRA. The argument of those who introduced this legislation was that you could not allow people engaged in criminal or 'terrorist' activity to have access to the air-waves where they could justify their cause, or, by implication, incite and encourage others to bomb and to shoot. Where is the line to be drawn?*

NC Well, people who argue like that are expressing a fear that there's a justification, and they don't want that justification to be heard. I mean, if you don't think there's any justification for their acts, it costs you nothing to allow the proposed justification to be expressed. It's only if you think there may be a justification for their acts, and you don't like the acts, that you impose a ban. But then you are the fascist. I think that *acts* should be prevented; for example, a person shouldn't be allowed to get up on television and pronounce a coded message which informs a bomber to set off a bomb. But if the IRA says 'here's why we put the bomb there – here are our reasons', and if you want to block that, it could only be because you're afraid that the reasons will be convincing.

RK *But that's rational discussion, persuasion, and debate. What about somebody who stands up on television and says: 'Bomb the Brits!'*

NC If that's convincing, we want to deal with the problem of *why* it's convincing. We have a real problem there. First of all, you're not going to stop that sentiment by preventing the person speaking on television. If an irrational and violent sentiment like that is persuasive to people, there are reasons, and then you have to go after the reasons. You don't achieve anything by just preventing the expression of what people are evidently believing in their hearts. That kind of authoritarianism is not only ineffective, but unjust. A person should be allowed to say 'Bomb the Brits!', appealing to a background understanding that will make that communicate something that the person wants to communicate. It is the same principle that allows public figures to say on television 'Bomb the Iraqis' (or the Vietnamese, or the Serbs). That's a form of persuasion – it should be allowed, and indeed is allowed (in fact facilitated by the powerful when it suits them). If you don't want it to be persuasive, then go after the *cause* of the persuasiveness of that message.

RK *Let's take another, equally controversial example: the prohibition against schoolgirls wearing the veil in France. Muslims were told 'you now belong to the established system of French republican education and you are not allowed to act* differently *in our schools. If you come here you speak our language, you behave as we do'. Do you think in the libertarian society that you envisage people should be allowed to act differently in that way, symbolically or ritualistically?*

NC If a child of an Iranian family comes to a school where there is a school uniform, and wants to wear a veil, why not?

RK *Even though that veil is seen in the West as a symbol of the suppression of women?*

NC That's their right to decide. I am opposed to it, but I'm not God. People have to decide for themselves.

RK *You are opposed to the wearing of the veil?*

NC To the extent that it symbolises the suppression of women, yes, I'm opposed to it, like thousands of other things in social life that I can think of. But just to be opposed to it doesn't give me any authority to stop it. That's for people themselves to figure out.

RK *To take a more vexed example – the mutilation of women according to certain religious rites . . .*

NC That's terror.

RK *And you think at that stage there should be intervention to stop it?*

NC Well, you know 'intervention' is a funny word . . .

RK *But one has a right to morally condemn it?*

NC One certainly has a right to morally condemn it. When you get to the mutilation of women, that's like torture, and the question is, do you have a right to intervene to prevent torture. Well, at this point, as in many human situations, there are conflicts of rights and conflicts of principles. Morality isn't geometry. There are simply contradictions, and you have to work your way through conflicting situations. And it's sometimes not easy, but you just do it by some sort of intuitive morality. Torture should be stopped if there's a way of stopping it that does not cause even greater evil.

RK *Even if certain women, because of religious indoctrination, are* willing *victims of ritual mutilation?*

NC Or other forms of torture. I mean, people who are willing victims of torture shouldn't be punished for that. But you should try to act in such a way to induce them not to be subjected to torture. If people are willing to subject themselves to torture it's because of severe distortions of their nature which should be changed, just like malnutrition should.

RK *Talking of intervention, you have been one of the most vociferous critics of US intervention in foreign countries, going so far as to talk about international terrorism. Could you envisage any situation, whether in Europe in the Second World War or in Bosnia today, where the US would be morally right to intervene in order to save a community from fascism?*

NC First of all, the United States did not intervene in Europe to save anybody from fascism. The US was supporting Mussolini, they supported Hitler, they supported Japan. They intervened because the interests of domestic groups were harmed. Period. In fact, they moved very quickly to reintroduce something like fascism after the war. And throughout history, it is very hard to find examples of actual humanitarian or moral intervention. I can't think of any to tell you the truth. In modern history one which maybe came close to this standard was the Vietnamese invasion of Cambodia. It's not that the Vietnamese invaded for humanitarian reasons; they didn't. They invaded largely because of violent Khmer Rouge attacks against Vietnamese border villages, which the West would never have tolerated for a moment. But they invaded and they overthrew Pol Pot and they drove him out of the country, and that did stop an ongoing terror. But that intervention was universally condemned and the Vietnamese are still being punished for it by the United States, and that means Europe and most of the First World, which follows US orders. That is a case in history that probably comes closest to something that could be called humanitarian intervention, not by design but by consequence, and it's condemned.

RK *But is it not conceivable that the US might occasionally intervene for moral reasons, say sending in paratroopers to stop a concentration camp operating in Bosnia where Muslim women are being raped, mutilated, and tortured . . .*

NC Yes, I could imagine it, but you're starting with what is almost an entire contradiction. For the United States, or any other power under its current institutional structure, the idea of intervening for humanitarian reasons is very remote from reality. States are not moral agents. Their populations can press them to refrain from immoral acts – that's usually the most you can hope for. It's imaginable that they might press them to act in a moral way, and a case of the kind you're describing could happen. For example, Iran has offered to send troops to defend Bosnia, but the offer is not even considered, because of what we know about Iran. Only ideological fanatics would refuse to raise similar questions about ourselves, and if they are capable of minimal honesty, the answers will not be pretty. If we are thinking about 'humanitarian intervention', there are a lot of easier cases to think of. Take one really close to home for the US, Haiti – 800 miles away. The United States would not have to send in Marines to stop terror in Haiti, they could make a couple of phone calls to the commanding generals. They're not doing it. In the case of Indonesia, which has been carrying out a near-genocidal slaughter in Timor, it's unnecessary to send the RAF to bomb Jakarta. It's enough for British Aerospace to stop sending them arms. And in fact, all over the world there are all kinds of ways of acting, far short of intervention, that could be extremely helpful to huge numbers of people. Take the example I mentioned before, debt-service in Africa. Saving the lives of half a million children a year is not a small thing, and, according to UNESCO at least, that's one consequence of debt-service. Well, you know what that means? Some Western banks will have undetectably less profit – that's the only intervention that's required there. If we really look in the mirror and ask 'Can we act in humanitarian ways?', there are a lot of ways that we can do it, which will save huge numbers of people and be very benign, short of intervention. Now, when we raise the question, shall we intervene for humanitarian reasons in the face of this reality, we should have the honesty to recognise that we're not talking about humanitarian intervention, we're talking about something else. Going back to your case of Bosnian concentration camps: it's not to say that one shouldn't intervene there (maybe we should), but let's recognise the context in which we're making this decision, let's be honest with ourselves at least.

RK *So most of the humanitarian rhetoric issuing from Western or European socities has been deceitful, to put it mildly?*

NC The only thing I would question is 'most'. If you could think of anything that isn't I'd like to hear it.

RK *What about the humanitarian rhetoric of someone like Kennedy? In your* Managua Lectures *Kennedy doesn't come out as a very saintly figure. You argue that his administration was responsible for establishing the basic structure of death squads in El Salvador, supporting the military gangs in Guatemala, and the coup in Brazil, etc. What are the facts on Kennedy?*

Was it that he was a bad person? Or was it that he was just part of a bad administration?

NC Kennedy represented a certain sector of American life which is a sort of mixture of Leninist and corporate capitalist influences. If you read someone like Robert MacNamara, Kennedy's appointment to the Department of Defence, his statements are virtually Leninist. I've often paired them in writing. These are people who call themselves the 'action intellectuals', they are going to take command, whip people into the right directions, control the world because they're smart. They're terribly arrogant, not very bright, with a lot of power at their command. They are also closely linked to the corporate community and strong believers in state power. What comes out of that is what you would expect. If you take a look at the electoral campaign in which Kennedy won, the people around Kennedy were attacking Eisenhower because he was passive, quiescent, a wimp; he was letting the Russians get ahead of us, frittering away our resources on trivialities while the Russians were striding the globe in a 'monolithic ruthless conspiracy', as Kennedy called it. We had, therefore, to be strong, violent. We had to organise ourselves into a unified state that was going to act powerfully to overcome this global conquest. We were going to have 'grand designs' abroad. Kennedy's campaign was very much like the Reagan campaign against Carter. In fact, my strong suspicion is that the Reagan PR people simply mimicked the Kennedy campaign. The programmes were also similar: both came in and had a very substantial expansion of state power, including the military budget. The military budget in the United States means two things: on the one hand, it's the basis for Third World intervention, on the other, it's pump-priming for the domestic economy. That's the way you keep high-tech industry going. Domestically, the Kennedy administration introduced regressive fiscal measures with programmes that supported investors, and so on.

RK *But what about the Kennedys' civil rights legislation and the battle with the Mafia?*

NC Yes, Robert Kennedy went after the Mafia, but he went after them the same way he did when working under the McCarthy committee: in illegal, improper, and anti-civil libertarian ways. That administration was not a civil libertarian administration. The Civil Rights movement was going on at the time and they didn't like it.

RK *The* Ku Klux Klan *didn't like the Kennedys either, did they? They must have been doing something right!*

NC A lot of people didn't like them. As far as the Ku Klux Klan were concerned, they liked Johnson even less because Johnson pushed through the civil rights legislation that the Kennedy people only reluctantly talked about. The Kennedy administration invaded Cuba; it built up the military system; after the invasion of Cuba failed it launched a huge terrorist war against the Cubans of an unparalleled character. There had never been international terrorism like 'Operation Mongoose', the Kennedy terrorist operation against Cuba. It set the basis for what were later called the 'National Security States' in Latin America. Kennedy's people made a crucial decision, a historically important decision in 1962: they shifted the mission of the Latin American militaries, which the US controlled. They shifted it from 'hemispheric defence' to 'internal security'. A 'hemispheric defence' was a residue of the Second World War, the Germans coming, and so on. 'Internal security' is just a euphemism – it means war against your own population. And that shift to internal security for the Latin American military missions set in motion the neo-Nazi national security states, which swept the continent and introduced a plague of repression unheard of even in the bloody history of that continent. The biggest and most important one was in Brazil, where the coup actually took place under Johnson, but the basis for it had been laid under Kennedy. In Southeast Asia, the United States under Kennedy moved to bombing South Vietnam; he sent the US airforce to start bombing South Vietnamese villages. There were other elements too, but all in all, I always felt that he was one of the most dangerous figures in American history.

RK *So would you advise Irish people to remove the photograph of JFK that sits beside the Pope over the mantelpiece?*

NC I would advise taking down any picture of any authoritarian figure, meaning anyone who has had any position of privilege, because they all have ugly records or they wouldn't be there.

Part two

RK *In several of your books, whether on politics, philosophy, or linguistics, you argue that there is a specific quality of human nature which distinguishes us from animals and, indeed, from machines. What is this specific nature?*

NC That there is a specific nature does not seem in question; humans are radically different from any other living organism. For instance, they are the only living organisms with a history. Just in terms of proliferation they're incomparable. The only other large organisms that come close are those that humans cultivate like sheep or chickens, etc. Humans just behave totally differently; the language capacity, for example, is almost certainly unique to humans. Remarkably, there doesn't seem to be anything remotely similar or close to it in even very closely related organisms.

RK *Would you identify that as the most distinguishing feature – language?*

NC It's certainly a dramatically distinguishing feature but I suspect that at the root of it is something quite different and here we move into areas where not much is understood, so we are in a zone now of speculation and even hopes, rather than firm understanding. But there is a traditional view which seems to be plausible – at least it conforms to experience and understanding – that what differentiates humans in a fundamental way from the rest of the animal world, and obviously from machines, is the difference between causation of behaviour and appropriateness of behaviour. So if you have a machine, for example, and you arrange its parts in a particular fashion and you put it into particular environmental situations, what it does is *determined* – the machine has no choice about it. It could have a random element which says it does any arbitrary thing, but that's the same as being determined, it is a menial act. On the other hand, in traditional terminology, unlike machines, humans may be *inclined* to act in certain ways, or induced to act in certain ways, but they're not *compelled*.

RK *But are we born with this capacity – is it innate?*

NC It must be an innate capacity if it's true of us, that we're inclined, but not compelled; and certainly our experience indicates that this is the case. For example, you and I know that we are going to sit here and talk for a period of time, but we also know perfectly well that we could stand up and say 'this is nonsense, I'm going to go out and take a swim!' We could do that – the machine couldn't, except as a random act, irrelevant here. We know we have that capacity; we have the capacity to harm ourselves voluntarily if we choose, and so on. If that indeed is true of us, it has to be innate. I mean there's no way in which such a capacity can be acquired.

RK *But is it biologically predetermined?*

NC Well, it's part of our nature. To say it's biologically determined is just another way of saying it's part of our nature. 'Biologically determined' simply means how we're constituted. Now, how we're constituted may involve properties of which we have no knowledge.

RK *So is that another way of saying 'we are predetermined to be free'?*

NC If this is true, then that is correct. Incidentally, what it means to be free is not at all clear. If this traditional point of view is correct, then what we do is appropriate to situations – it's not some random incoherent action – it's appropriate to what's going on and to our internal state. But it is not *caused* by situations. Now that difference between being appropriate and being caused goes beyond our current understanding. Nobody can explain what that means. You can point to it; you can say 'here's a case of it – this is appropriate but uncaused'. But if you're asked to explain 'what do you mean by appropriate and uncaused', all you can do is point to other examples.

RK *So if we are predetermined it's not in terms of the environment, you would argue, or our society and training, it is, rather, in terms of certain predispositions to act in certain ways?*

NC It has to be. I mean, you can have a machine which has interactions with the same environment that we have, but it will not develop these properties. Just as you can raise a chimpanzee in a place where people are talking to each other and it's not going to speak English. Or similarly, you can raise a human in a bird's nest and it's not going to end up being a bird. What we become, in almost every respect, is determined by our intrinsic nature.

RK *But you have gone so far as to suggest that it's not just language or thought that is determined by a certain fundamental human nature, it is also our aesthetic and ethical sensitivity, our striving for justice and freedom – that this is something fundamental to our nature.*

NC Well, that's more a point of logic than a discovery. Let's take something that is considered uncontentious, like our physical shape – the fact that we have two ears instead of five, or two arms instead of two wings, or the fact that humans undergo puberty at a certain age, or even that they die at a certain age. Now, nobody really understands much about that. I mean, how a human germ cell goes through these processes is not at all understood, but we all take for granted that it is internally determined. So nobody assumes that you get arms rather than wings because of some special kind of nutrition that reaches the cell. Nobody assumes that you undergo puberty because you see other people doing it, or something like that. Without knowledge we take for granted that such developments are intrinsically determined in essence. Now there's a good reason for that, it's a reason having to do with the logic of the situation. A very complex and highly articulated state is achieved with very specific capacities. It's achieved in a, more or less, uniform fashion – that is, everyone does it and gets to it in a rather comparable state. For example, you and I have quite different experiences, but we can talk because we ended up in similar cognitive states somehow, and, in fact, all humans did wherever they are. Now, when a system of any kind passes through a long series of transitions, and ends up in a highly intricate state, you can study the environment, you can see what it is. Suppose that the environment has virtually no directive information, it has very limited directive information – nevertheless, this course of development still takes place. Well, there's only one possibility: it's coming from the inside. Then you have to decide *how* it's coming from the inside. Well, let's move to aesthetic judgement: people can make quite uniform and intricate aesthetic judgements, they can go through a course of experience in which they improve their aesthetic capacities. They don't go in random directions, they go in particular directions. They can enrich the experience, and study, for example, a new artistic genre and come to appreciate it. Not everyone's a creative artist, but normal people can appreciate creative art, and there are other configurations which they just don't ever appreciate. Now, we don't understand much about this, but the logic of the situation is the same as physical growth. If that happens, it must be that fundamentally it's coming from *inside*. And the same is true of moral judgement; I mean, we're constantly making moral judgements in new situations, we can't help it. In almost every aspect of our lives we're making decisions about what is right and wrong, what we should do and what we shouldn't do. Maybe we don't follow what we know is right; in fact very often we don't, but we know it, we can understand it, we can enter into moral discourse. If you and I have a disagreement about what's right, we don't have to beat each other up. We can enter into a discourse about it, and often find a core from which we can proceed. Now, that must be on the basis of something which is *internal* to us because we had no relevant instruction in this.

RK *Well, that sounds very logical and self-evident, and yet for the last two centuries there has been an onslaught on the very idea of a fundamental human nature. Whether it be empiricism, behaviourism, existentialism, or post-structuralism – the idea of a fundamental human nature – or to put it in your terms, the claim that 'man is fundamentally a creative searching self-perfecting being' – is interpreted by many as outdated Enlightenment optimism.*

NC It's outdated, like lots of correct ideas; it's not necessarily optimistic because our intrinsic nature may be destructive and evil.

RK *But you do say our nature is 'self-perfecting'?*

NC I think it is. I think, in fact, it's all these things. I mean, I think part of our nature is destructive and even self-destructive – you can look around the world and you can see plenty of examples of it. There are many capacities to our inner nature, and which of those capacities become realised will depend very heavily on environmental conditions. Just as whether we speak English or Chinese will depend on where we grew up, even though they're almost identical systems. Or how tall you are depends, in part at least, on the kind of nutrition you had. So what we are intrinsically is certainly shaped by the environment, but really in peripheral ways. I think these are truisms; they're just part of the logic of the situation. It's interesting that they're taken for granted in the case of visible physical growth. It's only when we turn to what makes the distinctively *human* aspects of our nature that these truisms are denied.

RK *Like freedom, language, and thought?*

NC Freedom, language, thought, moral judgement, aesthetic judgement, in all of these areas which are clearly and distinctively human – we don't find them in other organisms. In those areas the truisms are denied. Well there are a number of possible reasons for this: one reason is that there is something in our nature which makes us totally irrational when we deal with certain problems, in particular, questions of our own nature. It could be that part of our design is to be irrational about our own nature. That's not too surprising. In fact, one might imagine that's a biological truth. That would mean in a sense that people are fundamentally dualist. They're rational with regard to the natural world, but when they turn to their own nature they become totally irrational, mystical. That could be part of our design. I mean, if you look at a sunset, you may know all of relativity theory, but you still see the sun set, you can't help it. If you look at the moon near the horizon you see it bigger, you know it isn't, but no matter how much you know, it's still bigger. There are things which we cannot overcome about our nature, and a strong possibility, in fact, in my opinion, a likelihood, is that part of our nature is to be dualistic, and we just can't get out of it. Now, we can move ourselves outside of our nature. So, take the sun setting; though we see the sun setting, we can, through some other exercise of our imagination and reflective capacities, come to understand that it's not really setting, there's just two objects moving relative to one another – their positions are changing relative to one another.

RK *And you would encourage us to develop that understanding, to become more rational?*

NC If we want to understand ourselves, yes.

RK *Maybe you ruin the sunset if you understand how it works?*

NC I don't think so. Because you always react to the sunset from your own inner nature – however much you have enriched your understanding by viewing it from another perspective. To look at things from another perspective doesn't diminish the earlier perspectives.

RK *It doesn't mean 'you murder to dissect', as Wordsworth would say?*

NC No. Suppose you become immersed in Cubist art and you take a look at a French landscape, well you still see it the old way, but you see it more richly because you now see it through Cézanne's eyes too – that just enriches things. Similarly, when you look at the sunset through Einstein's eyes, it doesn't look less beautiful to you. Rather, you have a richer array of perspectives from which to appreciate it. Now I think we should try to understand ourselves in the same way. Maybe we can't get very far, but we should try. That's one possibility. Another I'm struck by is the fact that the people who develop dualist ideas are basically intellectuals. What's their social role? Well, their social role is usually social management of one kind or another – the management could be teaching or direction or politics or corporate managers, but the people we call intellectuals, the people who have the accumulating intellectual tradition in their hands are people who are generally in a directive role. Now when you are directing, it's satisfying to be able to feel that there is no moral barrier to your dominating other people; you're free to dominate them as you like.

RK *So this would be in conformity with a certain pernicious tendency towards social engineering and the production of social consent where you persuade people to behave in certain ways?*

NC If people have no fundamental human nature, then there's no barrier to social engineering, there's no moral barrier to it. So you can have Skinner's *Walden 2*, because there's no moral barrier to your moulding people in accordance with your will. By definition, the person who holds this view, is always good and has everybody's best interests at heart. Now, if the people have no intrinsic nature of their own, there is no moral barrier to the authority of intellectuals, to domination. On the other hand, if people have a fundamental nature, and if part of that nature is a need for and a right to freedom and independence, then the directive managerial role is an illegitimate interference with their rights, and that puts bounds on you, and in effect, restricts your own authority to command and dominate. It's obvious that people who accept the latter point of view will simply not be in domineering positions.

RK *I see the logic, yet I have a problem with it in the following respect: if this is true, why do not the mass majority resist by virtue of their human nature, and their desire for freedom and justice? Why do they not reject this indoctrination, this social management, or this engineering of consensus and consent? It is a question I have often raised while reading your books. There seems to be a sort of circle. On the one hand you're saying there is a freedom innate in us, and yet you're also saying there are these managerial classes, who for reasons of power and wealth and investment, are seeking to control us. You say things like – 'the United States is one of the most indoctrinated societies in the world', 'the free press in the United States serves propaganda interests', there's thought-control in operation, which conceals the truth (e.g. the concealing of the invasion of South Vietnam, or the Contra campaign in Nicaragua). Either we are pawns of a system and we are indoctrinated, or else we're not. But we can't be both, can we?*

NC Well, firstly, there are several facets to this. For one thing there is the question to what extent people succumb to external power. I think from the vantage point of the privileged sectors where we are, it looks as if they're succumbing, when in fact they are not. There are a lot of ways of resisting power and people find all kinds of ways of doing it (children in school, people on the streets, and so on). They may not be able to organise to overthrow authority or even be able to identify it very coherently, but it doesn't mean that they're not resisting it. A worker on a slow-down is resisting it, a child who finds a way not to obey some ridiculous instruction is resisting it. In fact, sometimes that resistance takes astonishing forms: take

Central America in the last ten years, popular organisations resisted extraordinary terror, violence, and slaughter. It reminds one of Rousseau's comments about complacent Europeans who have no right to talk about freedom, they do not understand what half-naked savages understand, and you can see that from their actions. There's certainly an attempt at indoctrination and there's a system of indoctrination, but the question of its success is another matter. I think it's generally the case that indoctrination is even more successful among the educated sectors. Take Vietnam as an example: to this day, despite all the indoctrination, which is uniform, about 70 per cent of the American population, when asked for an opinion on the war, say it was 'fundamentally wrong and immoral'. Now among educated sectors, virtually no one says that. If you try to find that position articulated anywhere in the spectrum of established expression, it's not there – nor was it ever there at the height of the anti-war movement. That's not the only case. The general public may be disorganised, uncontrolled, ineffective in their resistance, but they do resist. In his *Principles of Government*, David Hume asked the question: How come people can be governed? He observes that force is always on the side of the governed, that the general public has force on their side. He says that's true in the most despotic regime as it is in the most free. You can't control people unless they agree to it. So how does it happen that people are willing to be governed? He replies that it must be that their *opinion* is controlled, and in relatively free societies, like his own at that time, it is true. I mean, the freer the society gets the more necessary it is to control people's opinion.

RK *It sounds as if what de Tocqueville called 'soft despotism', has in fact come to pass, and that it is not so much in the order of coercion (restraint of movement and so on), as of* opinion. *Yet that doesn't seem to tell the full story; Salman Rushdie was a victim of a death decree, but nobody in the US has issued a death sentence on you and you have said things which are just as subversive of your culture and society as Rushdie has of his?*

NC Well, Iran is not a society that is free – there you control people by force. The United States is free, more than Hume anticipated, and there the other centres of power just don't have the means to coerce. They do, therefore, in much more sophisticated ways try to control thought, and that doesn't involve assassination. They don't have the capacity, nor is it an efficient way. It involves other means, and among the educated sectors it certainly works – there's little doubt about that. Among the general public it is not at all clear that it works. I think that the method of control of people in a country like the United States is, in a broad brush-stroke, something like this: the more educated, the more indoctrinated you are – the more you are immersed in the system of propaganda. The less educated you are, the more isolated you are. So if you look at the general public they're isolated from one another, they're alone. Each person is alone in front of the television set and there is very little in the way of associations among them or co-operative endeavours, and so on. One of the striking things about the United States is that almost every constructive development – whether it's ecological or Third World solidarity – goes back to the churches. One of the reasons is that's all there is.

RK *Is there any kind of social opposition?*

NC There's a total breakdown of social connections and I think that is very consciously done. The public relations industry, which is huge, has been dedicated since the early part of the century to trying to mould people in a certain fashion, and that involves situation comedies on television and sporting events, amongst other things. The mould is very clear: you're supposed to be an isolated atom of consumption. The only value in your life is to gain more goods that you don't want. There's tremendous commitment to an artificial creation of wants. It is understood, and it has been understood for centuries, that we are trying to force on people things they don't want, because we have to create an environment in which they'll aspire to things they don't want. And there is to be nothing else in their lives; there's nothing like constructive work, there's nothing like solidarity with your neighbours. The only thing is maximising your own accumulation of goods – goods which may not improve your life.

RK *What is to be done? How does one escape from this dilemma? Can we work – in addition to the church work – to produce some kind of political-social vision where people can connect or reorganise again?*

NC I think we should understand exactly what the public relations industry understands.

RK *And what have they understood – that to control you have to isolate people?*

NC Yes, and to oppose such isolation, we should bring people together to form exactly those organisations the manufacturers of opinion are trying to destroy. US labour history is interesting in this respect – it's a very violent labour history, much unlike Europe. There were hundreds of workers being murdered, literally murdered by security forces in a period when European workers had already gained basic rights. There's been a big assault on unions since. Now there are reasons for this: unions, however corrupt they may be, are one of the few means by which relatively powerless people can pool their resources (which means not their money but their intellectual and emotional resources) and act in voluntary association to induce change. American business is highly class-conscious: it sees itself as fighting a vicious class war and it wants to contain this. Those who want to change the world should recognise these truths and try to rebuild and reconstruct and strengthen popular grassroots organisations, whether they are in the workplace or regional or through some other common interest, say feminist interest, environmental interest, or whatever it may be. And they should also expand their own moral sphere. After all we're responsible for future generations, we're responsible for hundreds of millions of people suffering throughout the world, and we *can* act in ways which will change the structure of power, dissolve it, and expand this sphere of justice and freedom.

(Dublin, 1993)

VÁCLAV HAVEL

Plays and politics

VÁCLAV HAVEL is one of Europe's foremost living playwrights and essayists. Sentenced to four and a half years' hard labour in his native Czechoslovakia for his involvement in the 'Charta 77' human rights movement, Havel went on to become president of his country in 1989. His plays include *Memorandum*; *Largo Desolato*; *Temptation* and *Slum Clearance*. His prose collections include *Living in Truth* and *Letters to Olga*.

VH Politicians deceive people when they offer them a complete recipe for human happiness, and maintain that only their political decisions and measures can make humans happy. Man is not only an object of political measures. Man is something more. Politics can offer only a limited number of things. It can provide and develop conditions under which people can lead a more dignified life; it can guarantee certain liberties. However it cannot guarantee an earthly paradise; it cannot promise people will be happy without having to move hand or foot. This is the border, the threshold where the ideal ends and utopia begins. Taking into account today's changes, our society should and must have certain ideals but cannot and must not substitute another utopia for the Communist one.

RK *We are talking about positive and negative ideas – about ideals and visions. In your country, the intellectual has had an important role. When one looks back at your history, you had men of ideas who were national heroes, for example Comenius, the educator; and Jan Hus, the humanist theologian; and then in the twentieth century your first president, Tomas Masaryk, was a philosopher – as was Jan Patočka, one of the founder members of Charta 77 (in which you also played a very central role). In one of your essays, 'Six asides on culture', you mention Patočka and say it's not an accident that this 'victim in the struggle for civil and human rights' in your country was also a thinker. What is this special Czech tradition of the intellectual? And do you think it an accident that the Czech people chose as president someone like you, who is a leading writer and intellectual?*

VH In my case, more than one reason led to my election. It is true, however, that intellectuals – writers, philosophers – have traditionally played a more significant and important role in both Czech and Slovak public life than they have played in other countries. Our nation, our society, has constantly been oppressed and endangered, its political rights always restricted – during the Austro-Hungarian Empire as well as in the Communist era. In these situations, in which civil and political or national rights are restricted, chances that professional politicians will mature are limited and intellectuals naturally take over. Who else should take over? Telling the truth under oppression is itself a political phenomenon and the tellers automatically become public figures. It was mostly intellectuals who represented the outspoken opposition in the Communist era. This is why those intellectuals who had been telling the truth about the system aloud for many years were given public office when the regime fell. They were not representatives of professional political parties. There are many people like me in the government and in the parliament. Of course, following the stabilisation of democracy, a new generation of professional politicians will come – and is already coming – into the political and public life of our country. The public role of intellectuals is likely to diminish. They will play the role of a mirror which reflects public life but they will not be the main actors.

RK *You were first and foremost a playwright, working in the theatre; and the theatre played quite a central role in the 'Velvet Revolution' in your country in 1989. You mentioned in one of your writings that each new work of theatre weakened the repressive regime. What is there about theatre in the Czech situation that proved so subversive and so revolutionary?*

VH This question has several aspects. Firstly, to follow up what I was saying earlier: art, culture and intellectuals play an increasingly political role in oppressive conditions. This is what happened in our country in the sixties and – subject to some changes – in the seventies and eighties. Theatres were centres of resistance, even if the resistance was limited because all theatres were marked by censorship. However, theatres were spiritual focal points, enclaves in which certain liberties flourished, most obviously in the sixties. Ever since the National Revival in the beginning of the nineteenth century, when performances in the Czech language had been helping to support national self-realisation, theatres have played an important role in our lives. Secondly, theatres played an important role in our revolution. They supported the rioting students immediately after the massacre. Scheduled performances were cancelled and theatres became public places where discussions were taking place and where, at a certain stage, the revolution was actually happening. The third aspect is more general and metaphysical: the theatrical, dramatic dimension of those changes in our country. The dramatic structure was here: acts, peripeteia, crises, etc. The features of various dramatic genres were here too: tragedy, comedy, absurd theatre, farce and (very markedly) a fairy-tale. The events had their actors. Singers also played key roles at mass meetings and manifestations. Changes in our country had theatrical and dramatic dimensions.

RK *You have written that you are against '-isms' and ideologies and for the development of an individual moral conscience. But how does one develop an individual moral conscience that remains open to some notion of a common social good and does not return to the old classical liberalism of each-person-for-him-or-herself? What is the moral basis or motivation behind this kind of conscience?*

VH The era of ideologies seems to have come to an end. I think that we are entering an era of thinking now. Ideological systems and doctrines either wore out and failed, like Marxism, or became a danger, a threat. The alternative is a future rehabilitation of the human subject – conscience and thought as such: the rehabilitation of thinking which originates in the human subject and is not transmissible by some system of precepts or dogmas. Regarding the connection with classical liberalism: the rehabilitation of the subject includes something which has been neglected in the nineteenth century. The era of liberalism was in love with science and technology and in this era the conception of man as a sovereign master of the world was born. When I speak about the rehabilitation of the subject or about an 'existential revolution', I really mean something more: the renaissance or revival of human responsibilities, of a relation between man and something mysterious which is more than man, some metaphysical assurance. When I speak of the re-establishment of the human subject, I do not have in mind 'Man' at the top of an existential pyramid, man who has no master and therefore can do as he pleases.

RK *In your 'Open letter to President Husak' in 1975, you write about an order without history, without culture and without morality – an order of tyranny and fear that has been imposed on your society. And you say to President Husak: 'How profound a moral impotence will the nation suffer tomorrow following the castration of its culture today?' Seventeen years later you are now sitting where President Husak once sat, here in Prague Castle. Do you feel that there has been some profound damage done to your nation during the post-war period of oppression; and if so, how does one repair it? How do you bring back a sense of culture, a sense of morality?*

VH First of all, let me say that when President Husak was sitting here, the social circumstances were totally different from those of today. I am not a representative of an authoritative, totalitarian regime. In my office, I have been trying with the help of others to rebuild Czech democracy. Of course I feel that my duty is to keep stressing certain moral values – to lay the emphasis on the spiritual dimension of human life and to face the danger of commercialisation which comes hand in hand with the market economy: to emphasise constantly that consumer society alone cannot secure human happiness and the future of humankind. This has always been and still is my opinion.

RK *You have spoken about the possibility of a partyless politics, and even an 'anti-political politics'. But today you as president have a critical and central role in politics. How is it possible to reconcile your role as writer – where you say 'the primary function is to live within truth' – and your political function as leader of the land? Is it possible to combine the two? Or would you like, as soon as possible, to do yourself out of a job?*

VH I was given this job by fate. As long as I hold this office, I must try to work in harmony with myself, to live up to and act according to my convictions. I cannot put aside my identity and become somebody else in the course of my term as president. Even today I fight a battle against party dictatorship. Of course I do not oppose the existence of political parties. That would be nonsense. Pluralistic democracy cannot exist without the existence of political parties. I am against the dictatorship of a party, against the secret power of party secretariats, against the type of situation in which deputies have more duties to bureaucracies and secretariats than to the people who voted for them. I keep fighting unsuccessfully for a different electoral system in our country. I think that the personal guarantee must be stressed. Party anonymity leads to collective irresponsibility.

RK *Mikhail Gorbachev claimed that the revolutionary changes in Eastern Europe and in the Soviet Union could not have taken place if it was not for the Pope. Do you think that religion and religious sensibility have played a positive role in these changes? After all when you were elected you quoted Masaryk's famous phrase, 'Jesus not Caesar'.*

VH The renaissance of faith has played a certain role in recent changes, as well as the fact that it was Karol Wojtyla who became Pope. However, I do not think this was the chief and single reason for those big changes in our part of the world. The totalitarian system wore out, rotted from within. People were unable to bear the continuous pressure of the system any more, rioting and resistance started. The system was leading to crises in every aspect of our society. I do not think that the Pope or Gorbachev were the sole figures responsible for all these changes. Gorbachev played a very important role in the process and had he not become the General Secretary of the Communist Party in the Soviet Union, the changes would probably have come later and would have been different, but they were bound to come sooner or later. Perestroika obviously played a key role but the changes did not come as a result of perestroika alone. They were due to more than one reason.

RK *In Europe at the moment – particularly the ex-Soviet bloc and Yugoslavia – there seems to be a slide or degeneration into separatist nationalist movements. Is there a danger that in Czechoslovakia today a similar movement towards separatist nationalism could destroy the possibility of a genuine federation?*

VH I do not know how the constitutional law will develop in our country. I do not even know if this country is going to be divided into two independent states, although I don't think it is likely. Many nations, and also the Slovak nation, are going through a certain process of emancipation. But I do not think that what has happened in some parts of the former Soviet Union or in Yugoslavia will happen here. There was never a war between Czechs and Slovaks, they have never fought against each other, there was never a time when one of them conquered the other nation. I cannot see why our country should be afflicted with such dramatic and violent conflict.

RK *Finally a question about Europe. You once spoke about the possibility of a European federation, based on the Council of Europe, that would include the Middle or Eastern European countries. What is your vision for Europe in the years to come?*

VH I cannot know exactly what course the European integration process will take. It depends on many people, governments, parliaments, geopolitical interests, etc. It is not something which I myself could plan. However, I have said publicly before that the idea of a united, confederate Europe is a good idea, that this is the path Europe should take and does take. It is difficult to say which institution will become the leading one. There are many international organisations in Europe: the Helsinki Process, the Council of Europe, the EC, NATO, etc. At this moment, it is difficult to tell what role each of them will play in the future or how these existing multinational organisations will be linked. The Helsinki Process could give a basic frame to the continuing integration, the Council of Europe could get the upper hand in the field of political culture and the setting of legal standards, while the EC remains the driving force of economic and political unification. I suppose that they will all be gradually linked closer together and Europe will hopefully become a more united continent, based on a unity of diversity.

(Prague, 1992)

Section B

LITERARY THINKERS

UMBERTO ECO

Chaosmos: the return of the Middle Ages

UMBERTO ECO is an Italian novelist and theorist. He is Professor of Semiotics at the University of Bologna and his books include *The Name of the Rose*; *Foucault's Pendulum*; *James Joyce and the Middle Ages*; *The Aesthetics of Thomas Aquinas* and *Faith in Fakes*.

RK *You have argued that the 'Dark Ages' is a much maligned period of European history. Why?*

UE We can speak of the Dark Ages in the sense that the population of Europe fell by twenty million. The situation was really horrible. The only flourishing civilisation was the Irish one, and that's not by chance. Those Irish monks went to civilise the continent. But immediately after the millennium, we cannot speak any longer of Dark Ages. You know that, about the tenth century, they discovered a new cultivation of beans, all those vegetable proteins. One historian called the tenth century 'the century full of beans'; it was an enormous revolution. Now, the whole of Europe started to be fed with vegetable proteins. A real, biological change. And the centuries immediately after the millennium were called the First Industrial Revolution, because in those three centuries, more or less before the Renaissance, there was a larger-scale application of the windmills and the invention of the new collar for horses and for cattle. With the old collar, they were practically strangled. With the new one, on the chest, the force of the animal was four, five or six times greater. Then there was the invention of the posterior rudder. Until that time, ships had a lateral rudder and it was very difficult to move against the wind. With a back-moving rudder, the possibilities for shipping became enormous; the discovery of America by Columbus wouldn't have been possible without this technological innovation. And we can list many other miracles of discovery. So, it means that European culture,

European society, grew with the new feudalism and the new bourgeoisie, the birth of Italian and Flemish communes, the free cities, the invention of the bank, the invention of the cheque, of credit.

RK *In one of your essays, you actually talk about the return of the Middle Ages. Do you believe that there is some sort of cycle to history, and that we are now reliving some of the traumas of the Middle Ages?*

UE Well, in that essay I wanted to stress certain common elements in the sense in which our era is undoubtedly an era of transition, in a very accelerated way. It's enough to think of what happened in the last few years in Europe to understand the sense in which we are living in a new era of revolution. This is, as the Middle Ages was, an era of transition in which new forms, new social, technological, philosophical forms are invented. And at the time I wrote the essay I was also impressed by certain common patterns in the rise of terrorism: I saw the rise of groups like the Red Brigade and PLO etc. as a return of medieval millenariansm, informed by a sense of apocalypse and breakdown. The Atomic Age as a sort of reliving of the Middle Ages.

RK *If I could take an example from literature now – Joyce, somebody you have written much about, including your book,* James Joyce and the Middle Ages. *You seem to argue that Joyce represents a balance between a fidelity to the cosmic order of the Middle Ages (represented in particular by his fascination for Thomist aesthetics), and an avant-garde pioneering quality which you equate with the contingency and experimentation of modernity. Is there not a sense in which for you Joyce is an exemplar who combines a medieval aesthetic with a modern one?*

UE I think that Joyce is a paramount case of contrast and fusion, an incredible cocktail between those two aspects. They are present in his life in a Catholic milieu, the reading of St Thomas Aquinas, a deep understanding of it, and his interest in experimental literature, and this sort of destruction of language that he called in *Finnegans Wake* the 'abnihilation of the ethym'. Joyce's work, as well as his life, was an oscillation, or dialectic between opposites. Take *Ulysses*. In *Ulysses*, he destroys all the existing forms of narrative, destroys all the existing forms of language. In doing that, he has built from the structure of the Odyssey, but it could have been something else; it was this medieval idea of the cathedral-like structure, and without this structure he would have been unable to undertake his work of disruption, destruction, decomposition. I think that this dialectic is present in every author, but in Joyce it was especially evident and openly confessed by the author himself – the nostalgia for order and taste for adventure, the necessity of using order as a disruptive machine. That's absolutely new and Joycean.

RK *So, you would argue that there is a dialectic between the nostalgia for a medieval order and a modern sense of chaos in Joyce?*

UE Well, I chose as a subtitle of my book, *Chaosmos*, a word invented by Joyce in which you have this sandwich between *cosmos*, which means organised structure, and chaos. Obviously, an author who has invented the word *chaosmos* was a little obsessed by this possibility of creative opposition.

RK *I'm reminded here of an example from your novel,* The Name of the Rose, *where the hero, the monk, is wandering through the labyrinth of the library, and he comes across a forbidden section where books on comedy have been hidden away. The point seems to be that while the Western tradition, and the Western church in particular, allowed Aristotle's teachings on tragedy, it censored Aristotle's writings on comedy; and in this secret section of the library, you also have a series of commentaries by learned Gaelic monks full of the paraphernalia of the Book of Kells – humour and mischief, contradiction and conflict. Are you making a point here about a certain Irish openness to contradiction and humour?*

UE You know, the Middle Ages was a serious age, because it was an age of faith and such things, so that the subject-matter of every discourse was God. It had to be serious. But since it had also a great sense of humour, it was also an age of carnival and popular licence. One only has to read Chaucer or Boccaccio to understand that they were not as virtuous as it seems. They tried to exploit this. The margins. There is a form of decorative art called marginalia. The texts were dealing with divine martyrs, and the margins were a sort of amusement, inventing, quoting from fairy-tales, from popular legends. What happened with the Irish medieval culture was that *marginalia* became *centralia*. The Book of Kells is made only of marginalia, and that is the way in which Irish culture was already Joycean at that medieval moment, trying to introduce extraneous elements, to disturb the order of things, to find a different order.

RK *You've argued that* Finnegans Wake *recounts the quest for a universal language – or to be more accurate, a parody of the old traditional quest for an original tongue, some kind of alphabet that would pre-exist Babel and the division into multiple tongues that today make up our polyglot civilisation.*

Now, your point seems to be that there is no such thing as a return to a time before Babel, that we live in a post-Babellic age, to use your phrase, where it's the very multiplicity, plurality, confusedness, and complexity of languages, that makes us what we are and is perhaps our greatest virtue.

UE Well, the story is the following. For years I've been working on this extraordinary episode in the history of European civilisation – the quest for a perfect language. Before the birth of Europe, there was not such a preoccupation, because the Greek civilisation, or the Latin civilisation, had their own language, which was considered the right one, and all the rest was considered barbarian. (The term 'barbarian' originally meant stutterer, people unable to speak, without a language.) As soon as Europe discovered the plurality of new languages, they started dreaming of some kind of universal language. There were two options. One, to go back before the confusion of the Tower of Babel where, according to Genesis 11, God confused language. Before, there was a single perfect language. And so there is in European history this effort to return to the purity of the original Hebrew, or another pre-Hebrew language, the one used by God to speak to Adam. And the other attempt was, on the contrary, to build up a new language that would allegedly follow the rules of universal reason – a language that could be spoken by everybody. Both were attempts to heal the wound of Babel. But there are, in this history, other such efforts. I discovered recently, probably one of the first texts about the story of Babel is an Irish drama of the seventh century in which it is told that the Gaelic language, invented by seventy-two wise men, instead of trying to go back before Babel or to eliminate the plurality of the other languages, tried to pick up the best from every language to create an alternative language – Gaelic. This mythical idea seems to me very similar to the idea of Joyce, who dreamed all his life of an alternative poetical language – *Finnegans Wake* is a proof of it. He did not try to invent a new one, or to rediscover an old one. *Finnegans Wake* is not written in English, it is a sort of polyglot construction in which every possible type of language is contributing to a new kind of discourse. What is the meaning of this metaphor – which is a metaphor, obviously, because it's impossible to think of a future Europe speaking in Finneganese? It is probably that the future of Europe is not to be seen as a development under the standard of a unique language, such as Esperanto, but as a sort of acceptance of a civilisation made of various languages. In Europe something different can happen, unlike what happened in the United States where the unification was made under the heading of a single language.

RK *You mean English?*

UE Yes. There were French-speaking people, German-speaking people, Dutch-speaking people, and all of that, but English became the unifying tongue in America. In Europe, we are facing more and more a fragmentation of languages. Look at what is happening in Yugoslavia. Or in the former Soviet empire. Lithuania, Estonia and Croatia are becoming again official entities. If today we could think of a Europe with three, four, five languages, the Europe of tomorrow would have tens of different languages, each of them recognised in their own autonomy and dignity. And, so, the future of Europe is probably to acquire a sort of polylingual attitude. And there is in the universities, at present, an interesting prefiguration of this. It is the Erasmus project. I have always said that the most important feature of the Erasmus project is the sexual one. Because, what does it mean if every student is supposed in the future to spend one year at least in another country? It means a lot of mixed marriages. It means that the next generation will be largely bilingual, with a father and mother from different countries. That's the best chance for Europe.

RK *So, you're really talking about exchange, inter-change, confusion in the best sense of the word. It reminds me of something that Brian Friel, one of our Irish playwrights, once said in his play* Translations, *that confusion is not an ignoble condition.*

UE No. It's the original condition of the cosmos. Before the Big Bang there was a great order, and a great peace. The Big Bang was the beginning of the confusion in which we live.

RK *But isn't there actually a stronger claim in what you're saying. I'm thinking of your argument that if God spoke to Adam he spoke in Finneganese.*

UE It was again a metaphor. But yes, the idea of a perfect language is a utopia. If it is possible to think that evolution took place several times in the world in different places, it is also possible to think that language was born several times in several places. The idea of an ideal language is that there was first a speaking animal, then all the other languages derived from it. And so it was for centuries: they dreamt of Hebrew as the original one, and then of Indo-European, and so on. Humanity being a speaking species, it is probable that languages were plural from the beginning. And seeing that plurality is a natural condition, it would be artificial and inhuman to reduce this plurality to an impossible unity.

RK *To take this back again into the realm of Europe, aren't you really claiming that cultural contamination is a good thing, that we should be muddying the waters, mixing together different languages, different races, different nationalities, and that one of the great errors of Europe has been the attempt to fashion some kind of purity of culture or politics? Two indications of this might be, on the one hand, the tradition of the centralised nation state which suppresses its regional minorities and languages – in other words, refuses to acknowledge the existence of a plurality of cultures within; and on the other hand, the attempt to close the frontiers of Europe and see it as some kind of ethnocentric, privileged continent which seeks to deny all those influences from Asia, North Africa or the Americas, which have shaped us as we now are. So could it be said that your basic argument is for a Europe of open frontiers which would see the confusion of different identities and languages as something positive?*

UE I dislike the use of terms like 'should' or 'would' that imply will and intention. It is irrelevant what Europe wants or doesn't want. We are facing a migration comparable to the early Indo-European migrations, East to West, or the invasion of the Roman Empire by the Barbarians and the birth of the Roman–German kingdoms. We are not just facing a small problem of immigration from the Third World; if that were so, it would be a problem for the police, for the customs, to control. The new migration will radically change the face of Europe. In one hundred years Europe could be a coloured continent. That's another reason to be culturally, mentally ready to accept a multiplicity, to accept inter-breeding, to accept this confusion. Otherwise, it will be a complete failure.

RK *One thing that comes through in nearly all of your work – your fiction and your critical writing – is a wonderful sense of humour.*

UE I think that a sense of humour is a healing quality in every culture. When there is a total absence of humour, we have Nazism. Hitler was unable to laugh. It's not only a European problem. I think that there is in humour, in a serious practice of humour, a religious effect. We are small creatures, we need not take ourselves too seriously.

(Dublin, 1991)

GEORGE STEINER

Culture: the price you pay

GEORGE STEINER is internationally known for his writings on European literature, language and culture. He has held Chairs at the Universities of Cambridge and Geneva, and his books include *Real Presences*; *Language and Silence*; *After Babel*; *Tolstoy or Dostoevsky* and *Proofs and Three Parables*.

RK *Do you believe that there is such a thing as the 'whole mind of Europe'?*

GS I believe that there is in the history of Europe a very strong central tradition, which is by no means an easy one to live with. It is that of the Roman Empire meeting Christianity. Our Europe is still to an astonishing degree, after all the crises and changes, that Christian Roman Empire. Virgil was taken to be, rightly or wrongly, the prophet of this Empire, and Dante the great incarnation. It is very striking that when General de Gaulle, who really used to think hard about these things, was interviewed and asked: 'Are there three or four authors who are Europe to you?' he said immediately, without hesitating, 'Of course, Dante, Goethe, Chateaubriand'. The astonished interviewer, having fallen like an elephant into the pit, said, 'What, Monsieur? No Shakespeare?' And the icy smile came, 'You asked me about "Europe"'. In that joke there is a deep Roman Christian truth.

RK *Do you believe in de Gaulle's notion of a great Europe extending from the Atlantic to the Urals, as the slogan goes?*

GS Let me answer honestly, not to make a joke, but out of deep conviction: if you draw a line from Porto in western Portugal to Leningrad, but certainly *not* Moscow, you can go to something called a coffee-house, with newspapers from all over Europe, you can play chess, play dominoes, you can sit all day for the price of a cup of coffee or a glass of wine, talk, read, work. Moscow, which is the beginning of Asia, has never had a coffee-house. This peculiar space – of discourse, of shared leisure, of shared exchange of disagreements – by which I mean the coffee-house, does define a very peculiar historical space roughly from western Portugal to that line which runs south from Leningrad to Kiev and Odessa. But not east of it and not very far north.

RK *This culture of the coffee-house you speak of would appear to be located only in certain European cities?*

GS Yes. The shared culture we have is the culture of the *cities*. I mean, it strikes me that Europe is essentially a constellation of cities which no other place on earth, no other civilisation, not even the United States, has ever known. When you come to think of the Muslim cities, for instance, they are all holy shrines. They are tied to religion, with the results we know. When you come to think of American cities, they look to me, except for a few of them, like settlements, just put there on the large wide expanses, plains and so on, with no heart, with no core in them, and everybody living in the suburbs and so on, and the city just being the sky line. But when you come to Europe, what strikes you immediately is the great diversity of all the cities, each one with its historical moment of grandeur, its historical past being engraved in stone and there to be admired. And, therefore, this is our sharing, this is what we have in common. We all of us have developed and evolved from the cities, from the Italian cities and from the Flemish cities.

RK *But couldn't one object that it is precisely the European cities that are quintessentially national – Paris as the epitome of France, London the epitome of England, Dublin the epitome of Ireland, Rome the epitome of Italy – that these are expressions of nation states, not of some pan-European culture?*

GS Paris is the epitome of a national city. But I would say that Paris is an exception. My theory is that France, and Paris as representative of France, are exceptions in Europe, and the French will be a long time becoming aware of that; they will probably have to change their ambitions and to rethink their nation, their sense of nationality, in order to adjust to the new European demands. But as soon as you mention Rome, I start smiling, because immediately I think of Venice and Milan, which are as diverse as possible, as different as possible from Rome, and which opposed themselves in the first place to Rome. What about Florence as well? What is now happening is that cities are re-emerging, as it were, taking over from nations, and entering some sort of competition; I personally think this is good, quite sound and healthy, because it's going to displace national competition, which was so cruelly messy and bloody.

RK *So what do you make of all the recent talk about a 'Europe of regions' – of the argument that, as we enter a more united Europe, some would even go as far as to say a United States of Europe, we need a counterbalancing movement of devolution and a decentralisation from the centre back to the regions? Can a unified Europe also be a Europe of differences?*

GS Differences and diversities, yes. I love every dialect, I'm passionate. I eat languages like *hors d'oeuvres*. I just hate uniformity. In Switzerland, where I live and teach much of the year, blindfolded, you can say within ten kilometres where you are by the accent, the smell, almost the pace of the human beings you are hearing walking by you. But careful. Much of regionalism has a cruel, dark atavism. It lives by hatred: Fleming against Walloon, the Basque situation, the Irish: the bombs in the pocket of the local, small, agricultural fanatical movement. Regions do tend too often to define themselves, not by remembering in joy, but in hatred. And I think we have to be very, very careful lest that come back and that flame burn again.

RK *It seems to me that the Europe you champion is a Europe of high literacy, which lasted for so many hundred years, by your definition. It seems to be, in fact, a rather elitist concept of Europe: confined to the coffee-houses where intellectuals talk to each other; confined to universities, to reading rooms. But one could argue that this is not something shared by the great majority of people, and indeed, that your elite notion of culture is now coming under threat. Do you see any way in which your Europe of high literacy can be preserved today?*

GS You are quite right about the threat to this notion, and I think we could define it in very honourable terms. There is very great anger and bitterness from human beings who have felt left out, who were never elected to the club, and that anger and bitterness is increasing all around us. There is, I hope, among those of us who have been privileged, and very lucky to be in the club, some severe self-questioning: we must ask ourselves what the price for this privilege of discourse was. It did not prevent the collapse of European civilisation into ultimate barbarity: it did not prevent savagery. Instead, it may even have abetted it. We are really very vulnerable. And the question is, are we going to find something better than Disneyland?

Twenty-eight or thirty miles from Paris, there is a Disneyland, the second largest in the world, and it will be followed by other amusement parks. Apparently, Russia is now equally eager to get in on this. I look on this with despair. And yet you may ask me, do I have something better to offer? What am I going to do for human beings who don't think that reading Kant, or Joyce, or Goethe, is the be-all and the end-all of their lives, and who, nevertheless, want more leisure, want more elbow-room for sensibility? That is probably the most difficult question of all, and in a funny way, people like us, privileged intellectuals, have almost disqualified ourselves from answering it.

RK *There is of course the opposing argument, which would hold that the electronic media of television and radio have actually made the cherished works of European culture – Shakespeare, the great operas, the great concertos – more accessible to people, because on their Saturday or Sunday nights, they now have an opportunity to tune into these classic works, and have access to them in a way they never could have had before.*

GS This would be the optimistic point of view. It would depend on whether, having enjoyed the television programme, you might then like to buy the book, or read it to your children, or want to see the play you've liked in a living theatre. As you know better than I, this is one of the most vexed topics. Is it happening? Is there, what they call, carry-over or spill-over from the mass media? Some people argue that there is, without doubt, and indeed there have been classic books whose sales have rocketed after a television presentation. There is, unfortunately, a lot of evidence which goes the other way, indicating an inverse trend. The bad drives out the good gradually, and, if anything, it is the trash that is beginning to fascinate more and more. We have to guard against being both too pessimistic and too optimistic. McLuhan's idea that we knew what we were doing, doesn't seem to be quite accurate. We've out-guessed ourselves on some of it. I would not deny that certain human beings who, because of distance, economics or leisure, cannot get to concert halls let alone operas, have certainly been introduced to new possibilities. But can we follow this up? Can we convey these forms to them in a living mode? Unfortunately, as you know, in the British Isles, statistics show that an overwhelming number of theatres, music halls and serious film houses are closing and becoming bingo halls. If anything, television has driven out the alternative live forms.

RK *This is what you call the 'Culture of the Secondary' – parasitism, talk about talk, images of images, replacing the real presence of the works themselves. But is there any sense in which that real presence can survive in anything but a mystical, or sacramental, reverence for the unique work of art, something no longer really feasible today?*

GS Is it no longer feasible? Let's take the really ugly end of the stick. Historians will one day say that this culture went insane when it paid one hundred million pounds for a painting; when the whole world rivalled itself in auction for one Van Gogh, one Renoir, one Picasso. And you will say, what a vulgar and mysterious way of honouring great art. Of course it is. But it comes very near to deification. Let's not forget that half the great churches of the Renaissance in Europe were built by rich patrons, trying to eclipse their neighbours – built, in fact, for conspicuous, ostentatious consumption. So there is a queer, philistine craziness about very great icons of art which continues, it's also true, in the building of new museums, of new emporia. It's not quite clear yet that, in some kind of much crueller way, the worship is gone. There is some sort of complicated idolatry. But if I could do something about it, I would like to start at the most day-to-day level. Will mothers or fathers begin to read more again to their children? Sociologists give us some evidence on that. There seems to be a deep shock, particularly in the middle class, about the fact that the child has never heard its parents' voices reading to it, reading good books to it. We're beginning, perhaps, to go back to certain possibilities. I think we're in a stage of acute conflict and transition where on both sides of the ledger you can find evidence. But the picture is not all black. The most terrifying prospect would be that of the fragile structures of privacy and of leisure being broken down by starvation, by mass migration which could come from Eastern Europe, or by the breakdown of civil forms of organisation, legalism and economic exchange in some of the critical areas. If I had to choose some kind of insane dictatorship, it would be to try to bring back the little silence into our lives. The latest estimate is that about 87 per cent of adolescents cannot read without hearing a radio, a record-player, a cassette, a long-playing disc, or television in the background. That electronic noise has become the *sine qua non*, the condition, of any act of attempted attention. If that is true, then something is happening to the old cortex which we don't fully understand.

RK *This is what you call the 'Americanisation' of the planet, and indeed of Europe in particular, isn't it? And you do say, at one point in your recent book,* Real Presences, *that the American genius is the attempt to democratise eternity and domesticate excellence. Do you think we in Europe can face that kind of competition?*

GS The best of America, like the best of any culture, doesn't export very well. There are very great wines which spoil when you ship them to other countries. The best of America, which has a kind of largesse of generosity, of human experimental humour and relaxation, does not export well. What does export is McDonalds, Kentucky Fried Chicken, the comic book, and all the dreadful soap operas.

RK *So, you would say we get the worst.*

GS We are importing the worst. We have invested our passions in the worst.

RK *And would you support the German and French moves, particularly at a cultural level, to protect national languages and European culture from that onslaught by promoting native film-making, and publishing?*

GS It does not work. Walk the streets of Germany, see the presence of 'Franglais' in France, and you must recognise that the American language, as also in England, has been almost totally triumphant. With the exception of the Beatles, there has not been a major counter-statement with any kind of comparable explosive dynamic, in the English language. It's like Fairy Liquid – it comes over, it tides over, it deterges, it cleans, it purifies, it uniformises. It might go away. I see one hopeful alternative in northern Italy. There much of the best of America has been adopted – why should people not have laundromats, and proper clothes off the rack, and look better and feel better, and have decent shoes, and so on – but the double presence of socialism and Catholicism in Italy, and the tension between them, has preserved an enormously powerful sense of national and linguistic identity. In other countries, however, we find hardly any national self-consciousness left. If it tides over, we may be in for a hundred years, two hundred years, during which human beings will say, 'Oh, shut up with all your cultural talk, we want to live decently. We actually want to have an ice box'. And for a while, that's what we're going to try – happiness is a new idea in Europe. Suppose we're on a new threshold of domestic comfort and elbow-room, in which intellectual passions are not only curiously luxurious, but positively the enemy. That's why I think we should be studying more about what is wrongly called the Dark Ages, when small groups, particularly Irish monks, scholars, wanderers, lovers of poetry and scripture and of the classics, began copying texts by hand again, began founding libraries. We've been through difficult stages like this. I'm not at all pessimistic. I see a pendulum motion between a certain elitist rapture of excellence and the ordinary passion for just having a better day and night of it. One must be a sadistic, arrogant fool, ever to say to another human being, 'You have no right to live a bit better'. Of course they have that right.

RK *So, in defence of the American ideal, one could say that it did introduce a certain egalitarian hope for many human beings, and, indeed, perhaps also a culture of tolerance for diversity, for inclusion, for what we call the melting-pot.*

GS Very much so. It has not worked all that well in America. Ethnic problems are obstinate, resistant, intractable, beyond our hopes. That very great observer, the greatest we've ever had in America, de Tocqueville, in the nineteenth century, wrote that wholly prophetic sentence: 'Aristocracies create works in bronze, democracies in plaster'. This was his dictum of the American situation, to which the answer is, perhaps, 'that's the inevitable concomitant of an increase in humanity'. That is a very strong defence. My reserve is, I'm not in that business. I've given my life to teaching, to trying to say to a very small number of human beings, 'let's read Homer, and Virgil, and Dante, together. That's what life is about'. I may be wrong, but I can't fake it. And what horrifies me about the present climate is that some of my colleagues, some of those of the intellectual profession, want it both ways. That, I think, is a piece of cant which is becoming very expensive.

RK *Do you think in Europe we're much better? We have witnessed two World Wars this century based on the worst kinds of tribal nationalism, intolerance for the other, intolerance for diversity, which at least America has been able to accommodate with its notion of a pluralistic society. Also, in recent times, we have witnessed the resurgence of ethnic nationalism in Europe, which, some would say, augurs very badly for our immediate future. And we cannot forget, indeed, that if we are a continent and a civilisation that has produced great minds, many of those minds in our own century, such as Heidegger, Pound, de Man, Céline, proved to be very immoral people in their support for fascism. How does one answer that charge?*

GS One cannot answer it on the factual level, it is true. But you and I have taken a kind of oath of clarity. Doctors take the Hippocratic oath – if I'm going to sign that, I'm going to behave in a certain way for the rest of my life, whatever the circumstances. We have taken an oath, which is to try to transmit excellence, to try to transmit beauty, to try to transmit form. It often seems to come a little out of the corner of hell. That is a very central truth and enigma. But I can't fake it. A world without the figures you've mentioned, a world without the great classics, a world without the great paintings and music, would to me, if not to others, be an ash-heap. That is not to defend the Manichaean claim about the double, the blackness being a constant part of every great creation. Saints don't need to write poems. Illiterate people don't write poems, or very rarely. The cultivation of the highest powers of expression and thought does seem to go along very often with a real political inhumanity. It would be wonderful if these people were nice. They aren't. But you and I write books about them. We live by what they teach us. We live by the joy, the worry, the anguish they give us and, sorry, we're in a bit of a trap there. And I think one can be honest about the trap, not pretend that human love, egalitarian justice, liberal dispensations, are very great creators of absolutely first-class work. They aren't.

RK *This touches on one of the central concerns of your writing – the notion of answerability as an aesthetic openness to the text, to the otherness of the text, a certain mode of concentration, attention, vigilance, and there seems to be built into that word answerability, being responsible* to *the text, an element also of being responsible* for *the text, and by implication, for others. Now, this seems to me to be quite problematic – the claim that an aesthetic answerability to great works of art will lead, logically and emotionally, to a sense of* moral *responsibility. Yet the facts are otherwise. Very answerable people, in terms of artistic work, have been very morally suspect. How do you explain that contradiction?*

GS Since we have so little time, let me try to answer you in two very simple ways. And the hardest thing in the world is to try to be simple on problems like this. Very roughly, Thomas Jefferson, Matthew Arnold (still a great teacher), F. R. Leavis, really believed that if you read better, you would vote better and treat other human beings better. I am simplifying, of course, but they made the link passionately, confidently – saying, you can't but be a finer human being, because your sensibility will be richer, more delicate, more apprehensive of the condition of others. In all my early work, when trying to show that people who could play Schubert like angels and read Goethe couldn't then torture other people in concentration camps, I came to the conviction that this was not demonstrable. On the contrary, as you've hinted before, sometimes, most awfully, the contrary prevails, and great readers are sadistic human beings or vote for fascism, and so on. Where is the bridge? In my more recent work, I've narrowed, I've tightened. That dubious figure and Titan among thinkers, Martin Heidegger, who will, I think, dominate much of culture in the future, as did Hegel and Plato – not politically very reassuring either, by the way – Heidegger said, look, the great poet, the great artist, he isn't *speaking*, he is being *spoken*. Something we can express by a little English pun, he's being 'bespoken'. Something is passing through him. Something much greater than any individual. The language is greater than the individual, it chooses certain vessels to contain its glory and its radiant pressure. I'm now speaking in opposition to what is the prevailing fashion, the prevailing way of teaching, which says that anybody can rearrange what he reads. I'm protesting desperately against the posters on every single wall, where the conductors' names are much larger than those of the composers. I'm protesting against the producer thinking he's greater than Shakespeare, or Molière, or Aristophanes, when he has everybody naked, or in rubber masks, or on spaceships, doing classic plays. I'm pleading for a certain courtesy in the face of really great art. Put quite simply, the great poet doesn't need me. I need him. There is the picture of Pushkin in which he said, 'Look, I'm Pushkin. I'll give you the mail to carry. See that it gets to the right delivery box'. I love to do that. I'm not pushed when I can't do it, but I love to carry the letters, which is one way of teaching, one way of being, as you and I are, writers, critics, elucidators. It's a very modest function, but it has become a dangerous and, I think, essentially a difficult one – to get people to *listen* at all, to *look* at all. But if you were to ask me does this carry the liberal, confident hope that you will then behave a little better in the street or in your home, I could not say I really have that hope.

RK *If we could return to the notion of the European mind. You mentioned earlier that the Dark Ages of Europe was a misnomer, and you seemed to imply that pre-Enlightenment Europe was a time when people had a single culture, and that with the* lingua franca *of Latin, they could move across borders and boundaries, and enter into some sort of social and political unity . . .*

GS You use the phrase '*lingua franca*'. There is no more deeper witticism or irony of history, and history is much wittier and more ironic than we are. *Lingua*, Latin. *Franca*, French. The two great moments when Europe thought it had a single language. And what is the *lingua franca* now? Anglo–American or American Creole or commercial American which organises the computers from Vladivostok to Madrid, the language every young scientist has to publish in, and has to know. I see a terrific contradiction, almost a trap. Can there be this new Europe when it speaks American? I don't know the answer, and I don't know anybody who has even begun to think this one through, because it's such a fierce challenge to all past history. What could be the basis for an answer? Could it be a revival of religion? Tricky one that. Fundamentalism is rampant again, not only in Islam, but also in Christianity. The Ukraine, which is one of the biggest nations on the globe, could again become a passionate Catholic wedge driven into the very heart of the Slavic world. Will we again have great religious wars? It's not excluded. One doesn't need to say this in Ireland. Is there another basis? I see only one. It is that of a shared body of active remembrance. When you visit Leningrad, whatever your feelings, you have twelve kilometres – it's scarcely imaginable – of cemeteries, of more than a million people who died of starvation and suffering in the siege. Right to the frontiers of Asia, which I tried to say are at Moscow, Europe shares a body of error, of remembered sorrow, of unspeakable self-destruction to the brink of suicide, in which there is perhaps also some hope. History might become the passport of shared identity, an actively lived and known history – and history is in many ways at the moment the dominant discipline of sensibility. We have lived through something so unspeakable. We were so close to the possibility of there being no Europe at all. And there's the re-entry of Spain – after forty years of Franco, we have one of the power-houses of liberal thought, art, philosophy and painting among us again, with its eagerness to join Europe, we're one of you: we too have lived that hideous history, of inquisition, and civil war, and Napoleon, and fascism. There are shared memories which an American does not share, which an Asiatic and an African does not share. They have their own immensely rich empires and evidences of the past tense.

Ours is probably the most urgent, and there is at least a chance the young today are crossing borders as even you and I never were able to do, that there is somewhere a decision that the past *has* to have borne some very fragile fruit. Otherwise, the darkness at the back of us becomes even less endurable.

RK *But the remembrance is of our collective errors as much as our collective achievements.*

GS There is a marvellous remark by the German poet Rilke, that at the end of a good marriage one has to become the loving guardian of the other's solitude. I would say that at the end of an historic crisis one must become the loving guardian of one's own mistakes.

(Dublin, 1991)

MARINA WARNER

A European woman's heritage

MARINA WARNER is a novelist and cultural historian. Her books include *Alone of All Her Sex: The Myth and Cult of the Virgin Mary*; *Joan of Arc: The Image of Female Heroism*; *Monuments and Maidens: The Allegory of Female Form*; *The Lost Father*; *Indigo* and *The Beast and the Blond*. Born of an Italian mother and English father, she has lived and lectured in several European countries and was recently appointed Tinbergen Professor at Erasmus University, Rotterdam.

RK *As a writer with an Italian mother and English father who has lived much of your life in different European countries, how do you now register your particular sense of Europe?*

MW Well, I think, in a way, you can belong to something imaginatively, which then displaces you from a particular locale. This is perhaps a helpful experience for a writer. Writing, to some extent, is connected with feeling apart, because of the writer's role of observer, or if you want to put it more rudely, as a sort of voyeur. I mean, there is a way in which you belong to something and distance yourself from it.

RK *You mean being a part of, and apart from, at the same time?*

MW Yes. Because I had this rather European, scattered, childhood, I did feel different. I was at schools abroad, but the nature of the immediate post-war world meant I was never in an indigenous school. I was always in a foreign school in the countries where we lived. I was with the French nuns in Egypt, in Cairo. And, in fact, I was with several different orders of nuns, because, at that stage, I was rather unruly. But they soon crushed my spirit, and I then became very obedient, and docile, and good, and remained in the same convent, when I finally returned to England. But when I came back, I was immediately sent to Coventry, because my English was so peculiar.

I had only learnt it from grown-ups, and I also knew a bit of Arabic in those days. I also spoke a sort of Belgian French, because we'd gone to Brussels, where I had gone to another French convent. There was a distinction, or snobbish distinction, and, of course, it was not a Flemish convent. Again, this sense that the stranger comes into a place but doesn't ever fully belong to that place. And then, a woman who marries an Englishman as my mother did, loses her native identity too to some extent. And my mother was of a generation where that was possibly something that was done more; but she never lost her mother tongue, and indeed is still a teacher of Italian in England. She did offer up her Italianness to my father's Englishness. She did abdicate it. We did not speak Italian at home. And we were meant to be English. She was sort of absorbed into that. But we never were successfully English, because of having lived abroad so long. I'm rather proud of it. I liked being different. I didn't mind being sent to Coventry. It made me feel special. I mean, I minded it as pain, because I was being laughed at, but I also felt special.

RK *And this experience of cultural migration – do you see that as something positive, both for your work and your imagination?*

MW Yes. But I've left out something rather important – which is of course the one thing that my mother did not abdicate, her Catholicism. If I had been a boy, I would have been brought up a Protestant, because my father would have insisted on his line of the family continuing in the Church of England. But he felt that it was perfectly all right that my mother gave her religion to her daughters, and indeed he thought that it was a very good religion for a girl. He thought that Catholicism would particularly foster the feminine virtues. And of course this was extremely influential upon me, and has conditioned so much of the enquiry in my work.

RK *Particularly* Alone of All Her Sex, *the study of the cult of the Virgin Mary.*

MW Yes. Mary was the most dominant, symbolic figure of my whole childhood, not just at home with my mother, who is a practising Catholic, but, of course, in the various convents. And I wanted in that book to go on a personal journey of understanding; I had no idea how far it would take me. I mean, one of the things about writing it was that it was exciting, that I began thinking I knew it because I had been surrounded by it, because I'd been wrapped in it, because the whole year was defined by Mary's feasts, the geography of the world consisted of apparitions, of places where she'd appeared in a vision. I could have put these little flags on the map . . .

RK *On the map of Europe.*

MW Yes, on the map of Europe. Blue was the colour of my childhood. So, I thought I knew it. And then when I started work, I found that I knew nothing. That it was this extraordinary, complex history of the interaction of really every aspect of society.

RK *So, you seem to be describing a double attitude to the theme of the Virgin Mary. On the one hand, a devotional attachment and sympathy of the heart that goes back to your Catholic childhood, and on the other hand a necessary critical detachment as a scholar who is looking historically at the development of these different stories and images and representations of Mary. But what does it tell you, as you look at that story developing, about Europe?*

MW I think there is an inter-reaction between images of Mary and changing patterns of thought about men and women. After all, so often the definition of what is the proper function of a woman gives us an idea, by extension, of what we think about men, and how men think about themselves because very often it is they who wish women to be obedient or keep their sexuality under a certain control.

RK *And in many respects those images were projections of a male mind or imagination.*

MW Yes. I think the most painful, the most devastating illumination came when I realised that the enchantment of Mary, this ideal figure of beauty and grace, was actually predicated on an idea of the human as sinful, and, in particular, of the ordinary woman as peculiarly and inevitably sinful in some way in her flesh itself. So that Mary, far from being as it were the perfect path on which we were all to walk, was actually in her own *hortus conclusus*, her own enclosed garden, and the door was sealed to that. This was a way of placing the rest of us *outside* in some great untended garden, feeling as if we were in some wilderness where things were spoiled.

RK *You were all Eves.*

MW Yes, we were all Eves. I did rebel against that very strongly. And I have modified my views. The Church, of course, itself has gone through enormous changes since I finished the book. It was published in 1976. It's quite a while ago, and there have been many upheavals, different popes, and also, to go back to the question of

Europe, many changes in Europe which have, interestingly enough, thrown Mary again into a very important symbolic position. In Poland, for example, with Our Lady of Czestochowa. She was a national figure-head for the Solidarity movement and now, of course, has become part of this return to a kind of theocracy in which people's private lives are being ordered by the new government. I think they were even considering banning contraception in Poland.

RK *So, would you suggest that it's not the images of the Virgin themselves that are either good or bad, but the narratives we tell about those images?*

MW Yes. And it's the different emphases that are given. For instance in the Orthodox Church the emphasis falls differently. Its beliefs and practices are now re-entering our Western Eurocentric consciousness because of greater access to Eastern European countries. And they are returning to religious practice very strongly.

RK *Bulgaria, Romania, Russia.*

MW Yes. The Orthodox Church has rather a different history of representations of the Madonna. There is much less emphasis on virginity and the taint of the flesh. There is a married clergy which, of course, makes a huge difference to ideas about sexuality in many of the Orthodox churches; and there is Mary's role as intercessor, which is also tremendously important in Ireland and a very merciful aspect of her persona.

RK *Mater Miseriocordiae.*

MW Yes, the Mother of Mercy, the intercessor, the mediator who stands between the wrath of God and weak humanity, interposes herself, and her milk, her Mother's milk, as it were, to turn away this just wrath. That aspect has always been very strong in the Greek and Russian Orthodox Church. They have this beautiful image of what is called the *maphorion*, which is her stole. They have it as an actual object which she holds in her hand in front of her. And this is the stole with which she covers and protects sinners.

RK *Couldn't one argue that there's another positive side to this introduction of the Christian image of the Mother, which is that it introduced into a Europe of multiple cultural differences some notion of universal identification whereby people could transcend ethnic diversities and aspire toward some common origin or goal?*

MW I think that Incarnational thought and theology in Catholicism provides one of its most nourishing aspects because it offers an affirmation of the human. But the difficulty has been – if we take, for example, Ireland or Italy – that the ultimate aim or purpose of woman has been defined as motherhood, maternity. There are some very shocking asides in the Church Fathers, saying things like, a man would have been a better helpmate for Adam in every way had it not been that God needed women for procreation. There's this idea that woman is only for childbearing. And, of course, the curse in the Garden of Eden is, 'In sorrow thou shalt bring forth children'. This becomes the woman's only legitimate role.

So, the transcendental aspects that you are quite rightly bringing in have been rather forgotten when it comes to Mary's motherhood. It's a highly restrictive definition of what women are for. And its cruelty is that it sets aside to some extent the life of the mind. By that I don't mean simply intellectuals. I mean the whole thinking life of a woman, which I would say – though I know this is a very problematic area – can transcend gender and sexuality. And then, it is very tough on the old, and one of the most difficult roles in history that women have lived is that of the old woman. I think that you can trace prejudices that gave rise to the great witchhunts: a whole variety of social phenomena, the numbers of old women who are homeless, prejudices about dependants, and the entire iconography of prostitution, raddled old hags, toothless old bags. There's almost a vocabulary of derision of this sort. But a lot of this really depends on there being no place for the transcendent wisdom of women after the childbearing age. I mean, the menopause is a kind of 'curse' because it seems, in our culture, to abolish the purpose of woman. All this is very cruel. It runs against the Incarnational message which should be at the centre of Christianity, which is that all of the flesh was created, God-given, and is therefore good. But this is not how it has been borne out in practice.

RK *Could I bring in here two doctrinal events in the Catholic Church and the Eastern Orthodox Church – the Assumption on the one hand, and, secondly, the Greek dogma of the divinisation of the Virgin Mother. Couldn't one say that these two doctrines in a sense admit the possibility of woman achieving transcendence, being taken up into the transcendental realm from which she was traditionally excluded?*

MW In order to express the idea that Mary had been born without original sin – conceived in the mind of God as his perfect daughter, and exempt from this stain in which all humanity was steeped – in order to represent that, interestingly enough, the Christian Churches did not resort to any of the traditional imagery of *Sophia*, which after all is a feminine word for wisdom in the Bible. No, they went for a late nineteenth-century image of a very young, nubile girl – curiously often rather an eroticised image, nubility and innocence being intertwined as a concept of virginity. But beyond that point, beyond the dewy, rosy, bare-footed young girl who, after all, is the Madonna, the female human being enters a womanhood which cannot be identified with this pure and immaculate condition. The carnality starts at puberty, so that the Immaculate Virgin must be representative of a time before that. And, then, the Assumption. This doctrine generally holds that Mary had died but had not been corrupted, that her body had been taken to Heaven and laid at the foot of the Tree of Life in Paradise, and that it had remained there incorrupt, which is a slightly different idea than that of her not dying; but most people think that the Assumption means that Mary, rather than dying, rose heavenwards, ascended into heaven, as Jesus did in his resurrected body, that this is a sort of female resurrection. And that, of course, also overturns the idea of mortality and carnality, and there is a kind of sympathetic magic idea that the corruption of the flesh is corruption of the spirit. Again we are back into this rather barbaric Platonism by which the exterior form is a mirror of the interior form. Of course one of the other components that crushes women in the Catholic cult of purity is its connection with beauty. It is in Catholic countries like Spain where you have this extraordinary paradox between the cult of women's purity – guardianship of daughters, seclusion of women, no divorce – and the afternoon procession when men watch women and comment on their physical attributes, you know, the *passeo* in Spain, the *passeggiata* in Italy: these are Mediterranean customs, which have grown up and flourished in Catholic cultures. The sexuality of woman is her identity. It is therefore watched, assessed, praised or despised.

RK *So the cult of the Virgin Mary is for you essentially negative in the European tradition?*

MW Perhaps I sound very critical, harsh, vehement. As my father used to say, 'Don't be so vehement. It's very unseemly in a woman'. But I have come, now, in my forties, to wish to cut my cloth from what I have been given. I used to want to go barefoot, you know. I used to want to strip myself of all this baggage that I'd been left as a bequest, as a Judaeo-Christian heritage. But now I want to take it up and assemble it differently. I want to have a pair of shoes, but I want to cut them differently.

RK *To re-interpret it, to retrieve what is valuable and enabling for women and leave aside what is not?*

MW Yes, and I'm not alone in that. I think it is work that a lot of women writers, and indeed some men writers, are doing. And it is comparable to the work of many poets and novelists, returning to old stories and finding why they happened. An example would be Toni Morrison's *Beloved*, a very savage story about a young mother who kills a child. But by the time you've read the book, because it's set in a period just after slavery with the most extraordinary upheavals and dangers and sufferings, you really understand this terrible infanticide. The great myths and narratives are precious stores of experience and even if – as in many European myths – they affirm the order of the masculine state against female wildness these stories can be retold, either to explain the past or perhaps to create a new future.

RK *Can we understand who we are as Europeans today without retelling those stories of our foundation cultures, the Judaeo-Christian, on the one hand, which you've treated in several of your books about Western representations of women, and, on the other hand, our Graeco-Roman tradition? Is it indispensable that at least some people engage in the retelling of those stories?*

MW There is a tension here. I think we have lost some stories, because we associate them with faith. Though the pagan gods lived on, they were set aside because they were seen to be connected with pagan religion. Again, we have a situation now in which many children don't know Bible stories, or indeed don't know the saints' lives. The Church itself has collaborated with this to some extent because in 1969 it swept away a lot of saints that I was brought up to know. Now, these stories are not told. So we have a gradual falling-off of a body of story. At the same time though, I don't want to become some kind of apostle for cultural Eurocentricity, because I do very much believe that it's dangerous to constantly hark back to the past. I abhor the kind of *revanchisme* you find in Le Pen or other extreme nationalist and neo-fascist movements. One must stand in the present. It's a question of remembering, of having the voices behind one but keeping one's face to the times.

RK *Isn't it curious how Le Pen marches with the Virgin Mary in one hand and Joan of Arc in the other?*

MW Well, Le Pen's attempt to retrieve Mary or Joan of Arc for his nefarious causes is not new in France. Joan of Arc has been identified with an extreme form of patriotism since the end of the last century. Even during the Dreyfus affair, she was identified with pure Frenchness, as opposed to 'adulterated' Jewish Frenchness and used as a figure-head for the anti-Dreyfus movement. At the time, in the 1880s and 1890s, there was a much more powerful campaign to retain her for another vision of France, a more tolerant vision led particularly by the Socialist and Catholic poet Charles Péguy, who wrote many books of beautiful verse about Joan as an emblem of a bountiful, merciful France. That's a very good example of how the symbolic can define and redefine women, and how difficult it is for the individual voice of a person who is female to emerge from the historical morass. Another example is Raphael's painting of *Parnassus* in the Vatican. He has all the assembled sages and philosophers around Apollo, and they're recognisable because we know what Dante looked like, and we know vaguely what Socrates looked like, and so forth. There's one woman, who is Sappho, but in order for the viewers of this fresco to understand that she's Sappho, she's the only person who is labelled. Otherwise she would have been thought to be *Poesia* or *Musica* or some personification, but not an historical, individual person in history. And that is the philosophical axiom which women contend with, this sort of flight into the symbolic, this difficulty in remaining a person rather than just a persona.

RK *You mention somewhere that one of the great legacies of European culture is the handshake. What do you mean by that?*

MW Sometimes identity resides in very small things. Instead of saying that the Western world was united by the sign of the handshake, I could actually, in the modern world, have said that it's united by the suit. But I didn't say the suit. It's just that the idea of the handshake as a gesture of equality and alliance and friendship does seem to have begun in our part of the world. It was, of course, a sign of a pact, the joining of right hands, in Roman law. And it is in a way a symbol for Europe, because though it is offered in good faith, and has at times sealed pacts in good faith, it has also been tremendously betrayed.

(Dublin, 1991)

SEAMUS HEANEY

Between North and South: poetic detours

SEAMUS HEANEY is an Irish poet. Born in County Derry in Northern Ireland, he has taught in Dublin, Oxford and Harvard, where he holds the Boylston Chair of Rhetoric and Logic. His publications include several major collections of poetry, as well as *New Selected Poems*; *Preoccupations* and *The Government of the Tongue*.

RK *T. S. Eliot spoke about the concept of the whole mind of Europe. Do you think such a thing exists?*

SH If you grow up in Northern Ireland, you have the whole mind of Europe there around you. You have Iceland in the mission hall, the tin mission hall with the strains of Methodist song in the evening coming out over the fields. . . . When I went to Iceland I saw these little lonely tin huts in the middle of the tundra, and recognised Reformed Europe. So that Protestant dissenter's God is around you. The English God. A memory of the whitewashed chastity of Danish churches, all that. In Northern Ireland there is both this reformed Europe and then there is the pre-Reformation culture of Catholic repositories, the Virgin and Child, the tawdry, 'dolled-up Virgin', as MacNeice called her. So, the Northern Irish mind is divided, or certainly embattled – if you're Protestant embattled by the Republic, if you're Catholic embattled by the Protestant thing – and that mind seeks ways in which to rephrase itself, make sense of itself, engender meaning out of confusion. And I suppose one of the meaning-seeking ploys that I used was to say that certain Eastern European writers – Poles and Romanians and Czechs – seem to understand these things better than English writers do. They take for granted disjunction, they take for granted that life will disappoint, that the roof is off the cottage of the universe. And I was being a bit unfair, of course. W. H. Auden recognised the roof was off, but he put it on again. I would still say, however, that people in Ireland have a greater sense of affinity than the English with that unsettled, uneasy, slightly distrusting attitude to reality.

RK *So for you there is such a phenomenon as a 'European mentality'?*

SH Well, I think it can be brought into existence, and it's thought to have been in existence. I suppose Eliot talked about it to some extent as an Anglican, a monarchist and a conservative. People in English culture like Matthew Arnold and T. S. Eliot promoted the idea of a 'mind of Europe' as an antidote to what they would have called provincialism, or Low Church life. I think that the tussle since Reformation times is to some extent a protest by the dissenter, the revolutionary, the protestant, against the totalising whole mind, the Latin mind, the imperial, big overall thing. It was a protest which said, let us have our own language rather than Latin, let's have the Bible in translation, let's have democracy rather than monarchy, and so on. So that the idea of a European tradition, the idea of European civilisation, these terms that were once hallowed are now suspect, because they seem to be imperial, totalising and Roman Catholic in a dangerous way. What the spirit of the age has in general promoted is a decolonising of the mind, taking out the big mind of Europe, putting in the mind of Ireland, the mind of Denmark, the mind of Spain, and so on. And of course it's correct politically to be on the side of decolonising your mind, and liberating yourself, realising that your consciousness has been to some extent created politically by big, totalising ideas. But, on the other hand, if you take out, almost in a military sense, the forms of the inheritance, if you take out Greek, Hellenic, Judaic culture – after all, the literary and artistic culture is almost coterminous with our discovery of moral culture, I mean, justice, freedom, beauty, love: they are in the drama of Greece, they are in the holy books of Judea – and if you take out those things, what do you put in their stead?

RK *Well, you have local pieties, don't you? I mean, your own work started with a certain celebration of the county and country of Derry. Much of your early poetry was an exploration of the parish and all that it entails. Would you see a move in your recent work away from this dissident, territorial, regional Heaney to a more universal, European, cosmopolitan Heaney?*

SH I wouldn't apply adjectives to myself like 'dissident' or 'European'. I'm just describing a movement of consciousness, a coming to awareness of what different myths entail. The Ireland, and Irish literature, that I grew up with were based upon pride in a kind of Gaelic Catholic difference, pure and simple-minded truths which are 'pieties' maybe: for example, Ireland was not invaded by the Romans, we had a Celtic background, we Christianised Europe, we were not touched by the Renaissance, as Daniel Corkery proudly says. I did once regard all that as a sign of distinction in a good sense, but I'm not so sure any more.

RK *What about your gravitation towards the Nordic territory of imagination, particularly with the publication of* North*? Wasn't there a sort of retrieval of another European geography there which might in some sense correspond to or complement the Northern Irish thing?*

SH Well, I think so, yes. The desire that one has is that what is possessed intimately should resonate more generally. You don't want to be promoting the local in its own right. I mean, the local has to be radiant with something you call truth. And yet I'm not saying that when I began to use images of barbarous practices in Iron Age Europe, that I was self-consciously promoting the truth. I was just excited . . .

RK *You're talking now about the Bog People and the sacrificial rites of burial . . .*

SH In the early 1970s, I made, as you say, this match, it's almost an intellectual rhyme between the sacrifice, violence and intimate killing in Iron Age Europe of a territorial, religious nature, and the territorial visions and religion implicit in Irish republicanism. So, yes, at that time I was, I suppose, in the grip of what is a romantic mythology – a sort of half-acknowledged presupposition that the nativist, the barbaric, is as authentic if not more authentic than the civilised; and then a moment came when I got a salutary reminder of what I was into. This was a moment in Macedonia. I went to a poetry conference, in Struga, and there was a Danish poet there. One afternoon, we went across the waters of a famous clearwater lake to an island which had the most entrancing Byzantine churches, monasteries with mosaics, those sages standing in God's holy fire, as Yeats said, images of the Madonna, of the Christ. And the Dane said to me, 'This is you, isn't it? You aren't really black bogs and sacrificial Iron Age creatures.' In a way he was right.

RK *So your imagination started migrating from the North to the South of Europe.*

SH Well, if you want to you can make a myth out of the authenticity, and the otherness, and the desirability of the Protestant North. And that is salubrious and salutary if it is to correct a rather too-smug idea of the absolute virtue of Graeco-Roman civilisation. But, on the other hand, I do think that you cut yourself off from enabling heritages and from visionary forms if you shut off what traditionally is European civilisation.

RK *So, it's not an accident that your most recent book,* Seeing Things, *marks a certain return to the vision and idioms of Homer and Virgil and Dante. What is it exactly in that Mediterranean, southern European thing that most fascinates you?*

SH I think it's a steadiness and a durability, a sense, for example, that in the word Orpheus, in the word muse, in the word drama, in the word mystery, or whatever, in the etymologies and associations, there is what Louis MacNeice calls a mystical sense of value. He said a writer didn't need to be mystic, but it seemed to him that a writer needed to possess a mystical sense of value. And I do believe that in the English language, in the French language, in the Italian language, in the Greek language, and I'm sure in many other languages, these deposits do promote a quickening, a challenge. I'm not going to say a transcendent Europe of value, but the possibility of a hopeful, other, renewable, non-utilitarian, joyful spirit of being. Those promises, hopes and invitations reside in that Graeco-Roman-Judaic heritage, I think.

RK *To continue our magical mystery tour through the geography of Europe! Having traversed the Northern, Protestant, Viking landscape, and said something about the Southern, Catholic, Graeco-Roman, perhaps you could now say something about Middle Europe. In* The Government of the Tongue, *but also in other writings, you have shown a great interest in the work of poets like Mandelstam, Milosz, Holub, Herbert, Rósewicz and Sorescu. What is it about the East, and particularly the old Eastern and Middle Europe, that appeals to you?*

SH I think many writers there have spoken the word, the original spiritual word, in a very laconic, down-beat, hard-bitten way. They have combined, if you like, a Northern rhetoric which is saying no when it means yes, which is chaste, ironical and indirect, they have combined that with quite a radiant desire for the big old values which were hidden erstwhile in rhetoric. What you find in poets like Milosz, Sorescu or Holub is an invocation of classical mythology, not in a decorative, Miltonic way, but in a totally contemporary, angry way. I mean, Miroslav Holub has a poem called 'The Corporal Who Killed Archimedes'. Archimedes is working at the very edges, at advanced stages of mathematical and intellectual thought of his day, and the Corporal kills him, and then Holub says, 'And now he goes counting: one, two, one, two'. The Corporal has the power, but he doesn't have the creative capacities that Archimedes had. So for Holub, the classical past is a source of vivifying *exempla*. Again, Procrustes, the man who cut people to the same size to fit his bed, he's used by Zbigniev Herbert as an image of a totalitarian regime's ruthlessness in making everything uniform. Now, those are very snap examples. Much more important I think is the cherishing by those 'Easterners' of what the West has taken for granted. We have become anxious in Western Europe about being Eurocentric, we have become anxious about the sins of colonialism. Even though in Ireland we think of ourselves as colonised, we too have after all connived in the imperial enterprise with our foreign missions, you know, to Africa. Of course it was a religious outing, but it was also an imperial outing, hand in hand even with the British Empire there. Nobody is free of self-blame when it comes to the abuse of European vision and fervour; but I think that that self-blame and that self-destruction of heritage has gone very far, and the East, among other things, reminds you that when the forms of value, when the value-engendering language is under fire, that heritage, the religious heritage, the cultural heritage, remains a possession. It's not just a stone-walling possession, it's something that is necessary to keep – humanist values engendering themselves.

RK *This reminds me, Seamus, of one of the examples you touch on in* The Government of the Tongue, *where you speak of a Russian poet, called Kutzenov, who buried his poems in a jam-jar at the bottom of his garden. This seems to be an analogy for the cultural memory that the dissident poets of the East have managed to preserve. Would you go so far as to say that they have preserved a more authentic and enabling notion of Europe than we in the West, with all our great rhetoric of European unity and community? Perhaps we need this reminder of cultural memory from Middle and Eastern Europe?*

SH There's no doubt that over the last forty years, from Pasternak's *Dr Zhivago* and Mandelstam's poetry onwards, a certain voltage of joy about what is going on in the East came through. Of course, it may be letting yourself off the hook to say, 'Oh God, aren't they marvellous? Look how they're resisting there.' So there has been a natural suspicion of this adoration of Eastern literature because it's almost a nostalgia? 'Isn't it great to have oppression? Look what a good literature it breeds.' Now, that is a kind of vulgarising of something that is genuine. I think that the Western intelligentsia is enlivened by the reality of spirit under pressure, by the spectacle of artistic and intellectual integrity. Words which the West had become shy of were still speakable in the East; and because they were speakable and manifest, it gave a certain excitement to writers in the West. The problems of Westerners are, and were, different. It's a question of how to speak the utterly persuasive word in an atmosphere where no matter what you say it's not entirely persuasive. Our Europe stands between Eastern Europe and the United States of America, where the language has got a wide, wide weave, where the poetry, no matter how protesting – whether it's Ginsberg writing in the fifties in San Francisco or John Ashbery writing in New York in the seventies and eighties – their protest is authentic, yet disappointed and hopeless; they would be shy of using a word like 'spirit', and if Socrates came into one of their poems, he would either be totally romanticised as a forerunner of William Blake or turned into a Donald Duck figure and ironised out of existence. That kind of ironical consciousness is what the West is used to, and so it got an injection of joy and a challenge to renewal from the East where poetry still had a close relationship to danger.

RK *Several of these Eastern European poets have in recent history had quite an influential role to play in the reshaping of their own countries and nations. Havel is the obvious case in Czechoslovakia. But it's also significant that a poet like Dinescu was there in Bucharest when they took over the television station and proclaimed a free Romania to the world, or indeed that that particular rebellion was launched from Sorescu's own house, another poet. So, there seems to be a message coming through from so-called Eastern Europe that poets can play a reforming role in society. You have spoken about a tension between the command to engage actively in history and the need to contemplate the motionless point, to see poetry as its own reality. How do you respond to this message from Eastern Europe that the poet can have a public role?*

SH There's no doubt that the poet can have a public role, but I think that the moment when the role becomes inevitable and compulsory is a special moment. In England in the seventeenth century,

John Milton didn't bother his head with poetry for twenty years, it took second place to revolution, politics and religion. He wrote poetry as an exquisite attainment of a certain kind of civilisation up to his early manhood. Then, he put it away, and he was Cromwell's Latin secretary. Then, defeat, boom! – and he left. Milton is an example of the poet in public life yielding to an invitation to be a servant of something larger than art. In post-Romantic times, we have managed to unite the idea of poetic vision and national service. I mean, you had it in Ireland from 1890 until 1920. Poets made the 1916 Revolution. You had a sense of them being at the centre of power in a way that Havel and all these people are. But I think that when a society settles back (and, paradoxically, in spite of the Northern situation, you could say that there's an element of settlement about Irish society) then the role of the artist is oppositional. But it's oppositional in terms of modes of thinking, modes of apprehending. He or she can be the magical thinker, he or she can stand for values that aren't utilitarian. The artist can refuse history as a category, can say 'No. I prefer to dream possibilities'.

RK *And is that a disruptive activity, to dream possibilities?*

SH It is. It is a refusal of the terms. Take a poet in Ireland like Paul Durcan, who seems to be connected up with the times: of course he is, but he's refusing the terms. In Durcan's case, what is dream-refusal can be taken for social comment. Of course it includes social comment, but its *modus agendi*, its way of going on, is to say 'I don't believe any of this'. If you take a completely different kind of voice like Paul Celan, you get a hermetic poetry, a secluded poetry, a poetry that huddles itself into the smallest space of language and says poetically within that language 'I refuse what's going on. I hate it.' So, artistic action is not necessarily dialogue, the much prized dialogue with other ideas. It's a statement of 'Look. There is another way. We don't have to take this way of doing it.' Now, I'm not saying that all writing has to be like this, but I am saying that that's the nature of lyric for sure; it's the way a certain kind of abstract anger works in poetry, and it is sponsored by the dissident tradition in Europe also.

RK *So you would be as suspicious of the poet king – the poet in power with maps and blueprints and diktats – as you would of the philosopher-king.*

SH I think so. There's been no example of a successful one. The poet Orpheus sings to the creatures and entrances them, and everybody goes 'ooooh'; they just go into a trance. That's one kind of writing, the writer as entrancer. But that is not enough when it comes to the writer as an inhabitant of reality. And that's why Plato was against the poet, because of this entrancement factor, because the mind went to sleep and one went on automatic pilot as a human being. Now, the fully empowered artist, and the fully living response to art, goes beyond entrancement into what Yeats called the 'desolation of reality'. And there you have Orpheus, not as the puller of the harp string that puts everybody to sleep, but Orpheus confronting the fact of death and love, going to the underworld, always defiant but always failing to overcome death, always failing to absolutely make the perfection cohere. The possibilities within a culture, cultural inheritance if you like, are what mediate between the individual psyche and the uncontrollable size of the reality out there, the unknowable size of society. Cultural inheritance – European or otherwise – allows some form of negotiation to take place, to make sense of it all.

(Dublin, 1992)

JORGE LUIS BORGES

The European writer in exile

JORGE LUIS BORGES was an Argentinian writer, poet and critic. His books include *Seven Nights*; *Dream Tigers*; *Doctor Brodie's Report*; *Other Inquisitions*; *The Book of Imaginary Beings*; *Labyrinths*. Borges always insisted on the importance of his extended journeys abroad as a young man, particularly his sojourn in Geneva (1914–21), where he first discovered Conrad, Baudelaire and Joyce and joined, as he put it, the 'international modernism of letters'.

This dialogue between Borges, Richard Kearney and Seamus Heaney took place in Dublin in 1982.

RK *I think it would be appropriate, since today is Bloomsday and since you are here in Dublin for the Joyce Centenary celebrations, if you could begin by talking about your literary relationship with Joyce. In 1925 you declared yourself proud to be the 'first Hispanic adventurer to undertake the conquest of James Joyce'. How would you describe this adventure into the world of Joyce and modern European literature?*

JLB Let us go back to the early 1920s. A friend of mine gave me a first edition of *Ulysses* which had just been published by Sylvia Beach in Paris. I did my best to leaf through it. I failed, of course. However, I did recognise from the beginning that I had before me a marvellously tortuous book. But a book of what? I asked myself. Every time I thought of *Ulysses*, it was not the *characters* – Stephen, Bloom or Molly – that first came to mind, but the *words* which produced these characters. This convinced me that Joyce was first and foremost a poet. He was forging poetry out of prose. My subsequent discovery of *Finnegans Wake* and *Pomes Penyeach* confirmed me in this opinion. When I consider novelists such as Tolstoy, Conrad or Dickens, I think of their powerful characters or plots, of the content matter of their narratives. But with Joyce the focus had shifted to the forms and words of the language itself, to those unforgettably musical sentences that strive towards the condition of poetry. Looking back on my own writings sixty years after my first encounter with Joyce, I must admit that I have always shared Joyce's fascination with words, and have always worked at my language within an essentially poetic framework savouring the multiple meanings of words, their etymological echoes and endless resonances. My own characters are often no more than excuses to play with words, to enter the fictional world of language. Joyce's obsession with language makes him very difficult if not impossible to translate. Especially into Spanish – as I discovered when I first translated a passage from Molly's soliloquy in 1925. The translations of Joyce into the Hispanic or Romance languages have been very poor to date. His symphonically compound words work best in Anglo-Saxon or Germanic languages. Joyce used prose to produce poetry. And I think all of his works should be read as poetry.

SH I have often wondered about what constitutes the difference between Joyce's use of language in his poems, *Chamber Music* for example, and in his prose works, *A Portrait* or *Ulysses*. It seems to me that in the former Joyce is approaching language as a sort of ventriloquist, he remains its obedient servant, he rehearses a note caught from literature. Whereas in the prose, something cuts loose and comes alive in a new way. Whenever he tried to approach verse directly he seems to have been hampered. Yet it was the inveterate struggling poet in him which enabled him to play with prose in unprecedentedly creative forms.

RK *In an essay in 1941 you praised Joyce for having written some of the 'most accomplished pages in matters of style'. Do you think Joyce has influenced your own style as a writer?*

JLB I was very struck by the way in which Joyce dared in *Ulysses* to write each chapter or episode in a different style. My own work also uses a plurality of styles. I'm not sure, however, that there is a direct influence here. Or if there is it is an unconscious one. The writers whose literary influence I consciously assimilated were Stevenson, Chesterton, Kipling and Shaw, authors I read when I was still a young boy growing up in Buenos Aires and spending a considerable amount of my time in my father's library, which contained a remarkable collection of English books. I spent my childhood dreaming with these authors, with Kipling in India, with

Coleridge in Xanadu, with Dickens in London. This is perhaps where I first experienced literature as an adventure into an endless variety of styles. The library was like a single mind with many tongues. I have been fascinated by libraries ever since (as have many of my fictional characters). I longed, for instance, to work in the National Library of Buenos Aires which possesses over 900,000 volumes. But the year in which I was finally appointed director of this library – 1955, after the fall of Peron – was the year I went blind. There I was, surrounded by books I could no longer read. Sometimes I used to pretend I could still see. Even to this day, I occasionally go into a bookshop and buy some volumes so as to deceive myself that I can still read. But I feel uneasy when talking about influences on my 'writing' for I do not consider myself as a writer. I don't write very good stuff and whatever I do write I cannot bear to reread. Nor have I ever read a commentary on my work. My library does not contain one such commentary. I have become famous, it seems to me, in spite of what I've written, not because of it. There must be some mistake, I say to myself. Perhaps people mistake me for somebody else, for some other writer?

SH Perhaps it is Borges rather than you who writes your works?

JLB Perhaps indeed! There seems to be two of us, at least. The shy, private man and the celebrated, talkative, public man.

RK *In the* Argentine Writer and Tradition *you said you felt yourself to be an author 'outside of a cultural mainstream'. Joyce expressed a similar sentiment when he described 'home, fatherland and church' as restrictive nets he would try to fly by, or when he had Stephen admit that he could never feel at home in the English language, that he could never speak or write its words 'without unrest of spirit'. Do you experience such a cultural or post-colonial alienation in your use of the Spanish language?*

JLB It is true that as an Argentine I feel a certain distance from the Spanish mainstream. I was brought up in Argentina with as much familiarity with the English and French cultures as with the Spanish. So I suppose I am doubly alien – for even Spanish, the language I write precisely as an outsider, is itself already on the margin of the mainstream European literary tradition.

SH Do you think there exists such a thing as a Hispanic-American tradition – accepting the fact that all traditions have to be imagined before they emerge?

JLB It is true that the notion of tradition involves an act of faith. Our imaginations alter and reinvent the past all of the time. I must confess, however, that I was never very convinced by the idea of a Hispanic-American tradition. When I travelled to Mexico, for example, I delighted in their rich culture and literature. But I felt I had nothing in common with it. I could not identify with their cult of the Indian past. Argentina and Uruguay differ from most other Latin-American countries in that they possess a mixture of Spanish, Italian and Portugese cultures which has made for a more European-style climate. Most of our colloquial or slang words in Argentine, for instance, are of Italian origin. I myself am descended from Portugese, Spanish, Jewish and English ancestors. And the English, as Lord Tennyson reminds us, are themselves a mixture of many races: 'Saxon and Celt and Dane are we'. There is no such thing as a racial or national purity. And even if there were, the imagination would transcend such limits. Nationalism and literature are therefore natural enemies. I do not believe that there exists a specifically Argentine culture which could be called 'Latin-American' or 'Hispanic-American'. The only real Americans are the Indians. The rest are Europeans. I like to think of myself therefore as a European writer in exile. Neither Hispanic nor American, nor Hispanic-American, but an expatriate European.

SH T. S. Eliot spoke of the 'whole mind of Europe'. Do you feel you have inherited something of this mind through the Spanish detour?

JLB In the Argentine, we have no exclusive allegiance to any single European culture. We can draw, as I said, from several different European languages and literatures – perhaps even from the 'whole mind of Europe', if such a thing exists. But precisely because of our distance from Europe we also have the cultural or imaginative freedom to look beyond Europe to Asia and other cultures.

RK *As you do in your own fiction when you frequently invoke the mystical doctrines of Buddhism and the Far East.*

JLB Not to belong to an homogeneous 'national' culture is perhaps not a poverty but a richness. In this sense I am an 'international' writer who resides in Buenos Aires. My ancestors came from several different nations and races – as I mentioned – and I spent much of my youth travelling through Europe, particularly Geneva, Madrid and London, where I learned several new languages, German, Old English and Latin. This multinational apprenticeship enables me to play with words as beautiful toys, to enter, as Browning put it, the 'great game of language'.

SH I find it very interesting that your immersion in several languages in early childhood – and particularly Spanish and English – gave you that sense of language as a toy. I know that my own fascination with words was keenly related to my learning of Latin as a young boy. And the way words travelled and changed between languages, the Latin roots, the etymological drama; all that verbal phantasmagoria in Joyce also seems to be deeply involved with his conventional classical education.

RK *Are there other Irish writers, besides Joyce, that you particularly admired?*

JLB When I was still a young man in Buenos Aires I read George Bernard Shaw's *The Quintessence of Ibsenism*. I was so impressed that I went on to read all of his plays and essays and discovered there a writer of deep philosophical curiosity and a great believer in the transfiguring power of the will and of the mind. Shaw possesses that typically Irish sense of mischievous fun and laughter. Oscar Wilde is another Irish author who had that rare ability to mix humour and frivolity with intellectual depth. He wrote some purple passages, of course, but I believe that every word he wrote is true . . .

RK *Wilde once said that a 'truth in art is that whose contrary is also true'.*

JLB Yes, this is just what I meant by *comic truth*, the truth of fiction which is able to tolerate cyclical and contradictory representations of reality. This is why I say that every word that Wilde wrote is true. I too believe in comic truth. Perhaps it is no accident that my first literary venture as a young man was a translation of Wilde's fairy-tales. But there is another Irishman who also fired my imagination at an early age – George Moore. Moore invented a new kind of book, a new way of writing fiction, nourished by anecdotal conversations which he overheard in streets and then transformed into a fictive order. I learned from him too.

RK *And what of Beckett – perhaps Joyce's closest Irish literary disciple? He seems to share with you an obsession with fiction as a self-scrutinising labyrinth of the mind, as an eternally recurring parody of itself?*

JLB Samuel Beckett is a bore. I saw his *Waiting for Godot* and that was enough for me. I thought it was a very poor work. Why bother waiting for Godot if he never comes? Tedious stuff. I had no desire to go on to read his novels after that.

RK *Your works are peppered with metaphysical allusions and reflections. What is your relationship with philosophy?*

JLB For me Schopenhauer is the greatest philosopher. He knew the power of fiction in ideas. This conviction I share, of course, with Shaw. Both Schopenhauer and Shaw exposed the deceptive division between the writer and the thinker. They were both great writers and great thinkers. The other philosopher who fascinated me greatly was George Berkeley – another Irishman! Berkeley knew that metaphysics is no less a product of the creative mind than is poetry. He was no civil servant of ideas, like so many other philosophers. Plato and the pre-Socratic thinkers knew that philosophical logic and poetic mythologising were inseparably linked, complementary partners. Plato could do both. But after Plato the Western world seems to have opposed these activities, declaring that we either dream *or* reason, use arguments *or* metaphors. Whereas the truth is that we use both at once. Many hermetic and mystical thinkers resisted this opposition; but it was not until the emergence of modern idealism in Berkeley, Schelling, Schopenhauer and Bradley (whose wonderful book *Appearance and Reality* actually mentioned me in its foreword: I was so flattered to be taken seriously as a thinker!) that philosophers began to explicitly recognise once again their dependence upon the creative and shaping powers of the mind.

RK *How did you first become interested in Berkeley's metaphysics?*

JLB My father introduced me to Berkeley's philosophy at the age of ten. Before I was even able to read or write properly he taught me to think. He was a professor of psychology and every day after dinner he would give me a philosophy lesson. I remember very well how he first introduced me to Berkeley's idealist metaphysics and particularly his doctrine that the material or empirical world is an invention of the creative mind: to be is to be perceived/*Esse est Percipi*. It was one day after a good lunch when my father took an orange in his hand and asked me: 'What colour is this fruit?' 'Orange' I replied. 'Is this colour in the orange or in your perception of it?' he continued. 'And the taste of sweetness – is that in the orange itself or is it the sensation on your tongue that makes it sweet?' This was a revelation to me: that the outside world is as we perceive or imagine it to be. It does not exist independently of our minds. From that day forth, I realised that reality and fiction were betrothed to each other, that even our ideas are creative fictions. I have always believed that metaphysics, religion and literature all have a common source.

RK *Berkeley insisted that his idealism was not to be confounded with British empiricism and protested against Locke: 'We Irish think otherwise'. Yeats hailed this phrase as 'the birth of the national intellect'. Do you think it is just a happy accident that your early discovery of the creative power of the mind coincided with your admiration for Irish writers and thinkers such as Berkeley, Shaw, Wilde and Joyce, who had also made such a discovery? How would you account for this shared empathy?*

JLB Perhaps nothing is an accident? Perhaps all such coincidences obey some hidden law, the unfolding of some inscrutable design? The principle of Eternal Return? of a Universal Logos? of a Holy Ghost? Who knows? But as an outsider looking on successive Irish thinkers I have sometimes been struck by unusual and remarkable repetitions. Berkeley was the first Irish philosopher I read, from the *Principles* and the *Three Dialogues* to *Siris*, and even his Messianic poem about the future of the Americas: 'The course of Empire takes its sway . . . etc'. Then followed my fascination for Wilde, Shaw and Joyce. And finally there was John Scotus Eriugena, the Irish metaphysician of the 9th century. I loved to read Eriugena, especially his *De Divisione Naturae*, which taught that God creates himself through the creation of his creatures in nature. I have all of his books in my library. I discovered that Berkeley's doctrine of the creative power of the mind was already anticipated by Eriugena's metaphysics of creation and that this in turn recurred in several other Irish writers: in the last two pages of the foreword to *Back to Methuselah* we find Shaw outlining a philosophical system remarkably akin to Eriugena's system of things coming from the mind of God and returning to him. In short, what Shaw calls the life-force plays the same role in his system as God does in Eriugena's. I was also very struck by the fact that both Shaw and Eriugena held that all genuine creation stems from a metaphysical nothingness, what Eriugena called the '*Nihil*' of God, which resided at the heart of our existence. I doubt that Shaw ever read Eriugena; he certainly showed very little interest in medieval philosophy. And yet the coincidence of thought is there. I suspect it has less to do with nationalism than with metaphysics.

RK *Your own writing displays a continuous obsession with the world of fiction and dream, a universe of subconscious labyrinths. So dream-like is it on occasion that it becomes impossible to distinguish between the author (yourself), the characters of the fiction and the reader (ourselves).*

SH This interplay between fiction and reality seems central to your work. How does the world of your dreams affect your work? Do you consciously use dream material?

JLB Every morning when I wake up I recall dreams and have them recorded or written down. Sometimes I wonder whether I am awake or dreaming. Am I dreaming now? Who can tell? We are dreaming each other all of the time. Berkeley held that it was God who was dreaming us. Perhaps he was right. But how tedious for poor God! To have to dream every chink and every piece of dust on every teacup and every letter in every alphabet and every thought in every head. He must be exhausted!

RK *Several characters in your fictions suggest the possibility of a single Divine mind or Alphabet which conjures up the universe as an author conjures up his imaginary world. In* Aleph, *for example, you seem to be challenging the conventional notion of an individual ego or subject, implying that all human beings may be no more than the dramatis personae of a universal play. The hero of this fiction declares at one point: 'I have been Homer . . . shortly I shall be all men'. And in* Tlön *it is even stated that 'it has been established that all works are the creation of one author who is atemporal and anonymous'.*

JLB Schopenhauer spoke of '*das traumhafte Wesen des Lebens*' – the dream-like being of life. He wasn't referring to some oneiric unconscious sublimation as modern psychology might like us to believe. He was referring to the restless mind in its search for imaginative fulfilment. Though I discovered this metaphysical doctrine in Berkeley and Schopenhauer, I later learned, on reading Koeppen's *Religion des Budda*, that it was a central teaching of Eastern philosophy. This Buddhist teaching that reality is the recurring dream of a Godhead prompted me to write *Circular Ruins*.

SH I would like to come back to the relationship between your dreams and your fictions. Does your dream world actually nourish your writing in a direct fashion? Do you actually borrow and transpose the *content* of your dreams into literature? Or is it a narrative skill the gives the images their shape and form?

JLB The fictional retelling brings an order to the disorder of the dream material. But I cannot say whether the order is imposed or is already latent within the disorder merely waiting to be highlighted by its repetition in fiction. Does the writer of fiction invent an entirely new order *ex nihilo*? I suppose if I could answer such questions, I would not write fiction at all!

SH Could you give us some actual examples of what you mean?

JLB Yes. I will tell you of a recurring dream which interested me greatly. A little nephew of mine who often stayed with me and told me his dreams every morning, experienced the following recurring motif. He was lost and then came to a clearing where he saw me coming out of a white wooden house. At that point he would break off his summary of the dream and ask me 'Uncle, what were you doing in that house?' 'I was looking for a book,' I replied. And he was quite happy with that. As a child he was still able to slide from the logic of his dream to the logic of my explanation. Perhaps this is the way my own fictions work?

SH Is it then the *mode* rather than the actual *material* of dreams that primarily inspires and influences your work?

JLB I would say that it is both. I have had several recurring dreams over the years that have left their imprint on my fiction in one form or another. The symbols often differ, but the patterns and structures remain the same. I have frequently dreamt, for example, that I am trapped in a room. I try to get out. But I find myself back in a room. Is it the same room? I ask myself. Or am I escaping into an outer room? Or returning to an inner one? Am I in Buenos Aires or Montevideo? In the city or in the country? I touch the wall to try to discover the truth of my whereabouts, to find an answer to these questions. But the wall is part of the dream! So the question eternally returns, like the questioner, into his room. This dream provided me with the motif of the maze or labyrinth which occurs so often in my fictions. I am also obsessed by a dream in which I see myself in a looking glass with several masks or faces each superimposed on the other; I peel them off successively and address the face before me in the glass; but it doesn't answer, it cannot hear me or doesn't listen, impossible to know.

SH What kind of truth do you think Carl Jung was trying to explore in his analyses of symbols and myths? Do you think the Jungian archetypes are valid explanations of what we experience in the subconscious worlds of dream and fiction?

JLB I have read Jung with great interest but with no conviction. At best he was an imaginative, exploratory writer. More than one can say for Freud: such rubbish!

RK *Your suggestion here that psychoanalysis has worth as an imaginative stimulant rather than as a scientific method, reminds me of your claim that all philosophical thought is 'a branch of fantastic literature'.*

JLB Yes, I believe that metaphysics is no less a product of imagination than is poetry. After all, the ontological idea of God is the most splendid invention of imagination.

RK *But do we invent God or does God invent us? Is the primary creative imagination divine or human?*

JLB Ah, that is *the* question. It might be both.

SH Did your childhood experience of the Catholic religion nourish your sensibility in any lasting way? I'm thinking more of its rites and mysteries than its theological precepts. Is there such a thing as a Catholic imagination, which might express itself in works of literature, as it did in Dante for example?

JLB In the Argentine, being a Catholic is a social rather than a spiritual matter. It means you align yourself with the right class, party or social group. This aspect of religion never interested me. Only the women seemed to take religion seriously. As a young boy, when my mother would take me to mass, I rarely saw a man in the church. My mother had a great faith. She believed in heaven; and maybe her belief means that she is there now. Though I am no longer a practising Catholic and cannot share her faith, I still go into her bedroom at four o'clock every morning – the hour of her death four years ago (she was 99 and dreaded being a hundred!) – to sprinkle holy water and recite the Lord's prayer as she requested. Why not? Immortality is no more strange or incredible than death. As my agnostic father used to say: 'reality being what it is – the product of our perception – everything is possible, even the Trinity'. I do believe in ethics, that things in our universe are good or bad. But I cannot believe in a personal God. As Shaw says in *Major Barbara*: 'I have left behind the Bride of Heaven'. I continue to be fascinated by metaphysical and alchemical notions of the sacred. But this fascination is aesthetic rather than theological.

RK *In* Tlön, Uqbar and Orbis Tertius, *you spoke about the eternal repetition of chaos gradually giving rise to, or disclosing, a metaphysical pattern of order. What did you have in mind?*

JLB I enjoyed myself very much in writing that. I never stopped laughing from beginning to end. It was all one huge metaphysical joke. The idea of the eternal return is of course an old idea of the Stoics. St Augustine condemned this idea in the *Civitas Dei*, when he contrasts the pagan belief in a cyclical order of time – the City of Babylon with the linear, prophetic and Messianic notion of time to be found in the City of God, Jerusalem. This latter notion has prevailed in our Western culture since Augustine. But I think there may be some truth in the old idea that behind the apparent disorder of the universe and the words we use to speak about our universe, a hidden order might emerge – an order of repetition or coincidence.

RK *You once wrote that even though this hidden cyclical order cannot be proved it remains for you 'an elegant hope'.*

JLB Did I write that? That's good, yes, very good. I suppose that in 82 years I am entitled to have written a few memorable lines. The rest can 'go to pot', as my grandmother used to say.

SH You spoke of laughing while writing. Your books are certainly full of fun and mischief. Have you always found writing an enjoyable task or has it ever been for you a difficult or painful experience?

JLB You know, when I still had my sight, I loved writing, every moment, every sentence. Words were like magic playthings that I would toy with and move about in all sorts of ways. Since I lost my sight in the fifties, I have not been able to exult in writing in this casual manner. I have had to dictate everything, to become a dictator rather than a playboy of words. It is hard to play with toys when one is blind.

SH I suppose that the physical absence of pen and being hooped to the desk makes a big difference . . .

JLB Yes, it does. But I miss being able to read even more than being able to write. Sometimes I treat myself to a little deceit, surrounding myself with all sorts of books – particularly dictionaries – English, Spanish, German, Italian, Icelandic. They become like living beings for me, whispering to me in the dark.

SH Only a Borges could practise such an act of fiction! Your dreams have, quite obviously, always been important to you. Would you say that your capacity or need to inhabit the world of fiction and dream was in any way increased by your loss of sight?

JLB Since I went blind all I have left is the joy of dreaming, of imagining that I can see. Sometimes my dreams extend beyond sleep into my waking world. Often, before I go to sleep or after I wake up, I find myself dreaming, babbling obscure and inscrutable sentences. This experience simply confirms my conviction that the creative mind is always at work, is always more or less dimly dreaming. Sleeping is like dreaming death. Just as waking is like dreaming life. Sometimes I can no longer tell which is which!

(Dublin, 1982)

MARTHA NUSSBAUM

Ethics of literature

MARTHA NUSSBAUM is Professor of Philosophy, Classics, and Comparative Literature at Brown University. Her books include *Love's Knowledge*; *The Fragility of Goodness*; *Luck and Ethics in Greek Tragedy and Philosophy*; *Essays on Philosophy and Literature*; *Greek Tragedy and Philosophy*; *Aristotle's De Motu Animalium*; *The Therapy of Desire*.

RK *The guiding question of your work, by your own admission, is how we should live? Why the primacy of this ethical question?*

MN That question has had a long history in my life, because I grew up in an upper-class world on the East coast of the US that was very sterile, very preoccupied with money and status. And I grew up at a time of tremendous change in American life – the civil rights movement, changes in women's lives. This forced me to notice the contrast between the life I was being brought up to lead, which was unreflective, which never posed the question of what was really worth caring for, and the changes that were taking place all around me. That contrast led me to focus on the ethical question.

RK *Why did you choose ancient Greek culture, the source of European civilization, as privileged hunting-ground for an answer to this question? Surely that seems like escapism, having recourse to some ancient exotic hinterland?*

MN In fact, I found the Greeks very immediate. Unlike a lot of the modern ethical views which seemed to me to be somewhat parochial, addressed to people who belonged to one religion rather than another, the Greek views seemed to grapple in a very powerful and dramatic way with the basic question 'How shall I live?' They confronted the question of what really has value head on, in a very undogmatic and intuitively powerful way.

RK *And how did you find your way into that? Was it at school or university?*

MN It was through acting actually! I wanted to be an actress when I was that age, and I acted the parts of the heroines in Greek tragedies. Through the imagining that I was doing to play those parts, I felt the force of the way they posed those questions. Then I developed a great passion for it and I wanted to understand it better.

RK *When did you leave acting for philosophy?*

MN When I realised that it wasn't really acting that I wanted to do, that it was not a way of life that I could sustain. I realised that what I wanted to do was to think and write about these plays because I thought they were so wonderful. I got more and more preoccupied with that idea.

RK *Some people might say, looking at those in the last century or so who have gone back to the Greeks – I'm thinking of the famous nostalgia for the Greeks in thinkers like Nietzsche, Hölderlin, the German Romantics and Heidegger – that there is an attempt to obviate the Judaeo-Christian tradition and return to a neo-paganism which has at times been allied to a conservative or reactionary position. This is clearly not your position. But could you say something about that return to what seems like a conservative Eurocentric agenda in the face of an America which is teeming with multiculturalist debate?*

MN From the very beginning, I noticed a gulf between the way the Greeks had been received in the Judaeo-Christian tradition and what I found in the texts themselves. Aristotle, for example, is very different from the Aristotle of the Catholic tradition. For one thing, he is continually thinking about the problems of poverty in a country that needs fresh air, clean water – problems that are facing developing countries today. The Greeks also offer some useful correctives and supplements to some of the abstractness of Enlightenment thinking because of the tremendous interest in personal relationships, relationships within community, the interest in the role of the emotions and the Good Life. But at the same time, I think it's very clear that the Greek philosophers had a passion for giving a universal account of the Good, asking what is the best way to live for any human being the world over. Aristotle does indeed ascribe to personal relationships great importance, but he also thinks that paying attention to the Good and the virtues is something that all human beings should do, and do in a very similar way. And I think one reason that his account of this is so different from a lot of contemporary 'neo-pagan' accounts is because his account of the emotions makes them rational. This is something that I am actually working on. Aristotle insists that emotions such as love, grief and anger are based upon reasoning about what's valuable, and in fact are suffused with reasoning. Emotions are ways of perceiving something as invested with value – you would not grieve for a loss if you don't see the person or thing you've lost as invested with value. But what this means is that philosophical reflection need not just sit on the emotions, or control them. It can actually enlighten and modify them. And that means that philosophical enlightenment can reach straight down into the most intimate quarters of human life, into the most allegedly personal and private parts of human life. So to me the Greeks carry the Enlightenment project (this is putting it very anachronistically) further than Kant was able to do. Kant thought the emotions were rather brutish and couldn't ever be enlightened, but the Greeks think that the whole of one's personal and public life can be enlightened by reflection.

RK *So you would see the return to the Greeks as a progressive movement that can develop the European Enlightenment rather than abrogate it?*

MN Yes, I really do. I think that it can show how the European Enlightenment can solve certain problems that seem to some modern thinkers very intractable. For example, the problem of how you deal with destructive passions in public life. The Greeks have fascinating accounts about how anger can be not just reined in, but actually modified by education. And I think these are accounts of great value for a world that's now torn by particularism and the angers that go with it.

RK *Given the movement of multiculturalism we spoke about earlier and the openness to a pluralism of different traditions and values, couldn't one object that the return to basic emotions can also lead to a relativism which sometimes degenerates into irrationalism? Isn't there a sort of soft-centred leniency towards that kind of irrationalism in your notion of the 'fragility of the Good' – a view that somehow vulnerability and messiness and tolerance of all these different multiple views is a good thing?*

MN I think that what I'm saying, when I talk about the fragility of the Good, is that there are some parts of life that are terribly important, without which your life is going to be impoverished, that make you vulnerable to fortune on a large scale. If you really love another person, if you really care about the political developments in your country, if you really love children, then losses will give you great grief and will threaten to derail you. But it doesn't seem to me at all to follow from that, that the more vulnerable you are the better, that if a child in Bangladesh lacks food, and is vulnerable towards daily food supply, that's a better way of life. I think only a ludicrous travesty of my position would say that all forms of vulnerability are good, and I think the Greek project interests me precisely because it's preoccupied with what forms of need are really worthwhile, are constitutive of a rich and worthwhile life. It distinguishes these from other needs for status, honour, reputation, excessive needs of money, and so on, those needs that are not very worthwhile. And also from forms of need, such as the need for food, which are quite important but ought to be guaranteed stably to the person by the society in which he or she lives. So, as far as multiculturalism goes, I love the Greeks because I think they offer great insights that are applicable to many societies.

RK *Are they better than the Africans, the Asians, the Chinese?*

MN I think that every student should try to find out the richness of thought in many different cultures; and of course, sometimes it doesn't take place in philosophical texts. Sometimes it will be expressed through musical works, through works of visual art, through oral traditions. And so I'm all in favour of a curriculum that takes very seriously the multiplicity of the sources of value in the world, because I think that otherwise you rest on your laurels, you pride yourself on your own tradition, and you think of it as better than other traditions. Obviously we have to talk together, we have to be able to understand one another across cultural gulfs, and we're not going to do that if we are as blankly ignorant as most American students are of what goes on in India, of what Chinese and African traditions have to offer. So I'm all in favour of this renovation of the curriculum, and I think that loving the Greeks, thinking that their works are very powerful, is not at all incompatible with saying that one had better learn quite a lot about the rest of the world.

RK *In your books there's a cultivation of story-telling, a celebration of the powers of the narrative imagination and the sympathetic imagination. But the examples you take are Greek and, to some extent, the nineteenth-century novel, particularly in* Love's Knowledge. *They aren't examples taken, for example, from the story-telling tradition of the native Americans, or the black story-telling tradition. Does that matter, or is it just that that's your own particular story and tradition?*

MN I think it's something I need to change a certain amount in my writing. I think it's always better to write about works you love and that you know very well. My own education was pretty one-sided, so I didn't come to know until much later in my life works from the Indian or Chinese tradition. I also find that these stories have a tremendous universality. I don't want to say that truths about human life generally can't be expressed by a work that is written in the European tradition – I think that's a very silly claim to make. On the other hand, I think that to show respect for people you're talking to, when you work as I have in an international development agency, it's a very good thing to read and care for the works in those traditions as well. I find when I talk to people from Sri Lanka, from Africa, from Latin America, that the story of *Antigone* resonates powerfully and there is something of universal importance that elicits a strong response. After all, it's as foreign to me as it is to them. It's a culture that's as distant from modern America as any of us is from one another, and one can get quite far by noticing the samenesses and the differences. But I also think that for a good undergraduate education one wants to learn something about these other traditions, or at least to become aware of the diversity of traditions, because otherwise you are too likely to show disrespect inadvertently, through blank ignorance.

RK *The titles of your books,* Love's Knowledge *and* The Fragility of Goodness, *are very suggestive. There is a critique of a certain mainstream rationalist approach to knowledge and technology, and public administration, and social science, and economics, which seems to stem from your belief that knowledge is not just a matter of cold, hard facts –* à la *Gradgrind in Dickens's* Hard Times *– but is a matter of* love. *That is a brave, audacious and radical statement to make?*

MN Well, I think the main opponent here – let me put the opponent squarely on the scene – is utilitarian economic reasoning. In the West, this is becoming more and more dominant in the public culture, in law schools. It's also gaining increasing ascendancy in development policy – in every area of public life. This involves the idea that all values are commensurable in a very crude sense – that we just ask one question: what will maximise something? Now, sometimes that's understood as satisfaction, sometimes as utility. But all the values of human life are funnelled into that one formula. And the distinctness, not only of the values, but of the different persons in the society who hold the values, is effaced. I think Dickens is a wonderful precursor of the modern critique, because he does show, very vividly in *Hard Times*, the contrast between the way the economist sees the world and the way the novel reader sees the world. In the Gradgrind schoolroom what the children are taught is that everyone in the room is a parcel of human nature to be weighed and measured, and all of their satisfactions are not just qualitatively indistinguishable, but they are aggregated in such a way that the separateness of one person from another is lost in the overall calculus of average utility. And what it is for one person to lead a life of terrible misery, is lost in a general social equation where the good fortune of one cancels out the misery of another. The novel reader, by contrast, is introduced to figures who have lives that are both qualitatively distinct, and separate from one another, who just have one life to lead from birth to death. And it doesn't buy off Stephen Blackpool's misery that Mr Bounderby is extremely fortunate. The whole averaging strategy of utilitarianism is criticised in the very act of reading, because you sympathise with that character and you say 'no! that life is a distinct life, and it doesn't matter to him that this guy over there is very well-off'. You are therefore led to focus on the plight of the worst off, and to wish it to be as good, other things being equal, as it can be.

RK *How does that relate to your analysis of development policy?*

MN Up until very recently when you turned to a developing country and you asked 'how are the people doing?', the technique used by economists was simply to ask 'What is the GNP per capita?' Now that is very much what goes on in *Hard Times*, just looking at this single figure, which isn't even very well correlated with averages of other sorts, like average life expectancy, average years of education and so on. But it certainly doesn't take into account either the bottom, as it were, of society; the fact that in a society with a reasonably high GNP per capita, let's take Saudi Arabia, you can have extreme inequalities in health, in education, in mortality statistics of all sorts, and so the average really doesn't get you very far in asking how human beings are doing.

RK *So you need a moral imagination, a literary imagination?*

MN Yes. In the development project I've been working on in the *World Institute for Development Economics Research*, Amartya Sen and I started our book on the quality of life with *Hard Times*, in order to suggest that economics needs that kind of moral imagination. It's really able to get inside a life and ask what are the various functions that matter to people who are trying to live well, and how is society really doing in making them capable or not capable of living as they really wish to live – and not only, as it were, wish now, but would wish had they had enough information about the possibilities for being human.

RK *One might object that that's all very utopian. It's all very well for you and other do-gooders to get together and think that you can introduce 'quality of life' to what is essentially a calculation about the quantity of life, and that you can have seminars and conferences and write wonderful books on it, but it's not going to make one bit of difference, is it? I mean, is there* any *possibility that these arguments – which of course I agree with – have any chance of* changing *things?*

MN I think they already have. Of course, it was Amartya Sen in economics who started making critiques of this sort, and we've worked together on this. This year's *Human Development Report*, that comes out from the United Nations, has a measure of well-being that's very responsive to the Development Program critique that we've been making. Instead of just looking at GNP per capita, it looks at a whole range of other human functions, and it's a very complicated report and it's not going to appeal to any economist who wants extremely simple forms of modelling. It asks how well people are actually doing in a lot of different areas, and yet, it is also able to model and measure and gather information in a digestible form that is actually useful to public policy. I think the consequence of that is going to be much more attention to specific areas of human well-being across the board, and not just to GNP per capita.

RK *How likely is it that such reports will have an effect when our universities keep literature, philosophy and the humanities in separate compartments from economics, public policy, public health, and so on? The very structure of our minds seems in some sense deformed and preconditioned by this academic apartheid.*

MN I think it's very hard, especially with economics, because economics has very sophisticated forms of mathematical reasoning that have been developed over a long period of time, and the sort of criticism that we have been making entails that a lot of those mathematical models would be radically changed. Now, that isn't going to appeal to people who are primarily interested in doing exclusively mathematical work, and who think of foundational criticism as the business of another discipline. I've found that very difficult. I have much more optimism about a field like law. There's a tremendous amount of back and forth between philosophy and law.

RK *They're open to each other?*

MN Yes, because they're always dealing with real human beings. Even legal thinkers who have been very committed to economic reasoning as normative, are also dealing with real cases; and if they can be brought to see that a simple way of reasoning is inadequate to the complexities of a real case, then that would be sufficient reason for them to look elsewhere, and I think they are looking elsewhere.

RK *So they're very Aristotelian in that respect, thinking of practical reasoning as distinct from deductive scientific reasoning?*

MN Yes. The whole common law tradition is very Aristotelian, because it is after all a tradition which says 'use rules, yes, but look always to the particular case, and remember that rules are often not adequate to the complexities of a particular case'. Now the Law and Economics Movement was an attempt to supplant that with something much more schematic, something much more formulable in advance. But I think that legal thinkers who are raised in the common law tradition always remember the historical complexity of reasoning in that tradition. After all, if they go and judge a particular case – if they're either litigating or judging in a case – they're confronted with the human facts, and often their sympathies are a lot broader than the technical mode of reasoning they are using. Therefore, they can be prevailed on by this sort of argument, and I think they're very eager to look for philosophical alternatives to economic reasoning – very eager to have this debate really thrashed out. So I'm optimistic about law.

RK *Your invocation of the literary imagination in* Love's Knowledge *is one I find persuasive, and yet it has problems for me. You seem to suggest that the literary imagination is intrinsically ethical because it makes us as readers more attentive to the singular, the circumstantial, the particular. Rather than reducing everything to an abstract model or to our own particular mind-set or prejudice, we become open, we wander, we allow ourselves to be astonished by the otherness of these particular people. And yet, while I can see that there's a certain moral sympathy induced by that kind of imagining, many of the great writers, and one might add many of the great readers, were also very immoral people. So does* good reading *necessarily lead to* good living?

MN Obviously it doesn't. It's all too evident that many lovers of art have been evil people. The first thing I want to say is, I am talking about what happens in the time that you're reading, and, of course, there may be all sorts of forces that will prevent you from enacting that in your life. So I'm talking about the morality of the *act* of reading, not the morality that's *caused* by reading. If you exercise this kind of sympathy in the act of reading, and yet you're part of a culture that asks you to be obtuse, that threatens you with penalties if you aren't obtuse in certain ways, then of course you might not carry that out in your life. One of the things that I was very struck by in Raoul Hilberg's *The Destruction of the European Jews* was the case of the evil art lover, which covered, of course, many of the Nazi leaders. But Hilberg shows that whenever such Nazi leaders actually approach a particular life in the manner of a reader, whenever, instead of applying generalisations – that these are cargo, that these are vermin and so on – where a particular life leapt out at them with a narrative force, there was what Hilberg calls a 'breakthrough', and suddenly they responded with the sympathy they previously reserved for their reading. I would say here that the habits of reading do have force, but very often can be eclipsed by other social forces. Then, I also want to say – and I am here agreeing with some of the things that you have written – it isn't just reading literature: there has to be, from the start, some sort of directedness towards other human beings and the good and ill that motivates that. Otherwise, the reading itself will never take place in an ethically satisfactory way. I think that a very good example of this is Dickens's *David Copperfield* – a novel that I love to talk about. There is a wonderful contrast here between the two story-lovers, Steerforth and David. Steerforth loves to listen to stories, loves to tell stories, but because from the start he's been brought up to believe that he's the only one in the world, and because, from the start, the world has been catering to his every whim and demand, he is a self-centred and, ultimately, quite evil story-teller who really doesn't have the sympathy that the reader of Dickens's novel quite naturally does for the fates of the characters that he is engaged with. Now, I think that means Steerforth also has limitations as a reader, I don't think he could understand the novel in which he figures . . .

RK *He is very seductive . . .*

MN He is very seductive as an adventure story-teller. David, by contrast, starts towards stories because of his love of his particular parents, and he has early experience of his parents as figures who are both extremely generous to him and who claim his love and generosity in return, who claim his protection in return. I think one sees in his relationship with his mother a combination of romantic storytelling with an impulse towards loving protectiveness that comes from very primitive and early elements of his childhood development. So, one of my concerns now in writing about the emotions is to try to talk about early child development and what makes possible that outward turning of the imagination, and the kind of reading of which David becomes capable, because I think you're absolutely right – you can't just say 'reading is a great thing no matter how it's done'. It has to be linked to an account of the development of the child's emotions.

RK *There is a view that there is a certain temptation in the literary imagination to express a will-to-power over fictional characters, to make of the fictional world one's kingdom. When translated into the real world, the political world, when one passes from text to action, this can lead to a certain megalomania or wilfulness. One thinks of Ezra Pound, T. S. Eliot, and indeed of Yeats, all tempted by fascism. Mainly by Mussolini interestingly, because Italian Fascism allied itself with the aesthetic movement of Futurism for a time, in the thirties. One can extend the argument to Céline and Heidegger. There is an embarrassing number of great imaginations who produced great works and yet were sometimes very immoral people. So how does one counteract the imperial will which seems to be as much part of the literary imagination as moral sympathy?*

MN I think the defender of the literary imagination doesn't have to defend all actual artists, or all actual readers. After all, I am talking about what is embodied in the work, and on the side of the reader, what happens in the act of reading. I'm not talking about all the other things that may or may not be part of a human being's life, who is a member of society that may have very bad social forces pressing in on the person. I'm also not talking about the ways in which writers make their living and do and don't have to become famous, and so on. All of those things may impinge on the moral action of the writer, but that doesn't necessarily negate the moral value of the work. I also don't want to say that all works of art are exemplary in the way that I've described. I've focused on the novel, and particularly on novels which have a distinct social and political dimension. I've focused on writers like Dickens, Henry James, for whom there's a certain kind of generosity and yielding quality in the imagination, a quality that makes it a powerful exemplar for the reader of how social imagining can work.

RK *So imagination is not,* per se, *an ethically good thing. Are you saying there are different kinds of imagination which one needs to discriminate between?*

MN I think that's absolutely right. Dickens's whole stance towards his creation as a child for which he tenderly cares – he said David Copperfield was his favourite child – it's that kind of tenderness and responsiveness that one sees also embodied in the work, in which there is a kind of romantic exuberance that can lead into error, and he shows of course how David is led astray by Steerforth. But he also shows that that very romantic exuberance is an essential constituent of his morality, that he is more generous in his good-doing than a lot of the more strictly rule-abiding characters. Far more generous and adequate as a moral agent than, for example, the Murdstones, who simply have a gloomy religion that forbids them all sympathetic identification with particular lives.

RK *What do you make of Noam Chomsky's view that education is something that largely impairs people's minds; that there is an innate predisposition in people towards liberty and freedom which education deforms as it feeds them, Gradgrind-like, with information, so they end up* less *free than before they went into the system? Presumably you would argue against that and claim that the reading of certain good novels – good literary education – is something that brings out the good in people?*

MN Yes. I would agree with Chomsky in his view that the innate instinct of a person is towards the good, and that this is brought out in the first place by relations with loving parents, and of course can be blighted by lack of parental love. But I think that the way this begins to develop early in a child's life is by asking 'what's it like to be that other person over there?', and that story-telling enters in at a very early stage, even with early nursery rhymes, like 'twinkle, twinkle little star, how I wonder what you are?' In that simple act of wonder you learn to invest a shape, which otherwise would seem a blank physical object, with life and with an inner world. And I think that's a moral ability which is absolutely crucial for all kinds of relations with human beings in later life, because after all, what do you see? You see a physical shape that's in motion, but how do you learn to respond to it? You could respond to it as just a parcel of human nature. But story-telling of an increasingly complex kind invests these shapes with a more and more complex, social and personal world, and teaches you to ask the questions that you need to ask of another person in your life – 'what is it like to feel pain of a certain kind?', 'what have I just inflicted on that person by my thoughtlessness?', and so on. So I think the story-telling which all societies share, and which they all use in their different ways to develop these abilities, is crucial. But I agree with Dickens that the circus, as it were, is not sufficient (he uses the 'circus' in *Hard Times* as a wonderful metaphor for the instinctual artistry of story-telling in a relatively uneducated person). Dickens shows that if you give somebody who has good instincts the wrong education, it can be very destructive. There's no doubt about that. I'm sure that's what Chomsky is talking about. On the other hand, you can't really translate this instinctive sympathy into social action without a great deal of historical knowledge, economic knowledge, and also without a much more complex form of story-telling. Dickens's own novel is not like the nursery rhymes that he mentions as very valuable; it depicts social classes, depicts economic differences among classes, depicts ways of life in concrete and very complex detail. That's what you need to be able to do if you're going to be a good citizen in a complex society.

RK *Aren't you making a plea for the re-introduction of what you call 'love's knowledge'? A knowledge which begins with the story-telling of children, and is later developed, and exemplified and rendered richer by the reading of novels. Isn't there a plea in your argument that this narrative ability be extended and reintroduced into the sciences?*

MN Yes. I think it should be reintroduced into economics, for example, not in a way that, of course, says get rid of models and measurement – that would be ludicrous – but in a way that informs the choice of starting-points in making models. I think it should be reintroduced into law, and I think there is a false ideal of what judicial neutrality is (e.g. if you get too close to anyone's life-story, you're likely to be derailed). Well, I think the best judges have always known that's *not* the case (even though you need to keep your own life-story out of it when you're judging about somebody else's life). But seeing what, for example, the damages of segregation really were to a black child in the American South, and seeing how that kind of separate schooling was very different – led to a different story from that of the white child – that's absolutely crucial to getting the right judgment in those cases. If you compare the actual judicial writing of some of these judges, who are trained in the law and economics movement, with what they write about legal reasoning – I'm thinking particularly of Richard Posner, one of the most famous examples of the idea that judging should be like economic reasoning – if you look at what he does when he's a judge, it's much more informed by his reading of novels than it is by economic practice. It shows tremendous sympathy and imagination. It's very revealing, since he is in fact a great reader of novels, to see how it's this habit that comes to the fore when he's actually trying to reach a good result in a particular case.

RK *Do you think it is significant that the Clinton administration wanted to appoint a woman as Supreme Court Justice in the States? Love's knowledge and the fragility of goodness – are these qualities which women are more likely to bring to the understanding of the world, the understanding of law, than men?*

MN I think this is a cultural matter, not anything about women's nature. I don't see any reason to think that there are natural differences. But I do think women are more often brought up to be willing to acknowledge that they need other people, and to think in those terms. Whereas men are very often brought up with an ideal of stern self-sufficiency, that can often lead in the direction of rather lofty, frosty ideals of neutrality, and an unwillingness to admit that an emotion of sympathy could play a legitimate and even a rational role in informing judging. Now this is complicated, because women who go into law often feel that they need to be more male than the male. In fact, the biggest opponent of emotion in judgment in recent US Supreme Court writing has been Justice Sandra May O'Connor, who actually has written that moral responses are altogether distinct from emotional responses.

RK *Somewhat like Margaret Thatcher in politics?*

MN Yes. By contrast, Justice Ruth Bader Ginsburg, from what I have read of her, seems to be a person of tremendous decency, warmth, and sympathy – so I have great admiration for that appointment, and I think she is also a distinguished legal thinker.

RK *Are there feminist implications to your books, to your writings?*

MN I think there are. One of the implications of focusing on human need is that it is important for all human beings to live in such a way as to acknowledge that they have needs for one another and for the world. The ideal of extreme self-sufficiency is a bogus and damaging ideal for social life. On the other hand, I want to say that there are some forms of need that no individual should have. If you focus on the unequal needs of people in different parts of the world, you notice that when it comes to needs for basic goods – like food, shelter, medical care and so on – women in many societies often fare very badly. That women are not guaranteed the basic needs of life by many societies is a cause for tremendous concern and urgent social action. So I think focusing on need, and also asking which needs should society guarantee the individuals, and what forms of need are really valuable and what forms are not, can take you in a number of different directions on feminist issues.

(Dublin, 1993)

MIROSLAV HOLUB

Middle Europe and the disestablished mind

MIROSLAV HOLUB, from Czechoslovakia, is internationally known as a doctor and immunologist, as well as a poet and essayist. His publications in English include *The Fly*; *Poems Before and After*; *On the Contrary* and *Vanishing Lung Syndrome*. His bridge-building between the arts and sciences is virtually unique in European literature.

RK *Has the role of the intellectual changed in Czechoslovakia since the 'Velvet Revolution' of '89?*

MH Our activity may be different to the extent that we can now identify with the present establishment, which by definition is the intellectual establishment, it's a literary establishment. The President, and the most important personality of the country is a playwright, Václav Havel, and many writers and artists became very important personalities during the recent events in Prague.

RK *And what does this do to you? Surely one of the roles of the poet in Czechoslovakia has been contestation and critique? What happens when that role of the poet as dissident, who says 'no' – as evidenced in the title of one of your poems,* On the Contrary – *what happens when the naysayer becomes part of the establishment or leader of the country?*

MH Well, I don't know about the others, but for me the situation has shifted a little – there is no reason for me to say no to the present establishment, because I deeply believe this is a democratic establishment which has been freely elected, and is continuing to develop democratically.

RK *But isn't there some sense in which the imagination – the poetic or the scientific imagination – should always remain disestablished?*

MH Oh yes, 'disestablished' is a beautiful word. Disestablished in relation to the old intellectual establishment and the reaction against the

Marxist, Leninist, materialist 'science' of the fifties, sixties, seventies and eighties. There is a sense now that we are switching or shifting a little too far towards the anti-scientific humanistic side of things. And science becomes almost a dirty word. Because I am not only a practising but also a believing scientist, I am in a position where I must disagree sometimes with the mainstream direction in the literary world.

RK *Given the fact that science was the official language and discourse of Marxist–Leninism and dialectical materialism in the Soviet bloc, as in Czechoslovakia, what can someone in your position do to retrieve the name of science, and the positive role that science might play in the future?*

MH Well, just to recall some concrete facts. What was the real history? Of course the regime, the Communist regime, was using scientific or pseudo-scientific slogans at every possible step. Marxism was labelled the science of sciences until science was all over the place. And of course the organisation of science, the academy of science, was Party-dominated and Party-directed. The regime had the heaviest possible upperhand on the 'scientific' approach to things. It was amazing – this is not well known – but we had a division between the bourgeois, Western science, the 'wrong' science, and our own *people's* science – the Russian, Czech, and Bulgarian sciences. This was the official attitude. In reality, of course the regime or the police disregarded the materialistic 'sciences of the people'. They always tried to steal some new technologies from the West. And what they also supported, under the surface, was all kinds of pseudo-science, occultism, alternative medicine, and so on. I know this because I was employed in a hospital, and some of the Party bosses always asked for healers, not for the official medical men, and they deeply believed in them. So, actually, the whole scientific approach of the regime was by this definition a counter-scientific movement.

RK *In opposing those pseudo-sciences, and occult sciences, are you advocating a narrow description of science, mere analysis or mere description, or a broader approach?*

MH By a scientific approach I would define something that asks all the questions, not just some questions. You have to be, not cynical, but slightly sceptical about everything, including science itself. Actually, science is the only human achievement which is, by definition, by structure, *autocritical* – redefining, restructuring itself by its own free will.

RK *But isn't that the point where philosophy and science become reconciled again? It is certainly a challenge to the modern tendency to separate them into two separate cultures – science on the one hand and the humanities (philosophy, poetry and the arts) on the other. In your attempt to bring together the scientific and the poetic imagination, do you see yourself as retrieving a lost tradition, which in the Renaissance, the Middle Ages, or going right back to the Greeks and the origin of Western Europe, was a happy relationship between reason and imagination?*

MH Well, in the Renaissance definitely, in the Aristotelian tradition, or in the Graeco-Roman tradition, to put it broadly, it was just one thing – the fables of fables, science alongside types of rhetoric or literature.

RK *When exactly did that separation take place in the West, in your view? And do you think there's any hope of undoing that discrepancy?*

MH It may have happened during the first Industrial Revolution. In the nineteenth century, it was already shifting apart. But obviously it was very much dependent on the structure of society, on the basic economy of the society, where it was more pronounced.

RK *Science became identified with the industrial devastation of nature. I'm thinking of the critique of science as alienating and inhuman by people like the Romantic poets, Blake and so on.*

MH Actually, I would say in a slightly cynical way that the split between science and the arts was pronounced in societies which could *afford* it. With our Czech enlightenment, with its national upsurgence at the end of the eighteenth and the beginning of the nineteenth century, there was no such feeling because the nation was fighting for some type of survival. I wouldn't say we were almost exterminated, but the language was retreating into the villages, into the country, and educated language almost didn't exist any more. And under this condition, the redefinition of the nation came in the same way in art, in poetry, and in science. So that science was something which was deeply identified with the national life. But the more we became a modern society, the more we began setting these things apart, which is obviously the 'two cultures' problem; it's a problem of affluent societies, those that can afford it.

RK *It's interesting that some of the founding fathers of modern Czechoslovakia, I'm thinking of Jan Hus, the humanist theologian, and later again Comenius, and later again Masaryk, the founding father of the present Czechoslovak nation, were all to some extent questioning minds. They were all scientists in whatever particular domain they worked – theology, philosophy, education, art.*

MH That is a nice way to put it, the 'questioning mind'. I think that the tradition of Czech Protestantism that developed with Hus and Comenius, and continued into the late nineteenth century, was something which the various Czech forms of reasoning had in common, and only in this century was it split into Romantic feelings on the one hand and scientific consciousness on the other. I would think the peak of Czech thinking has been the questioning mind.

RK *Up until this century then, science in your country was part and parcel of the general culture?*

MH The man in the street would think of science in terms of the Czech scientific tradition, the existence of the scientific establishment, like the National Museum, the Czech University. Even in the late nineteenth century, the main struggle in science was the struggle for Czech work in science, for a Czech science, in a way. Now we are, of course, in the late twentieth century and we are just going in the opposite direction. It's very hard to keep your national or minority language in science, because there is the one world language which is well adapted for scientific purposes, even for the very essence of grammar and information – English. The rules of information are simplest in English. Therefore, it's the international scientific language. It's computer-friendly.

RK *Czechoslovakia has been witnessing a conflict of national identities and cultures, the Czech on the one hand, the Slovak on the other. What do you think should be the primary locus of identity? Nations, regions, or the European federation that seems to be emerging now in the extended European Community?*

MH This is a rather personal question. For me, it's not a geographical position, it's not even the deep roots of Bohemia or Slovakia, or the Czech kingdom, or whatever. For me it's the Czechoslovak *idea*. Maybe it's not too rational, but I love Czechoslovakia without a hyphen. I just like all Czechoslovakia. Of course, I can't be against the federalisation of Europe, that would be very foolish and very conservative. Our aim and our hope is to be integrated, but to be integrated not as Czechs and Slovaks, I would prefer to be integrated as Czechoslovaks. We have Czech literature and Slovak literature. And in some instances we know the British or the Irish literature better than the Slovak literature, and vice versa. And we still translate between Czech and Slovak. It's not necessary, it's like Scottish–English and English–English. It's not so different. But we still translate. We have the news in both languages, for example.

RK *Are you Czech or Slovak?*

MH I am a Czech. My second wife was a Slovak. But who knows what we are? I discovered one of my ancestors was a Mores. By definition a Mores was a Jewish name, so I don't know what I am. I don't care whether I am Czech or Slovak. For me, it's all the same. I regard being a Czechoslovak as my broader identity, but still a very definite identity, and, therefore, I would like to keep it as it is.

RK *So, you're as mixed up as most Europeans today?*

MH Yes, this is even a biological rule – the hybridisation, the change of the species is what counts. And, in this sense, even the diversification of the national identities in a unified Europe would be a positive biological trait.

RK *You're suggesting that Czechoslovakia should be opened to this multiplicity of national and cultural identities. But would you go further than that and say that Europe itself, as an entity or entirety, should be open to other cultures, to cultural differences that reside outside of its borders?*

MH Europe is in a way all over the place. Europe is everywhere. Australia is not everywhere, Asia is not everywhere, China is not everywhere; but Europe is almost everywhere. And that's the trouble, how to define it. There are not clear European boundaries: this may be part of the legacy of Europe's colonial history. Europe is a very complex notion, and it is very hard to say how it will be influenced by other cultures. Europe has already influenced all the world, except for the most remote isolated corners. As America has influenced the cultures of the world. Recently, I had the opportunity to see India, China, Turkey, and I was amazed that there are increasing numbers of American hotels, and of course, American tourists. The tourist pilgrimage is more or less an American phenomenon. In Istanbul, for instance, what is left of Turkey is the Blue Mosque, or the smaller mosques, and some of the poor of the street – the rest is Marlboro cigarettes and other American consumer goods.

RK *How does one deal with this omnipresence of America in the world today?*

MH There are two alternatives. We may conserve our state, the face and the heart of the country, and stay poor, as in Asian countries. Or we will be Americanised, get all the dollars from the tourist traffic, and look like some kind of Disneyland.

RK *But is there a sense in which your Czech culture could retrieve its traditional position as Mittel Europa, as the middle of Europe, both geographically and politically, and find a 'third way' beyond the polarities of East and West?*

MH Years ago, even under the Russian boot, there was a Hungarian magazine which asked the question – is there a *Western* culture and is there an *Eastern* culture; is there an *American* type of superpower and a *Russian* type of superpower; and is there not something, a *third way*, a third type of culture, a Middle Europe? The answer to the last question was, yes, there is. Because everybody in Hungary, in Poland, in Czechoslovakia would say: we are different from both sides for good or for bad.

(Dublin, 1991)

JACQUES DARRAS

Bankers and poets: geniuses of the North

JACQUES DARRAS is a French poet and Professor of Literature at the Universities of Paris and Amiens. His books include *Beyond the Tunnel of History* (1989, BBC Reith lectures); *Le Génie du Nord; Conrad and the West* and *Autobiographie de l'espèce humaine.*

RK *With what particular moment would you identify the birth of modern Europe?*

JD With the time of the bankers, the time of the traders, people risking themselves with their currency, their coins. They came from Lombardy, from northern Italy, crossing the Alps, being protected by guards and reaching the first stage, Lyons, the central city, what we call in French *La plaque tournante* of all the conquests of Europe by the Italians. And then, travelling north, avoiding Paris, going to places like Reims and Troyes and ending up in that city of all cities, which is very dear to my own name, to my own feelings – Arras in Northern France – where the greatest fair of them all was at the time. But traders, because of their mobility, because of the mobility that is in money itself, in the exchange of goods, took along with them an exchange of ideas. You can't dissociate an exchange of goods from an exchange of ideas. I think that Europe developed from that sort of trading of ideas, currencies and fashions, over the counters, in the open air of an Arras square, for instance. Poets were there too. Of course they had no money. They were begging for money all the time, from the princes, from the bankers, from the traders: being fed on a free meal here and there, and giving in exchange a poem, or cracking a joke if the banker was not charitable to them. There you had poetry, scholarship, trading and banking as well.

RK *Today we seem to be moving towards a central European bank whose currency will be this famous* ECU. *We don't know what'll be on the cover of the*

ECU notes, but presumably it will be a variation on the round stars of Europe. And some people will feel that the old currencies where you had your king, queen, president, national hero or heroine, mattered to them in that that symbolism of money – the figure-head on the pound note or on the coin – gave some sense of attachment, some sense that they were governing their own lives. Moving from the world of the European ECU to a broad European ecumenism (to coin a phrase) you might say we are heading towards a lowest common denominator culture: one where the shared Europe would be precisely that banal, homogenous bit we all have in common, where instead of affirming our national and regional differences, we simply conform to the same kind of Eurospeak.

JD I'm no economist, but the little I know from history tells me that the ECU system was there already in the Middle Ages. I mean, you had your standard money, and what was standard money? It was gold. All the local monies, all the local currencies, operated by the gold standard. And, therefore, you could have spoken of a unification of money. Just as in the Middle Ages, Europe's gold standard, as far as language was concerned, was Latin. You could communicate with other people through Latin, as we are doing through English these days. No, I don't think the situation has changed tremendously. I'm quite sure that in the thirteenth and fourteenth centuries, people must have said, like you've just done, that there was a sense of uniformity and monotony being imposed upon them, resulting in a loss of diversity, of locality and localism. I think that's exactly what Europe is all about, trying to muster together, to bring together, throughout time, a sense of unity, while leaving chaos at the bottom. Well, this is democracy. What is democracy about, if not trying to restore, to impose, an order on top of a tremendous disorder crowding underneath?

RK *So, would you go along with T. S. Eliot's idea that there is a whole mind of Europe which is a unity of tradition?*

JD I think there is.

RK *And how would you define it?*

JD I would say it's cultural. The great price that is put on culture and scholarship has been an investment. I mean, I'm quite struck by the fact that some cities around the fourteenth century, Paris among them or the Italian cities such as Padua or Bologna, were cunning enough to understand that money as such was not enough, that they had to invest in learning. And old cities like Arras, for instance, declined almost overnight for not understanding that it had to put its money in knowledge, science and art. There was no university created in Arras, the university was created in Paris, in La Sorbonne. And all the nations of Europe flocked to La Sorbonne.

RK *And this investment in culture and learning was more than a cosmetic veneer?*

JD Indeed. That's why we see the rise to prominence of northern Flemish and Dutch cities, like Antwerp, especially with the coming of printing. And that's why we witness the collapse of those old medieval cities which lacked the lucidity that might have taken them towards learning instead of just making money as bankers and traders. The lesson of modern Europe is that you cannot separate economics and culture.

RK *Why are you so fascinated by the pan-European culture of the high Middle Ages? Again and again in your writings you come back to this, and your chosen example is often that of Burgundy. But you take various other parts of northern Europe as well to illustrate your point. What is it about the high Middle Ages that you feel we lost, and may be recovering again?*

JD What I feel is that there was at the time a sense of energy and dynamism in the making. The people realised that a feudal society, and feudal systems, were obsolete, on the way out, vanishing, that they were freeing themselves from that sort of order imposed upon them. They were beginning to discover the joy of freedom. This experience of freedom in Europe took place for the first time in the northern cities, not in the southern cities. And it actually happened when a few bold traders asked their freedom from the landlords, from the Church, or from the King, playing viciously and intelligently one against the other in order to acquire a real sense of liberty. A freedom for trade. Thus began a cross-frontier movement accommodating and accepting foreigners instead of levying taxes on them.

RK *So it was a Europe of open exchange and mobility.*

JD Absolutely. It was a Europe of free market exchange between those people of the North, and you can see that in the layout of the cities with their famous squares. The French word '*place*' is so beautiful in its simplicity, so open, enacting its image in Brussels for instance, or in Arras, those spaces surrounded by arcades under which the traders and the bankers sheltered themselves from the rain. You can still hear the noises of those crowds exchanging material, the clicking of the currency, and the punning of the Arras poets, who were quite numerous at the time. When I go to a place like the Place de Bruxelles, the Grand Marketplace, I can still feel that sense of openness, under the sky, with God residing where he should be, up there, not too close to Earth, leaving people, men and women, to their daily considerations, their everyday chores, letting them be governed by the life of the commons, the municipalities, that is, people elected from among the traders themselves.

RK *This is a symbol for you of the birth of European democracy?*

JD It is the birth of democracy. My contention is that actual democracy was born in the north of Europe, and this we tend to forget. We have strong misgivings about northern culture, owing to nineteenth-century cults of Germanic genius being unfortunately prolonged by Nazi history. But I think the North was once very joyous, very scholarly, open to all influences, very cosmopolitan, and it is this North that I want to recover.

RK *This is the Netherlands, this is Flanders, this is the North of France, Burgundy . . .*

JD And nothern Italy, of course. You have that extraordinary access route that links up cities like Venice, Genoa, and Lyons, leading up to Antwerp, and even London.

RK *But how do you account for the fact that when so many modern European nation states – you might say European modernity in general – looked for precedents they could invoke as an authority, they looked to* southern *Europe, to Greece and Rome?*

JD The concept of democracy may have been invented in Athens, but the actual life of democracy began in the North. I mean, French people don't want to be reminded that the name 'France' and 'French' come from the German tribe called the Franks.

RK *Why are they so embarrassed about this?*

JD They're embarrassed because of the successive wars, from 1870 onwards. We are supposed to be the privileged foes of the Germans; and that was unfortunately very true in the succession of bloody wars. But in France, in French, you have Franc, which is exactly the same root as freedom. I don't want to engage in some sort of pseudo-philology, but you had the sense of *breaking* in the very philological root, breaking free, breaking things in two or away from. French, Franc, freedom. I've come upon a very strange thing that I didn't know until quite recently: King Louis XI was the founder of our French state in the fourteenth century. That wily king played a very bad trick on my Arras compatriots at one stage, because they refused to be enlisted into the French kingdom. They looked towards Flanders, towards the Flemish people, and resisted Louis XI. He was very cunning, and started deporting the Arras people. My own name perhaps comes from the fact that my ancestors were deported at some stage and therefore called d'Arras, from Arras. The North was colonised by France. I would like my sort of decolonisation to be a gesture. Not a violent one at all, but giving the French a lesson in history, and reminding them of what French nationalism is based upon, what our nation state is made of, and saying to them: 'I'd rather revert to square one, or to *place* one', in order to start all over again, to replace the threads that made up the tapestry, that you so absurdly broke through, or tore apart. And this is part of my fascination for the north of France, because I think that it was the laboratory of a Europe to come, that never came, that never came to pass, because instead of that we had nationalities and nationalisms. We're beginning in the new Europe to return perhaps to that tolerant and creative tapestry of the late Middle Ages. That is my hope.

RK *If I could bring you back more specifically to the question of culture. You have argued that in the high Middle Ages we had a pan-European culture, which was decentralised into little city states or cultures which celebrated multiplicity, complexity, and produced works by printers like Bosch and Bruegel, who united high culture with popular culture. Was there a sense, at that time, that culture was available to the masses, to the people at large?*

JD I think that the painters, especially the Flemish painters, meant the paintings to be contemplated and to be seen by everybody. In the churches, of course, mainly. This is true as well as far as music was concerned; the main music of the times was polyphony, which, to me, is the realisation of democracy in song. It is very austere, very cold in a way, but just listening to all those voices criss-crossing each other, and creating a volume which little by little fills up those huge naves of the cathedrals, is something I find very, very beautiful indeed. The best of European art is something which is constantly active, which has a spiritual energy about itself, which people not only try to emulate but which brings new ideas, new concepts, into today's life, into present life.

RK *One could object that those modern artists and thinkers who tried to translate art into life often embraced some kind of reactionary politics – Céline, Pound and Heidegger . . .*

JD They are people of straw. They are the hollow men of T. S. Eliot's poem. But to take up the politics of modernism, my feeling is that what we call modernism, and praise greatly because it is the *ne plus ultra* of art, serving as a forerunner of the social movements, and so on, I think that basically was a sort of reactionary movement – but in the good sense of the word. Modernism was reacting against a society that led to the First World War, that led to a general massacre of human beings, of human life. Modernism says no to that. I mean, the best modernist movement of them all took place in Zurich, the place where Joyce was at the same time as the Dada movement, where those people who happened to belong to two cultures, German and French, saw their compatriots on either side of the trenches fight themselves to death. Those very people in Zurich said no to the war. In my opinion, modernism is a saying no. Now, we can't say no forever. We've been saying no for a whole century. My feeling is that that's enough.

RK *But writers and thinkers have a right to say no.*

JD Of course they have a right to say no. But can we go on living on a culture of negativity? I think that we are just, perhaps, emerging out of the wasteland culture. I've never thought actually that T. S. Eliot's poem was a great masterpiece in itself, except that it gave the keynote of the century. If you don't have poets, you don't have consciences, and you don't have that sort of aim to praise the world, to praise life, to say that life is good, life is pleasurable. That's exactly what the poet says, and the poet that never says that life is pleasurable is not a poet in my eyes. There is a pleasure in the simple energy of life that a poet is there to tell us about and keep telling us about. At the same time, pleasure is so akin to suffering, is so beset by danger all around, that you have to keep that sense of feeling alive, in touch with a greater truth, a cosmic, divine truth. That's what poets are here for and, therefore, they are very wary of political power, they dissent from political power because they say 'Your truth is not the truth'.

RK *What sort of European culture are we entering into?*

JD What we are entering into is very hard for me to say. What we are in need of is perhaps a new reconciliation of elite culture and popular culture, a retrieval of what is best in the Middle Ages. We are back again to that conception of the elite not dissociating itself from the people, from the population. I know it's very hard to achieve. I know it's very fashionable among the elite to have contempt for television – you still have those people in Paris who say to you, for instance, I won't let my children watch television; we have no TV set in our room. I don't agree with that at all. We have cable television, we have cable news, even if it's a zapping culture we're in, it's another type of freedom in a way. I can zap from Italian programmes to German programmes. Now, I'm not a born zapper but if I really want to apply my mind and put in the effort, for instance, to learn German, I can turn to my German news every night, and complement that by lessons in German. I think that culture for everybody is there. We are suffering from an excess, an over-abundance of culture. The problem is we need the guides, the guiding effort. People are talking of ethics, of an ethical renewal, and so on. I think that we shouldn't be taken in by those great words. Whenever somebody talks to me of ethics, I tend to become wary of it because I have the feeling that he wants to enlist me in his school, in his creed, in his camp. I think what we need are guidelines, guides, and perhaps people telling us where to apply our efforts, where best to apply our intelligence to acquire learning for ourselves. This is why the educational system is in such crisis.

RK *Who and where are those guides?*

JD I don't think they are yet there. They would probably be common-sense people who wouldn't despise scholarship and learning as such, who – taking the lesson from the Middle Ages – wouldn't be afraid of money, because if we really want to live in that type of society, well, it would cost a great deal. The people we want are new teachers, new minted teachers in a way. They're not in the market yet. They are to be found, they are to be turned into new preceptors. Like the elite during the sixteenth and seventeenth centuries taking their pupils on the *grand tour* through Italy and the continent, taking lessons on the very spot where the monuments were. We need such teachers today.

RK *So you're advocating more democracy in education . . .*

JD Yes, a more elitist democracy.

(Dublin, 1991)

INTRODUCTION II

These conversations will, I hope, articulate some central debates in modern European thought. The dialogue format affords the seven 'Continental' thinkers in question an opportunity to introduce, situate and clarify their own work, to speak for themselves. I have included short prefatory notes and bibliographies by way of providing the reader w]ith additional background information. Suffice it here to say something briefly about my selection of thinkers and then sketch out some common contexts and co-ordinates of their philosophies.[1]

My list is by no means exhaustive, but it does, I believe, include philosophers who articulate and illustrate significant and, for the most part, representative movements of contemporary European thought:

1) Derrida: deconstruction in debate with structuralism;
2) Lévinas: ethics in debate with metaphysics;
3) Marcuse: critical dialectics in debate with the Marxist–Hegelian Frankfurt school;
4) Ricoeur: critical hermeneutics in debate with the human sciences;
5) Breton: religious poetics in debate with Thomism, Neoplatonism and aesthetics;
6) Gadamer: an ontological hermeneutics in debate with the 'great texts' of tradition;
7) Lyotard: postmodern thinking in debate with the European 'project of modernity'.

The seven thinkers represent a variety of nations, cultures and religions. Derrida is a French Algerian of Jewish origin, educated in France, where he teaches at *l'Ecole des Hautes Etudes en Sciences Sociales*;

Lévinas is a Lithuanian Jew who has lived most of his life in Paris, though he has also worked in Germany and Israel; Marcuse is a German of Jewish background who began his philosophical work in Freiburg and Frankfurt, before moving to the United States; Ricoeur is a French Protestant who has lived and worked in Germany and Israel; Breton is a French Catholic who taught for many years at *l'Institut Catholique* in Paris; Gadamer is a German Protestant who taught at several universities, including Leipzig, Frankfurt and Heidelberg; Lyotard is a French thinker who has taught at the University of Paris, as well as at Emory in Georgia and Irvine in California.

In the preface to his novel *Roderick Hudson*, Henry James commented on the editorial procedure of establishing relations between themes, idioms and characters in his work: 'Really, universally, relations stop nowhere, and the exquisite problem of the [author] is eternally to draw, by a geometry of his own, the circle within which they shall appear to do so.' In these following paragraphs I will endeavour to sketch some circles of philosophical reference wherein our seven thinkers overlap or intersect.

Even though many of the writings of my seven philosophical interlocutors have been available in English for some time now, not a great deal has been written in the English-speaking world about the manner in which their respective intellectual projects derive from seminal movements of European thought. I am thinking particularly of the formative influence exerted upon these thinkers by three main schools of thought: first, the critical 'hermeneutics of suspicion' advanced by Hegelian Marxism, Nietzsche and Freud; second, the structural linguistics of Saussure, Jacobson, Lévi-Strauss; and, third, the phenomenological theories developed by Husserl and Heidegger. I confine most of my remarks to this third and I believe most influential movement.

* * * *

Phenomenology represents arguably the most persuasive influence for our seven thinkers. This is not surprising when one considers that phenomenological existentialism generated the main body of European philosophy between 1930 and 1960, especially in France and Germany, occasioning what many would regard as the 'golden age' of contemporary Continental thought.

The phenomenological movement was inaugurated by the German philosopher, Edmund Husserl, whose *Logical Investigations* was published in 1900–01. In this and subsequent works, Husserl outlined the primary aims and methods of phenomenology. His essential project was to address the 'crisis' of European science by initiating a philosophical 'return to the things themselves'. The future of European culture depended for Husserl on the recovery of meaning as constituted by human consciousness. Consciousness (*Bewusstsein*) was no longer to be understood in terms of traditional metaphysics or positivism as a given substance or objective fact. A new method, Husserl argued, must be advanced which would disclose and intuit its essential functioning as *an act of intentionality*. By this he meant that consciousness is always consciousness *of* something other than itself: a dynamic activity projecting itself beyond the idealist enclosures of the mind towards horizons of transcendent meaning. Husserl's phenomenological theory of intentionality led, furthermore, to the discovery that consciousness as a reflective operation already presupposes a *prereflective* lived experience of the world, what Husserl called the 'lifeworld' (*Lebenswelt*). Only by returning to this creative nexus *between* consciousness and world, where reality originally *appears* to us (qua *phenomenon*), can we arrive at an intuition of truth – the *essence* of things themselves.

Husserl's phenomenological investigations served as guide for subsequent works by Heidegger and Gadamer. Heidegger's *Being and Time*, published in 1927, registered a profound debt to his mentor Husserl (in addition to Kierkegaard, Nietzsche and Dilthey). Gadamer, in turn, developed phenomenology as a largely linguistic ontology of meaning. Whereas Husserl had tended to confine his analysis to an enquiry of the scientific and logical foundations of truth, Heidegger and Gadamer broadened the scope to include a concrete description of our finite being-in-the-world (*In-der-Welt-Sein*). Only by thus concentrating on the existential moods, cares and words of our being-there (*Da-Sein*) in historical time, might we eventually be in a position to ask the most fundamental of all philosophical questions: *what does it mean to be*? Human temporality as concretely lived and linguistically expressed emerged for Heidegger and Gadamer as the indispensable horizon of the question of Being itself.

The 'existential' version of phenomenology was further advanced by French thinkers like Sartre and Merleau-Ponty. Sartre's *Being and*

Nothingness (1943) offered a variety of vivid descriptions of human existence as project, choice and responsibility. He was to set the philosophical tone for his generation by declaring that our existence precedes our essence since we make ourselves what we are and are 'condemned to be free'.

Merleau-Ponty's *The Phenomenology of Perception* (1945) applied the method of phenomenology in a similarly *engagé* manner, its primary purpose being the description of our situated existence as 'body-subjects', who experience our world before we ever analyse it in abstract, scientific terms. Merleau-Ponty hailed phenomenology as being 'destined to bring back all the living relationships of experience, as the fisherman's net draws up from the depths of the ocean quivering fish and seaweed'.[2] He identified the compelling force of such an exploratory philosophy for the eager minds of his generation as follows:

> We shall find in ourselves and nowhere else, the unity and true meaning of phenomenology. It is less a question of counting up quotations than of determining and expressing in concrete form this phenomenology for ourselves which has given a number of present-day readers the impression, on reading Husserl and Heidegger, not so much of encountering a new philosophy as of recognizing what they had been waiting for . . . If phenomenology was a movement before becoming a doctrine or a philosophical system, this was attributable neither to accident, nor to fraudulent intent. It is as painstaking as the works of Balzac, Proust, Valéry or Cézanne – by reason of the same kind of attentiveness and wonder, the same demand for awareness, the same will to seize the meaning of the world or of history as that meaning comes into being. In this way it merges into the general effort of modern thought.[3]

Even though Lévinas, Ricoeur and Marcuse were already writing about the philosophy of Husserl and Heidegger in the thirties and forties, it was not until the sixties that they succeeded in transforming their research into works that proved original in their own right. Thus, for example, while Lévinas was the first to introduce Sartre to phenomenology with his *The Theory of Intuition in Husserl's Phenomenology*, published in 1930, it was the appearance in 1961 of his monumental *Totality and Infinity* that established Lévinas as a major contemporary thinker adjusting the intellectual tone for a second generation of European phenomenologists.

We find a similar pattern with Ricoeur. He began by publishing critical commentaries on Jaspers and Marcel (1948) and Husserl (1950), but it was undoubtedly with the publication of the second volume of his *Philosophy of Will* in 1960, followed by two works on phenomenological hermeneutics, *Freud and Philosophy: An Essay on Interpretation* (1965) and *The Conflict of Interpretations* (1969), that Ricoeur was ultimately acknowledged as one of the most significant European philosophers of the contemporary period.

For his part, Marcuse's seminal studies on phenomenological and critical theory in the late twenties and early thirties (when he studied with Husserl and Heidegger in Freiburg, before moving to the Frankfurt School), did not come to full fruition until the sixties and seventies, when his books, particularly *One-Dimensional Man* (1964) and *An Essay on Liberation* (1969), came to fascinate a new and rebellious generation.

Three other thinkers in dialogue here, Derrida, Breton and Lyotard, also acknowledge a debt to phenomenology. Since this debt is made explicit in the dialogues themselves, suffice it to mention here Lyotard's first book on Merleau-Ponty entitled *La Phénoménologie* (1954); Breton's phenomenological studies of the intentional relationship between consciousness and Being; and Derrida's 'deconstructive' reinterpretations of Husserl and Heidegger (beginning with his two first major publications: *Edmund Husserl's 'Origin of Geometry': An Introduction* (1962) and *Speech and Phenomena and Other Essays in Husserl's Theory of Signs* (1967)).

But whatever our seven Continental thinkers derived from phenomenology, they each refashioned this heritage according to their own image – often indeed to the extent of surpassing it altogether. One could perhaps venture a summary of their respective debts to the phenomenological movement in terms of the following broad descriptions: Gadamer and Ricoeur – hermeneutic phenomenology; Lévinas – ethical phenomenology; Breton – religious phenomenology; Marcuse – dialectical phenomenology; Derrida – deconstructive phenomenology; Lyotard – postmodern phenomenology. In short, despite their later differences, all seven would appear to share an initial phenomenological starting-point: namely, the conviction that an original interrogation of meaning requires us to penetrate beneath the established concepts of empirical, logical or scientific 'objectivication' (what Husserl called the 'natural attitude') to the 'lived experience' of our temporalising and signifying *being-in-the-world*.

I have confined my above remarks to the phenomenological movement, believing it to be the single most significant influence on the thinkers featured in this section. I do not underestimate, however, the critical impact exerted by other formative movements such as *structural analysis* or the *hermeneutics of suspicion*. The innovative theories of Saussure or Lévi-Strauss, for example, recur as critical references throughout the writings of Ricoeur and Derrida. Freud – as one instance of the 'hermeneutics of suspicion' – occupies a central place in the analysis of Marcuse, Ricoeur, Derrida and Lyotard; and the Marxist-Hegelian dialectic – as another instance of such a hermeneutics – plays a pivotal role in the critiques of ideology advanced by Marcuse, Breton, Ricoeur, Derrida and also, though less frequently, in the anti-totalitarian ethics of Lévinas and Lyotard. Once again, I refer the reader to my interlocutors' own remarks on these matters.

★ ★ ★ ★

Continental thinkers are often extremely difficult to understand. Part of this difficulty is, I believe, inherent in the very nature of the ontological and epistemological questionings in which these thinkers are engaged. Martin Heidegger acknowledged the essential difficulty raised by his own use of innovatory language in his Introduction to *Being and Time* (1927):

> With regard to the awkwardness and 'inelegance' of expression in the analyses to come, we may remark that it is one thing to give a report in which we tell about *entities* (i.e. familiar objects), but another to grasp entities in their Being. For the latter task we lack not only most of the words but above all, the 'grammar'.[4]

A one-dimensional language can only deal with a one-dimensional reality, whereas it is a critical task of philosophy to interrogate other, hitherto undisclosed, dimensions of existence.[5] The attempt to purge philosophical language of alternative dimensions in order to reduce it to the cut-and-dried clarity of formal logic or commonsense language is restrictive. The refusal to extend analysis beyond the parameters of 'ordinary discourse' bespeaks a refusal to open up new and qualitatively different meanings which contest our ordinary universe. As Marcuse remarked, adverting to the dangers of such reductionism: 'The metaphysical dimension, formally a genuine field of rational thought, becomes irrational and unscientific . . . The contemporary effort to reduce the scope and the truth of philosophy is tremendous and the philosophers themselves proclaim the modesty and inefficacy of philosophy. It leaves the established reality untouched; it abhors transgression.'[6] By attending exclusively to the facts of ordinary language, one risks ignoring the metaphysical or socio-historic factors which lie behind these facts.[7]

I have endeavoured in these dialogues to enable the thinkers in question to respond to critiques levelled against them and to spell out, where possible, the key concepts and arguments of their work. My intention here – and I have no doubt that of my interlocutors also – is to explain and simplify without being simplistic. I hope that this exegetical scruple might also serve to ensure that these exchanges will not be confined to university specialists or professional philosophers but will prove accessible to non-academic readers interested in knowing more about recent European thought. For those who remain sceptical of any discourse which transcends the 'analytic treatment of ordinary language', perhaps the best attitude to adopt in entering into these somewhat unfamiliar dialogues is that recommended by the poet Samuel Coleridge: 'a willing suspension of disbelief'.

1 There are many other influential thinkers from the European Continent whom one might reasonably expect to see included here – Barthes, Lévi-Strauss, Lacan, Foucault, Lefort, Habermas, Desanti, Althusser, Serres or Girard. But as Spinoza taught, *omnis determinatio est negatio*: any determination of inclusion necessarily involves exclusion. My particular selection in this section does not express a conviction that these seven thinkers are indisputably the most significant or the most representative of contemporary Continental thinkers. I do believe, however, that each of them is significant and representative in some important respect, and, of course, all share a common debt to a phenomenological formation and thereby represent a coherent grouping.

2 Maurice Merleau-Ponty, *The Phenomenology of Perception*, trans. C. Smith, Routledge and Kegan Paul, London, 1962, Preface, p. xv.

3 *Ibid.*, pp. viii, xxi. Parallel to this mainstream movement of phenomenological

existentialism emerged the 'Christian existentialism' of Karl Jaspers (whose three-volume *Philosophy* appeared in 1931) and of Gabriel Marcel (whose more 'personalist' study, *The Philosophy of Existence*, was published in 1936). This particular brand of existentialist thinking also held a profound attraction for several of the 'second generation' of Continental thinkers, perhaps most notably Paul Ricoeur and Emmanuel Lévinas.

4 Martin Heidegger, *Being and Time*, trans. J. Macquarrie and E. Robinson. Blackwell, Oxford, 1973, p. 63.

5 Herbert Marcuse, *One-Dimensional Man: Studies in the Ideology of Advanced Industrial Society*, Beacon Press, Boston, 1964, pp. 123 *et seq.*

6 *Ibid.*, p. 173.

7 The following passages from Marcuse's *One-Dimensional Man* identify the shortcomings of efforts to eradicate the novelty and unfamiliarity of much genuine philosophical discourse:

> The almost masochist reduction of speech to the humble and common is made into a program . . . Thinking (or at least its expression) is not only pressed into a straight-jacket of common usage, but also enjoined not to ask and seek solutions beyond those that are already there . . . One might ask what remains of philosophy? What remains of thinking, intelligence, without any explanation? However, what is at stake is not the definition or the dignity of philosophy. It is rather the chance of preserving and protecting the right, the *need* to think and to speak in terms other than those of common usage – terms which are meaningful, rational and valid precisely because they are *other* terms . . . An irreducible difference exists between the universe of everyday thinking and language on the one side, and that of philosophical thinking and language on the other . . . In its exposure of the mystifying character of transcendent terms, vague notions, metaphysical universals and the like, linguistic analysis mystifies the terms of ordinary language by leaving them in the repressive context of the established universe of discourse . . . In this analytic treatment of ordinary language the latter is really sterilized and anaesthetized. Multi-dimensional language is made into one-dimensional language, in which different and conflicting meanings no longer interpenetrate but are kept apart; the explosive historical dimension of meaning is silenced. (See pp. 177, 182, 184, 199.)

I have quoted Marcuse at length because I believe that his more ideological explanation of the difficulties involved in genuine thinking, coupled with Heidegger's ontological explanation, represents an essential caveat to any facile effort to 'explain away' the fundamental complexities of Continental philosophy.

Section C

PHILOSOPHICAL THINKERS

JACQUES DERRIDA

Deconstruction and the other

Prefatory note

Born in Algeria in 1931 to Jewish parents, JACQUES DERRIDA is considered by many to be one of the most innovatory thinkers working on the continent today. Along with Lacan, Foucault, Barthes and Lévi-Strauss, Derrida was largely responsible for putting the structuralist/post-structuralist controversy on the intellectual map. His influence has been paramount not only in France, where he studied and taught for many years at *l'Ecole Normale Supérieure* and *l'Ecole des Hautes Etudes*, but also in the Anglo–American world, where he has lectured widely in humanities and philosophy departments, serving as Visiting Professor at both Johns Hopkins and Yale Universities.

Most celebrated for his systematic and unremitting 'deconstruction' of Western metaphysics, Derrida hails originally from the phenomenological movement of Husserl, Heidegger and Lévinas; and it is within and around this particular philosophical framework, more than any other, that his thinking has evolved. Derrida's earliest works were *Edmund Husserl's 'Origin of Geometry': An Introduction* (1962), and a critical analysis of Husserl's theory of the sign entitled *Speech and Phenomena* (1967) – this latter work being, by his own admission, 'the one to which (he) feels most attached'. Already in these early texts, Derrida was working out his central notion of the irreducible structure of *différance* as it operates in human consciousness, temporality, history and above all in the activity of writing (*l'écriture*). By means of this *différance* – a neologism meaning both to 'defer' and to 'differ' – Derrida proposed to show how the major metaphysical definitions of Being as some timeless self-identity or presence (e.g. *logos, ousia, telos* and so on), which dominated Western philosophy from Plato to the present day, could ultimately be 'deconstructed'. Such a deconstruction would show that in each instance *différance precedes* presence rather than the contrary (as presupposed by what Derrida terms the 'logocentric' tradition of European thought).

In his more mature works, in particular *Of Grammatology* (1967), *Writing and Difference* (1967), *Dissemination* (1972) and *Margins of Philosophy* (1972), Derrida has applied his 'deconstructive' analysis to a wide variety of subjects – literary, scientific, linguistic and psychoanalytic, as well as strictly philosophical. Indeed, works such as *Glas* (1974), *Truth in Painting* (1978) and *The Postcard* (1980), freely experiment with new modes of thinking and writing in an attempt to overcome the traditional divide between aesthetic and philosophical discourse, a divide determined by the 'logocentrism' of Western metaphysics which sought to exile from the realm of pure reason (*logos*) all that did not conform to its centralising logic of identity and non-contradiction.

By redirecting our attention to the shifting 'margins' and limits which determine such logocentric procedures of exclusion and division, Derrida contrives to dismantle our preconceived notions of *identity* and expose us to the challenge of hitherto suppressed or concealed 'otherness' – the *other* side of experience, which has been ignored in order to preserve the illusion of truth as a perfectly self-contained and self-sufficient presence. Thus, for example, we find Derrida questioning and subverting the traditional priorities of speech over writing, presence over absence, sameness over difference, timelessness over time and so on. His work of rigorous deconstruction poses, accordingly, a radical challenge to such hallowed logocentric notions as the Eternal Idea of Plato, the Self-Thinking-Thought of Aristotle or the *cogito* of Descartes. For Derrida, there is nothing thought that cannot be rethought, nothing said that cannot be unsaid. Even deconstruction itself must be deconstructed.

The following dialogue took place in Paris in 1981.

RK *The most characteristic feature of your work has been its determination to 'deconstruct' the Western philosophy of presence. I think it would be helpful if you could situate your programme of deconstruction in relation to the two major intellectual traditions of Western European culture – the Hebraic and the Hellenic. You conclude your seminal essay on the Jewish philosopher,*

Emmanuel Lévinas, with the following quotation from James Joyce's Ulysses: *'GreekJew is JewGreek'. Do you agree with Lévinas that Judaism offers an alternative to the Greek metaphysics of presence? Or do you believe with Joyce that the Jewish and Greek cultures are fundamentally intertwined?*

JD While I consider it essential to think through this copulative synthesis of Greek and Jew, I consider my own thought, paradoxically, as neither Greek nor Jewish. I often feel that the questions I attempt to formulate on the outskirts of the Greek philosophical tradition have as their 'other' the model of the Jew, that is, the Jew-as-other. And yet the paradox is that I have never actually invoked the Jewish tradition in any 'rooted' or direct manner. Though I was born a Jew, I do not work or think within a living Jewish tradition. So that if there is a Judaic dimension to my thinking which may from time to time have spoken in or through me, this has never assumed the form of an explicit fidelity or debt to that culture. In short, the ultimate site (*lieu*) of my questioning discourse would be neither Hellenic nor Hebraic if such were possible. It would be a non-site beyond both the Jewish influence of my youth and the Greek philosophical heritage which I received during my academic education in the French universities.

RK *And yet you share a singular discourse with Lévinas – including notions of the 'other', the 'trace' and writing as 'difference', etc. – which might suggest a common Judaic heritage.*

JD Undoubtedly, I was fascinated and attracted by the intellectual journey of Lévinas, but that was not because he was Jewish. It so happens that for Lévinas there is a discrete continuity between his philosophical discourse *qua* phenomenologist and his religious language *qua* exegete of the Talmud. But this continuity is not immediately evident. The Lévinas who most interested me at the outset was the philosopher working in phenomenology and posing the question of the 'other' to phenomenology; the Judaic dimension remained at that stage a discrete rather than a decisive reference.

You ask if Judaism offers an alternative to the Greek philosophy of 'presence'. First we must ascertain what exactly we mean by 'presence'. The French or English words are, of course, neither Greek nor Jewish. So that when we use the word we presuppose a vast history of translation which leads from the Greek terms *ousia* and *on* to the

Latin *substantia*, *actus*, etc., and culminates in our modern term 'presence'. I have no knowledge of what this term means in Judaism.

RK *So you would account yourself a philosopher above all else?*

JD I'm not happy with the term 'philosopher'.

RK *Surely you are a philosopher in that your deconstruction is directed primarily to philosophical ideas and texts?*

JD It is true that 'deconstruction' has focused on philosophical texts. And I am of course a 'philosopher' in the institutional sense that I assume the responsibilities of a teacher of philosophy in an official philosophical institution – *l'Ecole Normale Supérieure*. But I am not sure that the 'site' of my work, reading philosophical texts and posing philosophical questions, is itself properly philosophical. Indeed, I have attempted more and more systematically to find a non-site, or a non-philosophical site, from which to question philosophy. But the search for a non-philosophical site does not bespeak an anti-philosophical attitude. My central question is: from what site or non-site (*non-lieu*) can philosophy as such appear to itself as other than itself, so that it can interrogate and reflect upon itself in an original manner? Such a non-site or alterity would be radically irreducible to philosophy. But the problem is that such a non-site cannot be defined or situated by means of philosophical language.

RK *The philosophy of deconstruction would seem, therefore, to be a deconstruction of philosophy. Is your interest in painting, psychoanalysis and literature – particularly the literary texts of Jabès, Bataille, Blanchot, Artaud, Celan and Mallarmé – not an attempt to establish this non-philosophical site of which you speak?*

JD Certainly, but one must remember that even though these sites are non-philosophical they still belong to our Western culture and so are never totally free from the marks of philosophical language. In literature, for example, philosophical language is still present in some sense, but it produces and presents itself as alienated from itself, at a remove, at a distance. This distance provides the necessary free space from which to interrogate philosophy anew, and it was my preoccupation with literary texts which enabled me to discern the problematic of *writing* as one of the key factors in the deconstruction of metaphysics.

RK *Accepting the fact that you are seeking a non-philosophical site, you would, I presume, still acknowledge important philosophical influences on your thought. How, for example, would you situate your strategy of deconstruction in respect to the phenomenological movement?*

JD My philosophical formation owes much to the thought of Hegel, Husserl and Heidegger. Heidegger is probably the most constant influence, and particularly his project of 'overcoming' Greek metaphysics. Husserl, whom I studied in a more studious and painstaking fashion, taught me a certain methodical prudence and reserve, a rigorous technique of unravelling and formulating questions. But I never shared Husserl's pathos for, and commitment to, a phenomenology of presence. In fact, it was Husserl's method that helped me to suspect the very notion of presence and the fundamental role it has played in all philosophies. My relationship with Heidegger is much more enigmatic and extensive: here my interest was not just *methodological* but *existential*. The themes of Heidegger's questioning always struck me as necessary – especially the 'ontological difference', the reading of Platonism and the relationship between language and Being. My discovery of the genealogical and genetic critique of Nietzsche and Freud also helped me to take the step beyond phenomenology towards a more radical, 'non-philosophical' questioning, while never renouncing the discipline and methodological rigour of phenomenology.

RK *Although you share Heidegger's task of 'overcoming' or 'deconstructing' Western metaphysics, you would not, presumably, share his hope to rediscover the 'original names' by means of which Being could be thought and said?*

JD I think that there is still in Heidegger, linked up with other things, a nostalgic desire to recover the proper name, the unique name of Being. To be fair, however, one can find several passages in which Heidegger is self-critical and renounces his nostalgia: his practice of cancelling and erasing the term in his later texts is an example of such a critique. Heidegger's texts are still before us; they harbour a future of meaning which will ensure that they are read and reread for centuries. But while I owe a considerable debt to Heidegger's 'path of thought' (*chemin de pensée*), we differ in our employment of language, in our understanding of language. I write in another language – and I do not simply mean in French rather than in German – even though this 'otherness' cannot be explained in terms of philosophy itself. The difference resides outside of philosophy, in the non-philosophical site of language; it is what makes the poets and writers that interest me (Mallarmé, Blanchot, etc.) totally different from those that interest Heidegger (Hölderlin and Rilke). In this sense my profound rapport with Heidegger is also and at the same time a non-rapport.

RK *Yes, I can see that your understanding of language as 'difference' and 'dissemination' is quite removed from Heidegger's notion of language as the 'house of Being', that which 'recalls and recollects' and 'names the Holy'. In addition, while Heidegger is still prepared to use such philosophical concepts as* Being *and* existence *to express his thought, you have made it clear that the operative terms in your language – e.g. deconstruction,* différance, *dissemination, trace and so on – are basically 'non-concepts', 'undecidables'. What exactly do you mean by 'non-concepts' and what role do they play in your attempt to deconstruct metaphysics?*

JD I will try to reconstitute the argument by means of which I advanced the notion of a non-concept. First, it doesn't have the logical generality which a philosophical concept claims to have in its supposed independence from ordinary or literary language. The notion of *différance*, for example, is a non-concept in that it cannot be defined in terms of oppositional predicates; it is neither *this* nor *that*; but rather this *and* that (e.g. the act of differing and of deferring) without being reducible to a dialectical logic either. And yet the term *différance* emerges and develops as a determination of language from which it is inseparable. Hence the difficulty of translating the term. There is no conceptual realm beyond language which would allow the term to have a univocal semantic content over and above its inscription in language. Because it remains a trace of language it remains non-conceptual; and because it has no oppositional or predicative generality, which would identify it as *this* rather than *that*, the term *différance* cannot be defined within a system of logic – Aristotelian or dialectical – that is, within the logocentric system of philosophy.

RK *But can we go beyond the logocentric system of metaphysics without employing the terminology of metaphysics? Is it not only* from the inside *that we can undo metaphysics by means of stratagems and strategies which expose the ambiguities and contradictions of the logocentric system of presence? Does that not mean that we are condemned to metaphysics even while attempting to deconstruct its pretensions?*

JD In a certain sense it is true to say that 'deconstruction' is still *in* metaphysics. But we must remember that if we are indeed *inside* metaphysics, we are not inside it as we might be *inside* a box or a milieu. We are still *in* metaphysics in the special sense that we are *in* a determinate language. Consequently, the idea that we might be able to get outside of metaphysics has always struck me as naive. So that when I refer to the 'closure' (*clôture*) of metaphysics, I insist that it is not a question of considering metaphysics as a circle with a limit or simple boundary. The notion of the limit and boundary (*bord*) of metaphysics is itself highly problematic. My reflections on this problematic have always attempted to show that the limit or end of metaphysics is not linear or circular in any indivisible sense. And as soon as we acknowledge that the limit-boundary of metaphysics is divisible, the logical rapport between inside and outside is no longer simple. Accordingly, we cannot really say that we are 'locked into' or 'condemned to' metaphysics, for we are, strictly speaking, neither inside nor outside. In brief, the whole rapport between the inside and the outside of metaphysics is inseparable from the question of the finitude and reserve of metaphysics as language. But the idea of the finitude and exhaustion (*épuisement*) of metaphysics does not mean that we are incarcerated in it as prisoners or victims of some unhappy fatality. It is simply that our belonging to, and inherence in, the language of metaphysics is something that can only be rigorously and adequately thought about from *another topos* or space where our problematic rapport with the boundary of metaphysics can be seen in a more radical light. Hence my attempts to discover the non-place or *non-lieu* which would be the 'other' of philosophy. This is the task of deconstruction.

RK *Can literary and poetic language provide this* non-lieu *or* u-topos*?*

JD I think so; but when I speak of literature it is not with a capital L; it is rather an allusion to certain movements which have worked around the limits of our logical concepts, certain texts which make the limits of our language tremble, exposing them as divisible and questionable. This is what the works of Blanchot, Bataille or Beckett are particularly sensitive to.

RK *What does this whole problematic of the closure of Western 'logocentric' philosophy and of the limits of our language tell us about the modern age in which we live? Is there a rapport between deconstruction and 'modernity' in so far as the latter bespeaks a crisis of scientific foundations and of values in general, a crisis occasioned by the discovery that the absolute origin that the*

Western tradition claimed to have identified in the 'logos' is merely the trace of an absence, a nothingness?

JD I have never been very happy with the term 'modernity'. Of course, I feel that what is happening in the world today is something unique and singular. As soon, however, as we give it the label of 'modernity', we inscribe it in a certain historical system of evolution or progress (a notion derived from Enlightenment rationalism) which tends to blind us to the fact that what confronts us today is *also* something ancient and hidden in history. I believe that what 'happens' in our contemporary world and strikes us as particularly new has in fact an essential connection with something extremely old which has been covered over (*archi-dissimulé*). So that the new is not so much that which occurs for the first time but that 'very ancient' dimension which recurs in the 'very modern'; and which indeed has been signified repetitively throughout our historical tradition, in Greece and in Rome, in Plato and in Descartes and in Kant, etc. No matter how novel or unprecedented a modern meaning may appear, it is never exclusively *modernist* but is also and at the same time a phenomenon of *repetition*. And yet the relationship between the ancient and the modern is not simply that of the implicit and the explicit. We must avoid the temptation of supposing that what occurs today somehow pre-existed in a latent form, merely waiting to be unfolded or explicated. Such thinking also conceives history as an evolutionary development and excludes the crucial notions of rupture and mutation in history. My own conviction is that we must maintain two contradictory affirmations at the same time. On the one hand we affirm the existence of ruptures in history, and on the other we affirm that these ruptures produce gaps or faults (*failles*) in which the most hidden and forgotten archives can emerge and constantly recur and work through history. One must surmount the categorical oppositions of philosophical logic out of fidelity to these conflicting positions of historical discontinuity (rupture) and continuity (repetition), which are neither a pure break with the past nor a pure unfolding or explication of it.

RK *How do you explain the way in which philosophy has altered and changed from one historical epoch to the next? How do you explain, for example, the difference between Plato's thought and your own?*

JD The difference between our modes of thought does not mean that I or other 'modern' thinkers have gone beyond Plato, in the sense of having succeeded in exhausting all that is contained in his texts. Here I return to what I was describing as the 'future' of a Heideggerian text. I believe that all of the great philosophical texts – of Plato, Parmenides, Hegel or Heidegger, for example – are still *before* us. The future of the great philosophies remains obscure and enigmatic, still to be disclosed. Up to now, we have merely scratched the surface. This opaque and inexhaustible residue of philosophical texts, which I call their 'future', is more predominant in Greek and German philosophy than in French. I have a profound respect for the great French thinkers, but I have always had the impression that a certain kind of rigorous analysis could render their texts accessible and exhaustible. Before a Platonic or Heideggerean text,, by contrast, I feel that I am confronting an abyss, a bottomless pit in which I could lose myself. No matter how rigorous an analysis I bring to bear on such texts, I am always left with the impression that there is something *more* to be thought.

RK *What exactly is the inexhaustible richness which these great texts possess and which continues to fascinate us throughout the centuries?*

JD The temptation here is to offer a quick and simple response. But having taught philosophy for over twenty years, I must honestly say that now, less than ever, do I know what philosophy is. My knowledge of what it is that constitutes the essence of philosophy is at zero degree. All I know is that a Platonic or Heideggerian text always returns us to the beginning, enables us to *begin* to ask philosophical questions, including the question: what is philosophy?

RK *But surely it must be possible to say* what *philosophy is by way of distinguishing it from other scientific disciplines such as economics, sociology, the natural sciences, or even literature? Why learn philosophy at all, in schools, universities or in the privacy of one's study, if it is impossible to say what it is or what function it serves? If deconstruction prevents us from asserting or stating or identifying anything, then surely one ends up, not with* différance, *but with indifference, where nothing is anything, and everything is everything else?*

JD It is as impossible to say what philosophy *is not* as it is to say what it *is*. In all the other disciplines you mention, there is philosophy. To say to oneself that one is going to study something that is *not* philosophy is to deceive oneself. It is not difficult to show that in political economy, for example, there is a philosophical discourse in operation. And the same applies to mathematics and the other sciences. Philosophy, as logocentrism, is present in every scientific discipline and the only justification for transforming philosophy into a specialised discipline is the necessity to render explicit and thematic the philosophical subtext in every discourse. The principal function which the teaching of philosophy serves is to enable people to become 'conscious', to become aware of what exactly they are saying, what kind of discourse they are engaged in when they do mathematics, physics, political economy, and so on. There is no system of teaching or transmitting knowledge which can retain its coherence or integrity without, at one moment or another, interrogating itself philosophically, that is, without acknowledging its subtextual premisses; and this may even include an interrogation of unspoken political interests or traditional values. From such an interrogation each society draws its own conclusions about the worth of philosophy.

RK *How, for example, can political economy interrogate itself philosophically?*

JD First, all of the major concepts which constitute the discourse of economics are philosophical, and particularly such concepts as 'property', 'work' or 'value'. These are all 'philosophemes', concepts inaugurated by a philosophical discourse which usually go back to Greece or Rome, and kept in operation by means of this discourse, which refers back at first, as does philosophy itself, to the 'natural languages' of Greece and Rome. Consequently, the economic discourse is founded on a logocentric philosophical discourse and remains inseparable from it. The 'autonomy' which economists might subsequently like to confer on their discipline can never succeed in masking its philosophical derivation. Science is never purely objective, nor is it merely reducible to an instrumental and utilitarian model of explanation. Philosophy can teach science that it is ultimately an element of language, that the limits of its formalisation reveal its belonging to a language in which it continues to operate despite its attempts to justify itself as an exclusively 'objective' or 'instrumental' discourse.

RK *Is the logocentric character of science a singularly European phenomenon?*

JD Logocentrism, in its developed philosophical sense, is inextricably linked to the Greek and European tradition. As I have attempted to demonstrate elsewhere in some detail, logocentric philosophy is a specifically Western response to a much larger necessity which also occurs in the Far East and other cultures, that is, the phonocentric necessity: the privilege of the voice over writing. The priority of spoken language over written or silent language stems from the fact that when words are spoken the speaker and the listener are supposed to be simultaneously present to one another; they are supposed to be the same, pure unmediated presence. This ideal of perfect self-presence, of the immediate possession of meaning, is what is expressed by the phonocentric necessity. Writing, on the other hand, is considered subversive in so far as it creates a spatial and temporal distance between the author and audience; writing presupposes the absence of the author and so we can never be sure exactly what is meant by a written text; it can have many different meanings as opposed to a single unifying one. But this phonocentric necessity did not develop into a systematic logocentric metaphysics in any non-European culture. Logocentrism is a uniquely European phenomenon.

RK *Does this mean that other cultures do not require deconstruction?*

JD Every culture and society requires an internal critique or deconstruction as an essential part of its development. *A priori*, we can presume that non-European cultures operate some sort of auto-critique of their own linguistic concepts and foundational institutions. Every culture needs an element of self-interrogation and of distance from itself, if it is to transform itself. No culture is closed in on itself, especially in our own times when the impact of European civilisation is so all-pervasive. Similarly, what we call the deconstruction of our own Western culture is aided and abetted by the fact that Europe has always registered the impact of heterogeneous, non-European influences. Because it has always been thus exposed to, and shadowed by, its 'other', it has been compelled to question itself. Every culture is haunted by its other.

RK *Did the arrival of Judaeo-Christianity represent such a radicalizing 'alterity' for the Graeco-Roman civilisation? Did it challenge the homogeneity of the Western metaphysics of presence?*

JD I'd be wary of talking about Judaeo-Christianity with a capital J and C. Judaeo-Christianity is an extremely complex entity which, in large part, only constituted itself *qua* Judaeo-Christianity by its assimilation into the schemas of Greek philosophy. Hence what we know as Christian and Jewish theology today is a cultural ensemble which has already been largely 'Hellenised'.

RK *But did not Judaism and Christianity represent a heterogeneity, an 'otherness' before they were assimilated into Greek culture?*

JD Of course. And one can argue that these original, heterogeneous elements of Judaism and Christianity were never completely eradicated by Western metaphysics. They perdure throughout the centuries, threatening and unsettling the assured 'identities' of Western philosophy. So that the surreptitious deconstruction of the Greek *Logos* is at work from the very origin of our Western culture. Already, the translation of Greek concepts into other languages – Latin, Arabic, German, French, English, etc. – or indeed the translation of Hebraic or Arabic ideas and structures into metaphysical terms, produces 'fissures' in the presumed 'solidity' of Greek philosophy by introducing alien and conflicting elements.

RK *The logocentrism of Greek metaphysics will always be haunted, therefore, by the 'absolutely other' to the extent that the* Logos *can never englobe everything. There is always something which escapes, something different, other and opaque which refuses to be totalised into a homogeneous identity.*

JD Just so – and this 'otherness' is not necessarily something which comes to Greek philosophy from the 'outside', that is, from the non-Hellenic world. From the very beginnings of Greek philosophy the self-identity of the *Logos* is already fissured and divided. I think one can discern signs of such fissures of *différance* in every great philosopher: the 'Good beyond Being' (*epekeina tes ousias*) of Plato's *Republic*, for example, or the confrontation with the 'Stranger' in *The Sophist*, are already traces of an alterity which refuses to be totally domesticated. Moreover, the rapport of self-identity is itself always a rapport of violence with the other, so that the notions of property, appropriation and self-presence, so central to logocentric metaphysics, are essentially dependent on an oppositional relation with otherness. In this sense, identity *presupposes* alterity.

RK *If deconstruction is a way of challenging the logocentric pretensions of Western European philosophy, and by implication of the sciences it has founded, can it ever surmount its role of iconoclastic negation and become a form of affirmation? Can your search for a non-site or* u-topos, *other than the* topos *of Western metaphysics, also be construed as a prophetic utopianism?*

JD I will take the terms 'affirmation' and 'prophetic utopianism' separately. Deconstruction certainly entails a moment of affirmation. Indeed, I cannot conceive of a radical critique which would not be ultimately motivated by some sort of affirmation, acknowledged or not. Deconstruction always presupposes affirmation, as I have frequently attempted to point out, sometimes employing a Nietzschean terminology. I do not mean that the deconstructing *subject* or *self* affirms. I mean that deconstruction is, in itself, a positive response to an alterity which necessarily calls, summons or motivates it. Deconstruction is therefore vocation – a response to a call. The other, as the other than self, the other that opposes self-identity, is not something that can be detected and disclosed within a philosophical space and with the aid of a philosophical lamp. The other precedes philosophy and necessarily invokes and provokes the subject before any genuine questioning can begin. It is in this rapport with the other that affirmation expresses itself.

As to the question of prophecy, this is a much more obscure area for me. There are certainly prophetic effects (*effets*); but the language of prophecy alters continually. Today the prophets no longer speak with the same accents or scenography as the prophets in the Bible.

RK *Lévinas has suggested that the contemporary deconstruction of philosophy and the sciences is symptomatic of a fundamental crisis of Western culture, which he chooses to interpret as a prophetic and ethical cry. Would you agree?*

JD Certainly prophets always flourish in times of socio-historical or philosophical crisis. Bad times for philosophy are good times for prophecy. Accordingly, when deconstructive themes begin to dominate the scene, as they do today, one is sure to find a proliferation of prophecies. And this proliferation is precisely a reason why we should be all the more wary and prudent, all the more discriminating.

RK *But here we have the whole problem of a criterion of evaluation. According to what criterion does one discriminate between prophecies? Is this not a problem for you since you reject the idea of a transcendental* telos *or* eschaton *which could provide the critical subject with an objective or absolute yardstick of value?*

JD It is true that I interrogate the idea of an *eschaton* or *telos* in the absolute formulations of classical philosophy. But that does not mean I dismiss all forms of Messianic or prophetic eschatology. I think that all genuine questioning is summoned by a certain type of eschatology, though it is impossible to define this eschatology in philosophical terms. The search for objective or absolute criteria is, to be sure, an essentially philosophical gesture. Prophecy differs from philosophy in so far as it dispenses with such criteria. The prophetic word is its own criterion and refuses to submit to an external tribunal which would judge or evaluate it in an objective and neutral fashion. The prophetic word reveals its own eschatology and finds its index of truthfulness in its own inspiration and not in some transcendental or philosophical criteriology.

RK *Do you feel that your own work is prophetic in its attempt to deconstruct philosophy and philosophical criteria?*

JD Unfortunately, I do not feel inspired by any sort of hope which would permit me to presume that my work of deconstruction has a prophetic function. But I concede that the style of my questioning as an exodus and dissemination in the desert might produce certain prophetic resonances. It is possible to see deconstruction as being produced in a space where the prophets are not far away. But the prophetic resonances of my questioning reside at the level of a certain rhetorical discourse which is also shared by several other contemporary thinkers. The fact that I declare it 'unfortunate' that I do not personally feel inspired may be a signal that deep down I still hope. It means that I am in fact still looking for something. So perhaps it is no mere accident of rhetoric that the search itself, the search without hope for hope, assumes a certain prophetic *allure*. Perhaps my search is a twentieth-century brand of prophecy? But it is difficult for me to believe it.

RK *Can the theoretical radicality of deconstruction be translated into a radical political praxis?*

JD This is a particularly difficult question. I must confess that I have never succeeded in directly relating deconstruction to existing political codes and programmes. I have of course had occasion to take a specific political stand in certain codable situations, for example, in relation to the French university institution. But the available codes for taking such a political stance are not at all adequate to the radicality of deconstruction. And the absence of an adequate political code to translate or incorporate the radical implications of deconstruction has given many the impression that deconstruction is opposed to politics, or is at best apolitical. But this impression only prevails because all of our political codes and terminologies still remain fundamentally metaphysical, regardless of whether they originate from the right or the left.

RK *In* The Revolution of the Word, *Colin MacCabe employed your notions of deconstruction and dissemination to show how James Joyce recognised and revealed the inner workings of language as a refusal of identity, as a process of* différance *irreducible to all of our logocentic concepts and codes. In* Ulysses *this process of* différance *is epitomised by Bloom, for instance, the vagrant or nomad who subverts the available codes of identity – religious, political or national. And yet, MacCabe argues, the Joycean refutation of all dogmatic or totalising forms of identity is itself a political stance – an anti-totalitarian or anarchic stance.*

JD This is the politics of exodus, of the emigré. As such, it can of course serve as a political ferment or anxiety, a subversion of fixed assumptions and a privileging of disorder.

RK *But does the politics of the emigré necessarily imply inaction and non-commitment?*

JD Not at all. But the difficulty is to gesture in opposite directions at the same time: on the one hand to preserve a distance and suspicion with regard to the official political codes governing reality; on the other, to intervene here and now in a practical and *engagé* manner whenever the necessity arises. This position of dual allegiance, in which I personally find myself, is one of perpetual uneasiness. I try where I can to act politically while recognising that such action remains incommensurate with my intellectual project of deconstruction.

RK *Could one describe the political equivalent of deconstruction as a disposition, as opposed to a position, of responsible anarchy?*

JD If I had to describe my political disposition I would probably employ a formula of that kind while stressing, of course, the interminable obligation to work out and to deconstruct these two terms – 'responsible' and 'anarchy'. If taken as assured certainties in themselves, such terms can also become reified and unthinking dogmas. But I also try to re-evaluate the indispensable notion of 'responsibility'.

RK *I would now like to turn to another theme in your work: the deconstructive role of the 'feminine'. If the logocentric domination of Western culture also expresses itself as a 'phallogocentrism', is there a sense in which the modern movement to liberate women represents a deconstructive gesture? Is this something which Nietzsche curiously recognised when he spoke of 'truth becoming woman'; or Joyce when he celebrated the 'woman's reason' of Molly Bloom in* Ulysses *and Anna Livia Plurabelle in* Finnegans Wake*? Is the contemporary liberation of woman's reason and truth not an unveiling of the hitherto repressed resources of a non-logocentric* topos*?*

JD While I would hesitate to use such terms as 'liberation' or 'unveiling', I think there can be little doubt that we are presently witnessing a radical mutation of our understanding of sexual difference. The discourses of Nietzsche, Joyce and the women's movement which you have identified epitomise a profound and unprecedented transformation of the man–woman relationship. The deconstruction of phallogocentrism is carried by this transformation, as are also the rise of psychoanalysis and the modernist movement in literature. But we cannot objectify or thematise this mutation, even though it is bringing about such a radical change in our understanding of the world that a return to the former logocentric philosophies of mastery, possession, totalisation or certitude may soon be unthinkable. The philosophical and literary discoveries of the 'feminine' which you mention – and even the political and legal recognition of the status of women – are all symptoms of a deeper mutation in our search for meaning which deconstruction attempts to register.

RK *Do you think then that this mutation can be seen and evaluated in terms of an historical progress towards the 'good', towards a 'better' society?*

JD This mutation is certainly experienced as 'better' in so far as it is what is desired by those who practically dispose of the greatest 'force' in society. One could describe the transformation effected by the feminine as 'good' without positing it as an *a priori* goal or *telos*. I hesitate to speak of 'liberation' in this context, because I don't believe that women are 'liberated', any more than men are. They are, of course, no longer 'enslaved' in many of the old socio-political respects, but even in the new situation woman will not ultimately be any freer than man. One needs another language, besides that of political liberation, to characterise the enormous deconstructive import of the feminine as an uprooting of our phallogocentric culture. I prefer to speak of this mutation of the feminine as a 'movement' rather than as an historical or political 'progress'. I always hesistate to talk of historical progress.

RK *What is the relationship between deconstruction and your use of poetic language, particularly in* Glas? *Do you consider* Glas *to be a work of philosophy or of poetry?*

JD It is neither philosophy nor poetry. It is in fact a reciprocal contamination of the one by the other, from which neither can emerge intact. This notion of contamination is, however, inadequate, for it is not simply a question of rendering both philosophy and poetry *impure*. One is trying to reach an additional or alternative dimension beyond philosophy and literature. In my project, philosophy and literature are two poles of an opposition and one cannot isolate one from the other or privilege one over the other. I consider that the limits of philosophy are also those of literature. In *Glas*, consequently, I try to compose a *writing* which would traverse, as rigorously as possible, both the philosophical and literary elements without being definable as either. Hence in *Glas* one finds classical philosophical analysis being juxtaposed with quasi-literary passages, each challenging, perverting and exposing the impurities and contradictions in their neighbour; and at some point the philosophical and literary trajectories cross each other and give rise to something else, some *other* site.

RK *Is there not a sense in which philosophy for you is a form of literature? You have, for example, described metaphysics as a 'white mythology', that is, a sort of palimpsest of metaphors (*eidos, telos, ousia*) and myths (of return, homecoming, transcendence towards the light, etc.), which are covered over and forgotten as soon as philosophical 'concepts' are construed as pure and univocal abstractions, as totalising universals devoid of myth and metaphor.*

JD I have always tried to expose the way in which philosophy is literary, not so much because it is *metaphor* but because it is *catachresis*. The term metaphor generally implies a relation to an original 'property' of meaning, a 'proper' sense to which it indirectly or equivocally refers, whereas catachresis is a violent production of meaning, an abuse which refers to no anterior or proper norm. The founding concepts of metaphysics – *logos, eidos, theoria*, etc. – are instances of *catachresis* rather than metaphors, as I attempted to demonstrate in 'White Mythology' (*Marges de la philosophie*). In a work such as *Glas*, or other recent ones like it, I am trying to produce new forms of catachresis, another kind of writing, a violent writing which stakes out the faults (*failles*) and deviations of language; so that the text produces a language of its own, in itself, which while continuing to work through tradition emerges at a given moment as a *monster*, a monstrous mutation without tradition or normative precedent.

RK *What then of the question of language as reference? Can language as mutation or violence or monstrosity refer to anything other than itself?*

JD There have been several misinterpretations of what I and other deconstructionists are trying to do. It is totally false to suggest that deconstruction is a suspension of reference. Deconstruction is always deeply concerned with the 'other' of language. I never cease to be surprised by critics who see my work as a declaration that there is nothing beyond language, that we are imprisoned in language; it is, in fact, saying the exact opposite. The critique of logocentrism is above all else the search for the 'other' and the 'other of language'. Every week I receive critical commentaries and studies on deconstruction which operate on the assumption that what they call 'post-structuralism' amounts to saying that there is nothing beyond language, that we are submerged in words – and other stupidities of that sort. Certainly, deconstruction tries to show that the question of reference is much more complex and problematic than traditional theories supposed. It even asks whether our term 'reference' is entirely adequate for designating the 'other'. The other, which is beyond language and which summons language, is perhaps not a 'referent' in the normal sense which linguists have attached to this term. But to distance oneself thus from the habitual structure of reference, to challenge or complicate our common assumptions about it, does not amount to saying that there is *nothing* beyond language.

RK *This could also be seen as a reply to those critics who maintain that deconstruction is a strategy of nihilism, an orgy of non-sense, a relapse into the free play of the arbitrary.*

JD I regret that I have been misinterpreted in this way, particularly in the United States, but also in France. People who wish to avoid questioning and discussion present deconstruction as a sort of gratuitous chess game with a combination of signs (*combinatoire de signifiants*), closed up in language as in a cave. This misinterpretation is not just a simplification; it is symptomatic of certain political and institutional interests – interests which must also be deconstructed in their turn. I totally refuse the label of nihilism which has been ascribed to me and my American colleagues. Deconstruction is not an enclosure in nothingness, but an openness towards the other.

RK *Can deconstruction serve as a method of literary criticism which might contribute something positive to our appreciation of literature?*

JD I am not sure that deconstruction can function as a literary *method* as such. I am wary of the idea of methods of reading. The laws of reading are determined by the particular text that is being read. This does not mean that we should simply abandon ourselves to the text, or represent and repeat it in a purely passive manner. It means that we must remain faithful, even if it implies a certain violence, to the injunctions of the text. These injunctions will differ from one text to the next so that one cannot prescribe one general method of reading. In this sense deconstruction is not a method. Nor do I feel that the principal function of deconstruction is to contribute something to literature. It does, of course, contribute to our epistemological appreciation of texts by exposing the philosophical and theoretical presuppositions that are at work in every critical methodology, be it Formalism, New Criticism, Socialist Realism or an historical critique. Deconstruction asks *why* we read a literary text in this particular manner rather than another. It shows, for example, that New Criticism is not *the* way of reading texts, however enshrined it may be in certain university institutions, but only one way among others. Thus deconstruction can also serve to question the presumption of certain university and cultural institutions to act as the sole or privileged guardians and transmitters of meaning. In short, deconstruction not only teaches us to read literature more thoroughly by attending to it *as language*, as the production of meaning through *différance* and dissemination, through a complex play of signifying traces; it also enables us to interrogate the covert philosophical and political presuppositions of institutionalised critical methods which generally govern our reading of a text. There is in deconstruction something which challenges every teaching institution. It is not a question of calling for the destruction of such institutions, but rather of making us aware of what we are in fact doing when we subscribe to this or that institutional way of reading literature. Nor must we forget that deconstruction is itself a form of literature, a literary text to be read like other texts, an interpretation open to several other interpretations. Accordingly, one can say that deconstruction is at once extremely *modest* and extremely *ambitious*. It is ambitious in that it puts itself on a par with literary texts, and modest in that it admits that it is only one textual interpretation among others, written in a language which has no centralising power of mastery or domination, no privileged metalanguage over and above the language of literature.

RK *And what would you say to those critics who accuse you of annihilating the very idea of the human subject in your determination to dispense with all centralising agencies of meaning, all 'centrisms'?*

JD They need not worry. I have never said that the subject should be dispensed with. Only that it should be deconstructed. To deconstruct the subject does not mean to deny its existence. There are subjects, 'operations' or 'effects' (*effets*) of subjectivity. This is an incontrovertible fact. To acknowledge this does not mean, however, that the subject is what it *says* it is. The subject is not some meta-linguistic substance or identity, some pure *cogito* of self-presence; it is always inscribed in language. My work does not, therefore, destroy the subject; it simply tries to resituate it.

RK *But can deconstruction, as the disclosure of language as* différance, *contribute to the* pleasure *of reading, to our appreciation of the living* texture *of a literary text? Or is it only an intellectual strategy of detection, of exposing our presuppositions and disabusing us of our habitual illusions about reading?*

JD Deconstruction gives pleasure in that it gives desire. To deconstruct a text is to disclose how it functions as desire, as a search for presence and fulfilment which is interminably deferred. One cannot read without opening oneself to the desire of language, to the search for that which remains absent and other than oneself. Without a certain love of the text, no reading would be possible. In every reading there is a *corps-à-corps* between reader and text, an incorporation of the reader's desire into the desire of the text. Here is pleasure, the very opposite of that arid intellectualism of which deconstruction has so often been accused.

(Paris, 1981).

Select bibliography in English

Speech and Phenomena and Other Essays in Husserl's Theory of Signs, trans. D. Allison, Northwestern University Press, Evanston, 1973.

Of Grammatology, trans. G. Spivak, Johns Hopkins University Press, Baltimore and London, 1977.

Positions, University of Chicago Press, Chicago, 1977.

Writing and Difference, trans. A. Bass, University of Chicago Press, Chicago, 1978.

Spurs: Nietzsche Styles, University of Chicago Press, Chicago, 1979.

Dissemination, trans. B. Johnson, Athlone Press, London, 1981.

Margins of Philosophy, trans. A. Bass, The Harvester Press, 1982.

Signéponge / Signsponge, trans. R. Rand, Columbia University Press, New York, 1984.

Glas, trans. J. P. Leavey, Jr. and R. Rand, University of Nebraska Press, Lincoln, 1986.

'Shibboleth', trans. J. Wilner, in S. Budick and G. Hartman (eds.), *Midrash and Literature*, Yale University Press, New Haven, 1986.

The Postcard: From Socrates to Freud and Beyond, trans. A. Bass, University of Chicago Press, Chicago, 1987.

The Truth in Painting, trans. G. Bennington and I. McLeod, University of Chicago Press, Chicago, 1987.

Limited Inc., trans. J. Mehlmann and S. Weber, ed. G. Graff, Northwestern University Press, Evanston, 1988.

The Ear of the Other: Otobiography, Transference, Translation: Texts and Discussions with Jacques Derrida, trans. P. Kamuf and A. Ronell, University of Nebraska Press, Lincoln, 1988.

Edmund Husserl's 'Origin of Geometry': An Introduction, trans. J. P. Leavey, Jr., University of Nebraska Press, Lincoln, 1989, rev. edn.

Memoires for Paul de Man, trans E. Cadava, J. Culler, P. Kamuf and S. Lindsay, Columbia University Press, New York, 1989.

Of Spirit: Heidegger and the Question, trans. G. Bennington and R. Bowlby, University of Chicago Press, Chicago, 1989.

The Other Heading: Reflections on Today's Europe, trans. P. A. Brault and M. G. Naas, Indiana University Press, Bloomington, 1992.

Acts of Literature, trans. D. Attridge, Routledge, London, 1992.

Aporias, trans. T. Dutoit, Stanford University Press, Stanford, 1993.

The Gift of Death, trans. D. Wills, University of Chicago Press, Chicago, 1995.

EMMANUEL LÉVINAS

Ethics of the infinite

Prefatory note

EMMANUEL LÉVINAS was born in Kaunas, Lithuania in 1906 to a Jewish family. He later moved to the Ukraine, where he lived through the Russian Revolution in 1917, before finally departing as a young man for France, where he spent most of his adult life. In 1923, Lévinas began to study philosophy at Strasbourg University, where he was taught by Blondel, Pradines and later by Héring, who first introduced him to phenomenology in 1927. During these student years, Lévinas also made the acquaintance of Maurice Blanchot and was deeply impressed by both the repercussions of the Dreyfus affair and the emergence of Zionism, which he described as 'the vision of a strange startling new advent of a people, on a par with all humanity'.

In 1928 Lévinas travelled to Freiburg University in Germany to pursue his studies of phenomenology with Husserl and Heidegger, whose monumental *Being and Time* had just been published. This brief apprenticeship with the 'masters' (Lévinas returned to France in 1929) was to prove a lifelong inspiration for Lévinas. His first three major publications – *The Theory of Intuition in Husserl's Phenomenology* (1930), *Existence and Existents* (1947) and *Discovering Existence with Husserl and Heidegger* (1949) - were written from an explicitly phenomenological standpoint.

Lévinas became a French citizen in 1930 and began to frequent the avant-garde philosophical groups of Gabriel Marcel and Jean Wahl in Paris. Indeed it was during the thirties and forties that he became familiar with the more 'existentialist' brand of phenomenology practised in France. Although he has lectured frequently in Israel and Belgium, Lévinas has worked and taught in France for most of his life, serving as Director of *l'Ecole Normale Israélite*

Orientale and as Professor of Philosophy at the Universities of Poitiers, Nanterre and the Sorbonne.

Lévinas's most influential work is undoubtedly *Totality and Infinity*, first published in 1961. Here Lévinas deploys the phenomenological method to describe two basic kinds of relationship to the world: (1) an 'ontological' relationship which centralises our experience in terms of Being-as-a-totality (be it the being of our subjective *cogito* or the being of the immanent, finite *cosmos*); and (2) a 'metaphysical' relationship which decentralises our experience and opens us to the infinite otherness of transcendence. While the former favours a *philosophy of nature*, whereby the human subject can be accorded its place in the totalising scheme of things, the latter endorses the primacy of an *ethical philosophy* which shows how the self's relationship to the other can transcend the natural rapport of possession, power and belongingness, in search of a Good beyond Being. Lévinas argues that the mainstream of Western European philosophy represents a totalising ontology, running from the pre-Socratics up to Hegel and Heidegger, which seeks to reduce 'difference' and 'otherness' to the category of the 'same'. Over against this ontological tradition, he champions the alternative and usually ignored counter-tradition of 'metaphysics' to which, he claims, Plato's notion of the Good, and Descartes 'Idea of the Infinite' belong in so far as they surpass the totalising categories of Being. In short, Lévinas's phenomenological descriptions of our finite being-in-the-world (*être-au-monde*) lead him ultimately beyond the limits of phenomenology to an ethics of transcendence based on the primacy of the *other* over the *same*.

While Lévinas remains cautious in his early work about identifying the relationship with the other as religious, from the sixties onwards he wrote a number of studies on Judaism – including *Difficile liberté* (1963), *Quatre leçons talmudiques* (1968) and *Du sacré au saint* (1977) – in which he argues that the Hebraic tradition differs from its Hellenic counterpart in affirming that God as the absolutely Other can only be encountered in and through our ethical rapport with our fellow humans (what he terms the 'face to face relationship'). The biblical and Talmudic texts, he claims, teach us that the 'I' does not begin with itself in some pure moment of autonomous self-consciousness but in relation with the other, for whom it remains forever responsible. The overall purpose of

Lévinas's thought is, accordingly, to turn knowledge into 'an act of unsettling its own natural condition' as power and violence in order to open it to the infinity of the other who transcends every attempt to reduce him/her to our totalising grasp. 'To exist', writes Lévinas, 'has a meaning in another dimension than that of the perduration of the totality; it can go beyond Being'.

The dialogue that follows took place in Paris in 1981.

RK *Perhaps you could retrace your philosophical itinerary by identifying some of the major influences on your thought?*

EL Apart from the great masters of the history of philosophy – in particular Plato, Descartes and Kant – the first contemporary influence on my own thinking was Bergson. In 1925, in Strasbourg University, Bergson was being hailed as France's leading thinker. For example, Blondel, one of his Strasbourg disciples, developed a specifically Bergsonian psychology quite hostile to Freud – a hostility which made a deep and lasting impression on me. Moreover, Bergson's theory of time as concrete duration (*la durée concrète*) is, I believe, one of the most significant, if largely ignored, contributions to contemporary philosophy. Indeed, it was this Bergsonian emphasis on temporality that prepared the soil for the subsequent implantation of Heideggerean phenomenology into France. It is all the more ironic therefore, that in *Being and Time* Heidegger unjustly accuses Bergson of reducing time to space. What is more, in Bergson's *L'Evolution créatrice*, one finds the whole notion of technology as the destiny of the Western philosophy of Reason. Bergson was the first to contrast technology, as a logical and necessary expression of scientific rationality, with an alternative form of human expression which he called creative intuition or impulse – the *élan vital*. All of Heidegger's celebrated analyses of our technological era as the logical culmination of Western metaphysics and its forgetfulness of Being came after Bergson's reflections on the subject. Bergson's importance to contemporary Continental thought has been somewhat obfuscated; he has been suspended in a sort of limbo; but I believe it is only a temporary suspension.

RK *Could you describe how, after Bergson, you came under the influence of the German phenomenologists, Husserl and Heidegger?*

EL It was in 1927 that I first became interested in Husserl's phenomenology, which was still unknown in France at that time. I travelled to the University of Freiburg for two semesters in 1928–29 and studied phenomenology with Husserl and also, of course, with Heidegger, who was then the leading light in German philosophy after the publication of *Sein und Zeit* in 1927. Phenomenology represented the second, but undoubtedly most important, philosophical influence on my thinking. Indeed, from the point of view of philosophical method and discipline, I remain to this day a phenomenologist.

RK *How would you characterise the particular contribution of phenomenology to modern philosophy?*

EL The most fundamental contribution of Husserl's phenomenology is its methodical disclosure of how meaning comes to be, how it emerges in our consciousness of the world, or more precisely, in our becoming conscious of our intentional rapport (*visée*) with the world. The phenomenological method enables us to discover meaning within our lived experience; it reveals consciousness to be an intentionality always in *contact* with objects outside of itself, other than itself. Human experience is not some self-transparent substance or pure *cogito*; it is always intending or tending towards something in the world which preoccupies it. The phenomenological method permits consciousness to understand its own preoccupations, to reflect upon itself and thus discover all the hidden or neglected horizons of its intentionality. In other words, by returning to the implicit horizons of consciousness, phenomenology enables us to explicate or unfold the full intentional meaning of an object, which would otherwise be presented as an abstract and isolated entity cut off from its intentional horizons. Phenomenology thus teaches us that consciousness is at once tied to the object of its experience and yet free to detach itself from this object in order to return upon itself, focusing on those *visées* of intentionality in which the object emerges as *meaningful*, as part of our lived experience. One might say that phenomenology is a way of becoming aware of where we are in the world, a *sich besinnen* which consists of a recovery of the origin of meaning in our lifeworld or *Lebenswelt*.

RK *Your second major work was entitled* En découvrant l'existence avec Husserl et Heidegger. *If Husserl introduced you to the phenomenological method, how would you assess your debt to Heidegger?*

EL Heidegger's philosophy was a shock for me, and for most of my contemporaries in the late twenties and thirties. It completely altered the course and character of European philosophy. I think that one cannot seriously philosophise today without traversing the Heideggerian path in some form or other. *Being and Time*, which is much more significant and profound than any of Heidegger's later works, represents the fruition and flowering of Husserlian phenomenology. The most far-reaching potentialities of the phenomenological method were exploited by Heidegger in this early work and particularly in his phenomenological analysis of 'anguish' as the fundamental mood of our existence. Heidegger brilliantly described how this existential mood or *Stimmung* revealed the way in which we were attuned to Being. Human moods, such as guilt, fear, anxiety, joy or dread, are no longer considered as mere physiological sensations or psychological emotions, but are now recognised as the ontological ways in which we feel and find our being-in-the-world, our being-there as *Befindlichkeit*.

RK *This phenomenological analysis of our existential moods was, of course, something which you yourself used to original effect in your descriptions of such human dispositions as need, desire, effort, laziness and insomnia in* Existence and Existents. *But to return to Husserl and Heidegger, how would you define the main difference of* style *in their employment of phenomenology?*

EL Husserl's approach was always more abstract and ponderous – one really had to have one's ears cocked if one wished to understand his lectures! Husserl was primarily concerned with establishing and perfecting phenomenology as a method, that is, as an epistemological method of describing how our logical concepts and categories emerge and assume an essential meaning. What is the relation between our logical judgements and our perceptual experience? This was Husserl's question – and phenomenology was his method of responding by means of rigorous and exact descriptions of our intentional modes of consciousness. Phenomenology was thus a way of suspending our preconceptions and prejudices in order to disclose how essential truth and meaning are generated; it was a methodical return to the beginnings, to the origins of knowledge. On the other hand, Heidegger, the young disciple, brought the phenomenological method to life and gave it a contemporary style and relevance. Heidegger's existential analyses possessed a poetic quality and force which enchanted and astonished the mind, while preserving all the while the rigorous contours of the master's method. So that I would say, by way of summary, that if it was

Husserl who opened up for me the radical possibilities of a phenomenological analysis of knowledge, it was Heidegger who first gave these possibilities a positive and concrete grounding in our everyday existence; Heidegger showed that the phenomenological search for eternal truths and essences ultimately originates in *time*, in our temporal and historical existence.

RK *Your first study of phenomenology,* The Theory of Intuition in Husserl's Phenomenology, *published in 1930, was the first complete work on Husserl in French. Your seminal study of Heidegger in* La Revue philosophique *in 1931 was another milestone in contemporary French philosophy. Sartre and Merleau-Ponty were soon to follow suit, exploring further possibilities of the phenomenological method known today as French existentialism. As the discreet inaugurator of the French interest in phenomenology, what exactly was your relationship with Sartre and Merleau-Ponty?*

EL I have always admired the powerful originality of Merleau-Ponty's work, however different from my own in many respects, and had frequent contact with him at Jean Wahl's philosophical meetings in the *Collège de Philosophie* in the thirties and forties, and also whenever I contributed to *Les Temps modernes* while he was still co-editor with Sartre. But it was Sartre who guaranteed my place in eternity by stating in his famous obituary essay on Merleau-Ponty that he, Sartre, 'was introduced to phenomenology by Lévinas'. Simone de Beauvoir tells how it happened in one of her autobiographical works. One day in the early thirties Sartre chanced upon a copy of my book on Husserl in the Picard bookshop just opposite the Sorbonne. He picked it up, read it and declared to Beauvoir, 'This is the philosophy I wanted to write!' Afterwards he reassured himself that my analysis was far too didactic and that he could do better himself! And so he applied himself to a sustained study of Husserl and Heidegger. The result was a host of enterprising phenomenological analyses ranging from *L'Imaginaire* (1940) to *Being and Nothingness* (1945). I was extremely interested in Sartre's phenomenological analysis of the 'other', though I always regretted that he interpreted it as a threat and a degradation, an interpretation which also found expression in his fear of the God question. In fact, Sartre's rejection of theism was so unequivocal that his final statements, in the *Nouvel Observateur* interviews just before his death, about the legitimacy of Jewish history as a belief in the existence of

God seemed incredible to those who knew him or had studied him. In Sartre the phenomenon of the other was still considered, as in all Western ontology, to be a modality of unity and fusion, that is a reduction of the other to the categories of the same. This is described by Sartre as a teleological project to unite and totalise the for-itself and the in-itself, the self and the other-than-self. It is here that my fundamental philosophical disagreement with Sartre lay. At a personal level, I always liked Sartre. I first met him in Gabriel Marcel's house just before the war and had further dealings with him after the war on the controversial question of Israel's existence. Sartre had refused the Nobel Prize for Literature and I felt that someone who had the courage to reject such a prize for ethical reasons had certainly conserved the right to intervene and to try to persuade Nasser, the Egyptian leader at the time, to forego his threats to Israel and embark upon dialogue. What I also admired in Sartre was that his philosophy was not confined to purely conceptual issues but was open to the possibility of ethical and political commitment.

RK *What are the origins of the religious dimensions in your own thinking?*

EL I was born in Lithuania, a country where Jewish culture was intellectually prized and fostered and where the interpretation and exegesis of biblical texts was cultivated to a high degree. It was here that I first learned to read the Bible in Hebrew. It was at a much later date, however, that I became actively interested in Jewish thought. After the Second World War I encountered a remarkable master of Talmudic interpretation here in Paris, a man of exceptional mental agility who taught me how to read the Rabbinic texts. He taught me for four years, from 1947 to 1951, and what I myself have written in my *Talmudic Lectures* has been written in the shadow of his shadow. It was this post-war encounter which reactivated my latent – I might even say dormant – interest in the Judaic tradition. But when I acknowledge this Judaic influence, I do not wish to talk in terms of belief or non-belief. 'Believe' is not a verb to be employed in the first person singular. Nobody can really say *I believe* – or *I do not believe* for that matter – that God exists. The existence of God is not a question of an individual soul uttering logical syllogisms. It cannot be proved. The existence of God, the *Sein Gottes*, is sacred history itself, the sacredness of man's relation to man through which God may pass. God's existence is the story of his revelation in biblical history.

RK *How do you reconcile the phenomenological and religious dimensions of your thinking?*

EL I always make a clear distinction, in what I write, between philosophical and confessional texts. I do not deny that they may ultimately have a common source of inspiration. I simply state that it is necessary to draw a line of demarcation between them as distinct methods of exegesis, as separate languages. I would never, for example, introduce a Talmudic or biblical verse into one of my philosophical texts to try to prove or justify a phenomenological argument.

RK *Would you go so far as to endorse Heidegger's argument that genuine philosophical questioning requires one to suspend or bracket one's religious faith? I am thinking in particular of Heidegger's statement in his* Introduction of Metaphysics *that a religious thinker cannot ask the philosophical question, 'Why is there something rather than nothing?' – since he already possesses the answer: 'Because God created the world.' Hence Heidegger's conclusion that a religious (in the sense of Christian or Jewish) philosophy is a square circle, a contradiction in terms.*

EL For me the essential characteristic of philosophy is a certain, specifically Greek, way of thinking and speaking. Philosophy is primarily a question of language; and it is by identifying the subtextual language of particular discourses that we can decide whether they are philosophical or not. Philosophy employs a series of terms and concepts – such as *morphe* (form), *ousia* (substance), *nous* (reason), *logos* (thought) or *telos* (goal), etc. – which constitute a specifically Greek lexicon of intelligibility. French and German, and indeed all of Western philosophy is entirely shot through with this specific language; it is a token of the genius of Greece to have been able to thus deposit its language in the basket of Europe. But although philosophy is essentially Greek, it is not exclusively so. It also has sources and roots which are non-Greek. What we term the Judaeo-Christian tradition, for example, proposed an alternative approach to meaning and truth. The difficulty is, of course, to *speak* of this alternative tradition given the essentially Greek nature of philosophical language. And this difficulty is compounded by the fact that Judaeo-Christian culture has, historically, been incorporated into Greek philosophy. It is virtually impossible for philosophers today to have recourse to an unalloyed religious language. All one can say is that the Septennium is not yet complete, that the translation of biblical wisdom into the Greek language remains unfinished. The best one can do by way of identifying the fundamental difference between the Greek and biblical approaches to truth is to try to define the distinctive quality of Greek philosophy before the historical incursion of Jewish and Christian cultures. Perhaps the most essential distinguishing feature of the language of Greek philosophy was its equation of truth with an *intelligibility of presence*. By this I mean an intelligibility which considers truth to be that which is present or co-present, that which can be gathered or synchronised into a totality which we would call the world or *cosmos*. According to the Greek model, intelligibility is what can be rendered present, what can be represented in some eternal here-and-now, exposed and disclosed in pure light. To thus equate truth with presence is to presume that however different the two terms of a relation might appear (e.g. the Divine and the human) or however separated over time (e.g. into past and future), they can ultimately be rendered commensurate and simultaneous, the same, englobed in a history which totalises time into a beginning or an end, or both, which is presence. The Greek notion of Being is essentially this presence.

RK *Would you agree then with Heidegger's critique of Western metaphysics as a philosophy of presence?*

EL I don't think Heidegger is entirely consistent on this point. For me, Heidegger never really escaped from the Greek language of intelligibility and presence. Even though he spent much of his philosophical career struggling against certain metaphysical notions of presence – in particular the objectifying notion of presence as *Vorhandenheit* which expresses itself in our scientific and technological categorisation of the world – he ultimately seems to espouse another, more subtle and complex, notion of presence as *Anwesen*, that is, the coming-into-the-presence of Being. Thus, while Heidegger heralds the end of the metaphysics of presence, he continues to think of Being as a coming-into-presence; he seems unable to break away from the hegemony of presence which he denounces. This ambiguity also comes to the surface when Heidegger interprets our being-in-the-world as history. The ultimate and most authentic mission of existence or *Dasein* is to recollect (*wiederholen*) and totalise its temporal dispersal into past, present and future. *Dasein* is its history to the extent that it can interpret and narrate its existence as a finite and contemporaneous story (*histoire*), a totalising co-presence of past, present and future.

RK *How does the ethical relation to the other, so central a theme in your philosophy, serve to subvert the ontology of presence in its Greek and Heideggerean forms?*

EL The interhuman relationship emerges with our history, with our being-in-the-world as intelligibility and presence. The interhuman realm can thus be construed as a part of the disclosure of the world as presence. But it can also be considered from another perspective – the ethical or biblical perspective which transcends the Greek language of intelligibility – as a theme of justice and concern for the other as other, as a theme of love and desire which carries us beyond the finite Being of the world as presence. The interhuman is thus an interface: a double axis where what is 'of the world' *qua phenomenological intelligibility* is juxtaposed with what is 'not of the world' *qua ethical responsibility*. It is in this ethical perspective that God must be thought and not in the ontological perspective of our being-there or of some Supreme Being and Creator correlative to the world, as traditional metaphysics often held. God, as the God of alterity and transcendence, can only be understood in terms of that interhuman dimension which, to be sure, emerges in the phenomenological-ontological perspective of the intelligible world, but which cuts through and perforates the totality of presence and points towards the absolutely Other. In this sense one could say that biblical thought has, to some extent, influenced my ethical reading of the interhuman, whereas Greek thought has largely determined its philosophical expression in language. So that I would maintain, against Heidegger, that philosophy can be ethical as well as ontological, can be at once Greek and non-Greek in its inspiration. These two sources of inspiration coexist as two different tendencies in modern philosophy and it is my own personal task to try to identify this dual origin of meaning – *der Ursprung des Sinnhaften* – in the interhuman relationship.

RK *One of the most complex and indeed central themes in your philosophy is the rapport between the interhuman and time. Could you elucidate this rapport by situating it in terms of the ethics/ontology distinction?*

EL I am trying to show that man's ethical relation to the other is ultimately prior to his ontological relation to himself (egology) or to the totality of things which we call the world (cosmology). The relationship with the other is *time*: it is an untotalisable diachrony in which one moment pursues another without ever being able to retrieve it, to catch up with or coincide with it. The non-simultaneous and non-present is my primary rapport with the other in time. Time means that the other is forever beyond me, irreducible to the synchrony of the same. The temporality of the interhuman opens up the meaning of otherness and the otherness of meaning. But because there are more than two people in the world, we invariably pass from the ethical perspective of alterity to the ontological perspective of totality. There are always at least three persons. This means that we are obliged to ask who is the other, to try to objectively define the undefinable, to compare the incomparable in an effort to juridically hold different positions together. So that the first type of simultaneity is the simultaneity of equality, the attempt to reconcile and balance the conflicting claims of each person. If there were only two people in the world, there would be no need for law courts because I would always be responsible for, and before, the other. As soon as there are three, the ethical relationship with the other becomes political and enters into the totalising discourse of ontology. We can never completely escape from the language of ontology and politics. Even when we deconstruct ontology we are obliged to use its language. Derrida's work of deconstruction, for example, possesses the speculative and methodological rigour of the philosophy which he is seeking to deconstruct. It's like the argument of the sceptics: how can we know that we can't know anything? The greatest virtue of philosophy is that it can put itself in question, try to deconstruct what it has constructed and unsay what it has said. Science, on the contrary, does not try to unsay itself, does not interrogate or challenge its own concepts, terms or foundations; it forges ahead, progresses. In this respect, science attempts to ignore language by constructing its own abstract non-language of calculable symbols and formulae. But science is merely a secondary bracketing of philosophical language from which it is ultimately derived; it can never have the last word. Heidegger summed this up admirably when he declared that science *calculates* but does not *think*. Now what I am interested in is precisely this ability of philosophy to think, to question itself and ultimately to unsay itself. And I wonder if this capacity for interrogation and for unsaying (*dédire*) is not itself derived from the pre-ontological interhuman relationship with the other. The fact that philosophy cannot fully totalise the alterity of meaning in some final presence or simultaneity is not for me a deficiency or fault. Or to put it in another way, the best thing about philosophy is that it fails. It is better that philosophy fail to totalise meaning – even though, as ontology, it has attempted just this – for it thereby remains open to the irreducible otherness of transcendence. Greek ontology, to be sure, expressed the strong sentiment that the last word is unity, the many becoming one, the truth as synthesis. Hence Plato defined love – *eros* – as only *half*-divine in so far as it lacks the full coincidence or unification of differences which he defined as divinity. The whole Romantic tradition in European poetry tends to conform to this Platonic ontology by inferring that love is perfect when two people become *one*. I am trying to work against this identification of the Divine with unification or totality. Man's relationship with the other is *better* as difference than as unity: sociality is better than fusion. The very value of love is the impossibility of reducing the other to myself, of coinciding into sameness. From an ethical perspective two have a better time than one (*on s'amuse mieux à deux*)!

RK *Is it possible to conceive of an eschatology of non-coincidence wherein man and God could coexist eternally without fusing into oneness?*

EL But why eschatology? Why should we wish to reduce time to eternity? Time is the most profound relationship that man can have with God precisely as a going towards God. There is an excellence in time which would be lost in eternity. To desire eternity is to desire to perpetuate oneself, to go on living as oneself, to *be* always. Can one conceive of an eternal life that would not suspend time or reduce it to a contemporaneous presence? To accept time is to accept death as the impossibility of presence. To be in eternity is to be *one*, to be *oneself* eternally. To be in time is to be for God (*être à Dieu*), a perpetual leavetaking (*adieu*).

RK *But how can one be for God or go towards God as the absolutely Other? Is it by going towards the human other?*

EL Yes, and it is essential to point out that the relation implied in the preposition *towards* (*à*) is ultimately a relation derived from time. Time fashions man's relation to the other, and to the absolutely Other or God, as a diachronic relation irreducible to correlation. 'Going towards God' is not to be understood here in the classical ontological sense of a return to, or reunification with, God as the

Beginning or End of temporal existence. 'Going towards God' is meaningless unless seen in terms of my primary going towards the other person. I can only go towards God by being ethically concerned by and for the other person. I am not saying that ethics presupposes belief. On the contrary, belief presupposes ethics as that disruption of our being-in-the-world which opens us to the other. The ethical exigency to be responsible for the other undermines the ontological primacy of the meaning of Being; it unsettles the natural and political positions we have taken up in the world and predisposes us to a meaning that is other than Being, that is otherwise than Being (*autrement qu'être*).

RK *What role does your analysis of the 'face'* (visage) *of the other play in this disruption of ontology?*

EL The approach to the face is the most basic mode of responsibility. As such, the fact of the other is verticality and uprightness; it spells a relation of rectitude. The face is not in front of me (*en face de moi*) but above me; it is the other before death, looking through and exposing death. Secondly, the face is the other who asks me not to let him die alone, as if to do so were to become an accomplice in his death. Thus the face says to me: you shall not kill. In the relation to the face I am exposed as a usurper of the place of the other. The celebrated 'right to existence' which Spinoza called the *conatus essendi* and defined as the basic principle of all intelligibility, is challenged by the relation to the face. Accordingly, my duty to respond to the other suspends my natural right to self-survival, *le droit vital*. My ethical relation of love for the other stems from the fact that the self cannot survive by itself alone, cannot find meaning within its own being-in-the-world, within the ontology of sameness. That is why I prefaced *Totality and Infinity* with Pascal's phrase, '*Ma place au soleil, le commencement de toute usurpation*'. Pascal makes the same point when he declares that '*le moi est haïssable*'. Pascal's ethical sentiments here go against the ontological privileging of 'the right to exist'. To expose myself to the vulnerability of the face is to put my ontological right to existence into question. In ethics, the other's right to exist has primacy over my own, a primacy epitomised in the ethical edict: you shall not kill, you shall not jeopardise the life of the other. The ethical rapport with the face is asymmetrical in that it subordinates my existence to the other. This principle recurs in Darwinian biology as the 'survival of the fittest', and in psychoanalysis as the natural instinct of the 'id' for gratification, possession and power – the *libido dominandi.*

RK *So I owe more to the other than to myself . . .*

EL Absolutely, and this ethical exigency undermines the Hellenic endorsement, still prevalent today, of the *conatus essendi.* There is a Jewish proverb which says that 'the other's material needs are my spiritual needs'; it is this disproportion or asymmetry which characterises the ethical refusal of the first truth of ontology – the struggle to *be.* Ethics is, therefore, *against nature* because it forbids the murderousness of my natural will to put my own existence first.

RK *Does going towards God always require that we go against nature?*

EL God cannot appear as the cause or creator of nature. The word of God speaks through the glory of the face and calls for an ethical conversion or reversal of our nature. What we call lay morality, that is, humanistic concern for our fellow human beings, already speaks the voice of God. But the moral priority of the other over myself could not come to be if it were not motivated by something beyond nature. The ethical situation is a human situation, beyond human nature, in which the idea of God comes to mind (*Gott fällt mir ein*). In this respect, we could say that God is the other who turns our nature inside out, who calls our ontological will-to-be into question. This ethical call of conscience occurs, no doubt, in other religious systems besides the Judaeo-Christian, but it remains an essentially religious vocation. God does indeed go against nature for He is not of this world. God is other than Being.

RK *How does one distil the ethico-religious meaning of existence from its natural or ontological sedimentation?*

EL But your question already assumes that ethics is derived from ontology. I believe, on the contrary, that the ethical relationship with the other is just as primary and original (*ursprünglich*) as ontology – if not more so. Ethics is not derived from an ontology of nature; it is its opposite, a meontology which affirms a meaning beyond Being, a primary mode of non-Being (*me-on*).

RK *And yet you claim that the ethical and the ontological coexist as two inspirations in some way?*

EL Already in Greek philosophy one can discern traces of the ethical breaking through the ontological, for example in Plato's idea of the 'Good existing beyond Being' (*agathon epekeina tes ousias*). (Heidegger, of course, contests this ethical reading of the Good in

Plato, maintaining that it is merely one among other descriptions of Being itself.) One can also cite in this connection Descartes' discovery of the 'Idea of the Infinite', which surpasses the finite limits of human nature and the human mind. And similarly supra-ontological notions are to be found in the pseudo-Dionysian doctrine of the *via eminentiae* with its surplus of the Divine over Being, or in the Augustinian distinction in the *Confessions* between the truth which challenges (*veritas redarguens*) and the ontological truth which shines (*veritas lucens*), etc.

RK *Do you think that Husserl's theory of temporality points to an otherness beyond Being?*

EL However radically Husserl's theory of time may gesture in this direction, particularly in *The Phenomenology of Internal Time Consciousness*, it remains overall a *cosmological* notion of time; temporality continues to be thought of in terms of the present, in terms of an ontology of presence. The present (*Gegenwart*) remains for Husserl the centralising dimension of time, the past and the future being defined in terms of intentional re-presentations (*Vergegenwärtigen*). To be more precise, the past, Husserl claims, is retained by the present and the future is pre-contained in, or protended by, the present. Time past and time future are merely modifications of the present; and this double extension of the present into the past (retention) and the future (protension) reinforces the ontology of presence as a seizure and appropriation of what is other or transcendent. Heidegger, who actually edited Husserl's lectures on time, introduced an element of alterity into his own phenomenological description of time in *Being and Time*, when he analysed time in terms of our anguish before death. Temporality is now disclosed as an ecstatic being-towards-death which releases us from the present into an ultimate horizon of possibles, rather than as a holding or seizing or retaining of the present.

RK *But is not Heidegger's analysis of temporality as a being-towards-death still a subtle form of extending what is* mine, *of reducing the world to* my *ownmost (*eigenst*) authentic (*eigentlich*) existence? Death is for Heidegger always* my *death.* Dasein *is always the Being which is* mine.

EL This is the fundamental difference between my ethical analysis of death and Heidegger's ontological analysis. Whereas for Heidegger death is *my* death, for me it is the *other*'s death. In *The Letter on Humanism*, Heidegger defines *Dasein* in almost Darwinian fashion as 'a being which is concerned for its own being'. In paragraph 9 of *Being and Time*, he defines the main characteristic of *Dasein* as that of *mineness* (*Jemeinigkeit*), the way in which Being becomes mine, imposes or imprints itself on me. *Jemeinigkeit* as the possession of my Being as *mine* precedes the articulation of the *I*. *Dasein* is only 'I' (*Ich*) because it is already *Jemeinigkeit*. I become I only because I possess my own Being as primary. For ethical thought, on the contrary, *le moi*, as this primacy of what is mine, is *haïssable*. Ethics is not, for this reason, a depersonalising exigency. I am defined as a subjectivity, as a singular person, as an 'I', precisely because I am exposed to the other. It is my inescapable and incontrovertible answerability to the other that makes me an individual 'I'. So that I become a responsible or ethical 'I' to the extent that I agree to depose or dethrone myself – to abdicate my position of centrality – in favour of the vulnerable other. As the Bible says: 'He who loses his soul gains it'. The ethical I is a being who asks if he has a right to be, who excuses himself to the other for his own existence.

RK *In the structuralist and post-structuralist debates which have tended to dominate Continental philosophy in recent years, there has been much talk of the disappearance or demise of the subject. Is your ethical thought an attempt to preserve subjectivity in some form?*

EL My thinking on this matter goes in the opposite direction to structuralism. It is not that I wish to preserve, over and against the structuralist critique, the idea of a subject who would be a substantial or mastering centre of meaning, an idealist self-sufficient *cogito*. These traditional ontological versions of subjectivity have nothing to do with the meontological version of subjectivity that I put forward in *Autrement qu'être*. Ethical subjectivity dispenses with the idealising subjectivity of ontology which reduces everything to itself. The ethical 'I' is subjectivity precisely in so far as it kneels before the other, sacrificing its own liberty to the more primordial call of the other. For me, the freedom of the subject is not the highest or primary value. The heteronomy of our response to the human other, or to God as the absolutely Other, precedes the autonomy of our subjective freedom. As soon as I acknowledge that it is 'I' who am responsible, I accept that my freedom is anteceded by an obligation to the other. Ethics redefines subjectivity as this heteronymous responsibility in contrast to autonomous freedom. Even if I deny my primordial responsibility to the other by affirming my own freedom as primary, I can never escape the fact that the other has demanded a response from me *before* I affirm my freedom not to respond to his demand. Ethical freedom is *une difficile liberté*, a heteronymous freedom obliged to the other. Consequently, the other is the richest and the poorest of beings: the richest, at an ethical level, in that it always comes before me, its right-to-be preceding mine; the poorest, at an ontological or political level, in that without me it can do nothing, it is utterly vulnerable and exposed. The other haunts our ontological existence and keeps the psyche awake, in a state of vigilant insomnia. Even though we are ontologically free to refuse the other, we remain forever accused, with a bad conscience.

RK *Is not the ethical obligation to the other a purely negative ideal, impossible to realise in our everyday being-in-the-world? After all, we live in a concrete historical world governed by ontological drives and practices, be they political and institutional totalities or technological systems of organisation and control. Is ethics practicable in human society as we know it? Or is it merely an invitation to apolitical acquiescence?*

EL This is a fundamental point. Of course we inhabit an ontological world of technological mastery and political self-preservation. Indeed without these political and technological structures of organisation we would not be able to feed mankind. This is the great paradox of human existence: we must use the ontological *for the sake of the other*; to ensure the survival of the other we must resort to the technico-political systems of means and ends. This same paradox is also present in our use of language, to return to an earlier point. We have no option but to employ the language and concepts of Greek philosophy even in our attempts to go beyond them. We cannot obviate the language of metaphysics and yet we cannot, ethically speaking, be satisfied with it: it is necessary but not enough. I disagree, however, with Derrida's interpretation of this paradox. Whereas he tends to see the deconstruction of the Western metaphysics of presence as an irredeemable crisis, I see it as a golden opportunity for Western philosophy to open itself to the dimension of otherness and transcendence beyond Being.

RK *Is there any sense in which language can be ethical?*

EL In *Autrement qu'être* I pose this question when I ask: 'What is saying without a said?' Saying is ethical sincerity in so far as it is exposition. As such this *saying* is irreducible to the ontological definability of the *said*. Saying is what makes the self-exposure of sincerity possible; it is a way of giving everything, of not keeping anything for oneself. In so far as ontology equates truth with the intelligibility of total presence, it reduces the pure exposure of saying to the totalising closure of the said. The child is a pure exposure of expression in so far as it is pure vulnerability; it has not yet learned to dissemble, to deceive, to be insincere. What distinguishes human language from animal or child expression, for example, is that the human speaker can remain silent, can refuse to be exposed in sincerity. The human being is characterised as human not only because he is a being who can speak but also because he is a being who can lie, who can live in the duplicity of language as the dual possibility of exposure and deception. The animal is incapable of this duplicity; the dog, for instance, cannot suppress its bark, the bird its song. But man can repress his saying, and this ability to keep silent, to withhold onself, is the ability to be political. Man can give himself in saying to the point of poetry – or he can withdraw into the non-saying of lies. Language as *saying* is an ethical openness to the other; as that which is *said* – reduced to a fixed identity or synchronised presence – it is an ontological closure to the other.

RK *But is there not some sort of 'morality' of the* said *which might reflect the ethics of* saying *in our everyday transactions in society? In other words, if politics cannot be ethical in so far as it is an expression of our ontological nature, can it at least be 'moral' (in your sense of that term)?*

EL This distinction between the ethical and the moral is very important here. By morality I mean a series of rules relating to social behaviour and civic duty. But while morality thus operates in the socio-political order of organising and improving our human survival, it is ultimately founded on an ethical responsibility towards the other. As *prima philosophia*, ethics cannot itself legislate for society or produce rules of conduct whereby society might be revolutionised or transformed. It does not operate at the level of the manifesto or *rappel à l'ordre*; it is not a *savoir vivre*. When I talk of ethics as a 'dis-interestedness' (*dés-inter-essement*), I do not mean that it is indifference; I simply mean that it is a form of vigilant passivity to the call of the other which precedes our interest in Being, our *inter-esse* as a being-in-the-world attached to property and appropriating what is other than itself to itself. Morality is what governs the world of political 'interestedness', the social interchanges between citizens in a society. Ethics, as the extreme exposure and sensitivity of one subjectivity to another, becomes morality and hardens its skin as soon as we move into the political world of the impersonal 'third' – the world of government, institutions, tribunals, prisons, schools, committees, etc. But the norm which must continue to inspire and direct the moral order is the ethical norm of the interhuman. If the moral–political order totally relinquishes its ethical foundation, it must accept all forms of society including the fascist or totalitarian, for it can no longer evaluate or discriminate between them. The state is usually better than anarchy – but not always. In some instances, fascism or totalitarianism, for example, the political order of the state may have to be challenged in the name of our ethical responsibility to the other. This is why ethical philosophy must remain the first philosophy.

RK *Is not the ethical criterion of the interhuman employed by you as a sort of Messianic eschatology wherein the ontological structures of possession and totality would be transcended towards a face-to-face relation of pure exposure to the absolutely Other?*

EL Here again I must express my reservations about the term eschatology. The term *eschaton* implies that there might exist a finality, an end (*fin*) to the historical relation of difference between man and the absolutely Other, a reduction of the gap which safeguards the alterity of the transcendent, to a totality of sameness. To realise the *eschaton* would therefore mean that we could seize or appropriate God as a *telos* and degrade the infinite relation with the other to a finite fusion. This is what Hegelian dialectics amounts to, a radical denial of the rupture between the ontological and the ethical. The danger of eschatology is the temptation to consider the man–God relation as a state, as a fixed and permanent state of affairs. I have described ethical responsibility as *insomnia* or *wakefulness* precisely because it is a perpetual duty of vigilance and effort which can never slumber. Ontology as a state of affairs can afford sleep. But love cannot sleep, can never be peaceful or permanent. Love is the incessant watching over of the other; it can never be satisfied or contented with the bourgeois ideal of love as domestic comfort or the mutual possession of two people living out an *égoisme-à-deux*.

RK *If you reject the term 'eschatology', would you accept the term 'Messianic' to describe this ethical relation with the other?*

EL Only if one understands Messianic here according to the Talmudic maxim that 'the doctors of the law will never have peace, neither in this world nor in the next; they go from meeting to meeting discussing always – for there is always more to be discussed'. I could not accept a form of Messianism which would terminate the need for discussion, which would end our watchfulness.

RK *But are we not ethically obliged to struggle for a perfect world of peace?*

EL Yes, but I seek this peace not for *me* but for the other. By contrast, if I say that 'virtue is its own reward' I can only say so *for myself*; as soon as I make this a standard for the other I exploit him, for what I am then saying is: be virtuous towards me – work for me, love me, serve me, etc. – but don't expect anything from me in return. That would be rather like the story of the Czar's mother who goes to the hospital and says to the dying soldier: 'You must be very happy to die for your country'. I must always demand more of myself than of the other; and this is why I disagree with Buber's description of the I-Thou ethical relation as a symmetrical co-presence. As Alyosha Karamazov says in *The Brothers Karamazov* by Dostoevsky: 'We are all responsible for everyone else – but I am more responsible than all the others.' And he does not mean that every 'I' is more responsible than all the others, for that would be to generalise the law for everyone else – to demand as much from the other as I do from myself. This essential asymmetry is the very basis of ethics: not only am I more responsible than the other but I am even responsible for everyone else's responsibility!

RK *How does the God of ethics differ from the 'God of the philosophers', that is, the God of traditional ontology?*

EL For ethics, it is only in the infinite relation with the other that God passes (*se passe*), that traces of God are to be found. God thus reveals himself as a trace, not as an ontological presence which Aristotle defined as a Self-Thinking-Thought and scholastic metaphysics defined as an *Ipsum Esse Subsistens* or *Ens Causa Sui*. The God of the Bible cannot be defined or proved by means of logical predictions and attributions. Even the superlatives of wisdom, power and causality advanced by medieval ontology are inadequate to the absolute otherness of God. It is not by superlatives that we can think of God, but by trying to identify the particular interhuman events which open towards transcendence and reveal the traces where God has passed. The God of ethical philosophy is not God the Almighty Being of creation, but the persecuted God of the prophets who is always in relation with man, and whose difference from man is never indifference. This is why I have tried to think of God in terms of desire, a desire that cannot be fulfilled or satisfied – in the etymological sense of *satis*, measure. I can never have enough in my relation to God for he always exceeds my measure, remains forever incommensurate with my desire. In this sense, our desire for God is without end or term: it is interminable and infinite because God reveals himself as absence rather than presence. Love is the society of God and man, but man is happier for he has God as company whereas God has man! Furthermore, when we say that God cannot satisfy our desire, we must add that the insatisfaction is itself sublime! What is a defect in the finite order becomes an excellence in the infinite order. In the infinite order, the absence of God is better than his presence; and the anguish of our concern and searching for God is better than consummation or comfort. As Kierkegaard put it: 'The need for God is a sublime happiness.'

RK *Your analysis of God as an impossibility of Being or being-present would seem to suggest that the ethical relation is entirely utopian and unrealistic.*

EL This is the great objection to my thought. 'Where did you ever see the ethical relation practised?' people say to me. I reply that its being utopian does not prevent it from investing our everyday actions of generosity or goodwill towards the other: even the smallest and most commonplace gestures, such as saying 'after you' as we sit at the dinner table or walk through a door, bear witness to the ethical. This concern for the other remains utopian in the sense that it is always 'out of place' (*u-topos*) in this world, always other than the 'ways of the world'; but there are many examples of it in the world. I remember meeting once with a group of Latin American students, well versed in the terminology of Marxist liberation and terribly concerned by the suffering and unhappiness of their people in Argentina. They asked me rather impatiently if I had ever actually witnessed the utopian rapport with the other which my ethical philosophy speaks of. I replied: 'Yes, indeed, here in this room.'

RK *So you would maintain that Marxism bears witness to a utopian inspiration?*

EL When I spoke of the overcoming of Western ontology as an 'ethical and prophetic cry' in 'Dieu et la philosophie' (*De Dieu qui vient à l'idée*), I was in fact thinking of Marx's critique of Western idealism as a project to understand the world rather than to transform it. In

Marx's critique we find an ethical conscience cutting through the ontological identification of truth with an ideal intelligibility and demanding that theory be converted into a concrete praxis of concern for the other. It is this revelatory and prophetic cry which explains the extraordinary attraction which the Marxist utopia exerted over numerous generations. Marxism was, of course, utterly compromised by Stalinism. The 1968 Revolt in Paris was a revolt of sadness, because it came after the Khrushchev Report and the exposure of the corruption of the Communist Party. The year of 1968 epitomised the joy of despair; a last grasping at human justice, happiness and perfection after the truth had dawned that the Communist ideal had degenerated into totalitarian bureaucracy. By 1968 only dispersed groups and rebellious pockets of individuals remained to seek their surrealist forms of salvation, no longer confident in a collective movement of humanity, no longer assured that Marxism could survive the Stalinist catastrophe as the prophetic messenger of history.

RK *What role can philosophy serve today? Has it in fact reached that end which so many contemporary Continental philosophers have spoken of?*

EL It is true that philosophy, in its traditional forms of ontotheology and logocentrism – to use Heidegger's and Derrida's terms – has come to an end. But it is not true of philosophy in the other sense of critical speculation and interrogation. The speculative practice of philosophy is by no means near its end. Indeed the whole contemporary discourse of overcoming and deconstructing metaphysics is far more speculative in many respects than metaphysics itself. Reason is never so versatile as when it puts itself in question. In the contemporary end of philosophy, philosophy has found a new lease of life.

(Paris, 1981)

Select bibliography

En découvrant l'existence avec Husserl et Heidegger, Vrin, Paris, 1949.
Difficile liberté, Albin-Michel, Paris, 1963.
Quatre leçons talmudiques, Editions de Minuit, Paris, 1968.
Humanisme de l'autre homme, Fata Morgana, Montpellier, 1972.
Existence and Existents, trans. Al. Lingis, Nijhoff, The Hague, 1978.
Noms propres, Fata Morgana, Montpellier, 1979.
Totality and Infinity, trans. Al. Lingis, Nijhoff, The Hague, 1980.
Otherwise Than Being or Beyond Essence, trans. Al. Lingis, Nijhoff, The Hague, 1981.

De Dieu qui vient à l'idée, Vrin, Paris, 1982.
Du sacré au saint. Cinq nouvelles lectures talmudiques, Editions de Minuit, Paris, 1982.
Ethics and Infinity, Duquesne University Press, Pittsburgh, 1985.
The Theory of Intuition in Husserl's Phenomenology, trans. A. Orianne, Northwestern University Press, Evanston, 1985.
Collected Philosophical Papers, Kluwer Academic Publishers, Boston, 1993.

HERBERT MARCUSE

The philosophy of art and politics

Prefatory note

HERBERT MARCUSE was born in Berlin in 1898 to a prosperous family of assimilated Jews. While still a youth he became an active member of the Social Democratic Party. It was only after the failure of the German Revolution in 1919 that Marcuse decided to devote himself to the study of aesthetics and philosophy, first in Berlin, then in Freiburg in 1929, where he submitted his doctoral thesis on Hegel's *Concept of History* and worked on phenomenological research under both Husserl and Heidegger. He published two major essays during this period, 'Contributions to a phenomenology of historical materialism' (1928) and 'Concrete philosophy' (1929). Fleeing from Nazi Germany in the early thirties, Marcuse became a close associate of Max Horkheimer's Institute for Social Research (exiled from Frankfurt), which sought to apply the dialectical theories of Hegel and Marx to the critique of such contemporary issues as mass culture, anti-Semitism, Enlightenment positivism, authoritarianism and fascism. His work with the Institute brought him into contact with Lukács, Fromm, Benjamin, Adorno and other humanist Marxist thinkers. It was in this middle period of his intellectual career that Marcuse launched a radical project to explore socio-cultural models of liberation as alternatives to the extremes of consumer capitalism and totalitarian Communism. After the war, Marcuse worked at both Columbia and Harvard on a critical analysis of Soviet Marxism (published in 1958). In the late fifties, sixties and seventies he taught at Brandeis University in Boston, *l'Ecole des Hautes Etudes* in Paris, and the University of California; and it was during this mature period that he developed and refined his multifaceted critique of advanced industrial societies, a highly influential analysis which proved a seminal source of ideas for New Left thinking. Marcuse died in 1978.

Though never claiming to be an original thinker in the strict sense of the word, Marcuse's work was singularly representative in that it provided a critical synthesis of three of the major movements of modern Continental thought: (1) the *phenomenological* movement inaugurated by Husserl and Heidegger to which the young Marcuse contributed as a research student in Freiburg (1928–32); (2) the *dialectical* movement of Hegelian Marxism, tailored by the humanism of the German Idealist tradition, which Marcuse espoused as a member of the Frankfurt School of Social Research after 1933; (3) the *psychoanalytic* movement based on a Freudian meta-psychology of unconscious drives which Marcuse refashioned in the sixties into a critique of the repressive strategies of contemporary culture.

Perhaps the keynote of Marcuse's philosophy was its insistence that the relation of modern thought and ideology to contemporary society be critically investigated. Hence the use of the term 'critical social theory' to characterise his thought. Marcuse's critical theory exerted a widespread influence on both the Continental and Anglo-American worlds of contemporary philosophical debate. His exile in the United States provided Marcuse with the opportunity to introduce some of the most significant modern European thinkers – particularly Hegel, Marx, Freud and Heidegger – to an English-speaking academia still largely conditioned by the 'one-dimensional' methodologies of behaviourism, positivism and common-sense empiricism. Since the forties, Marcuse's principal works – *Reason and Revolution* (1941), *Eros and Civilization* (1955), *One-Dimensional Man* (1964), and *Counter-revolution and Revolt* (1972) – were published in both English and German and served to conflate the author's critical responses to both cultures. One conspicuous result of this convergence was the manner in which Marcuse's critique of advanced technological cultures and his dovetailing of political and aesthetic discourse were able to function as a guiding inspiration for the 1968 student revolts in both the United States and Europe.

Marcuse's most significant contribution to contemporary thinking was undoubtedly his ability to combine the concerns of a formalist aesthetics of subjective transcendence with a liberal revolutionary politics. Indeed one of his first projects in the early thirties was to try to reconcile an existentialist hermeneutics of subjectivity with a Marxist-Hegelian dialectics of history. And throughout his works, one finds an unswerving emphasis on the capacity of critical individuals for free aesthetic consciousness and revolutionary praxis combined with a systematic critique of the technological domination and dehumanisation of 'one-dimensional' societies, East and West.

The dialogue that follows took place in San Diego, California, in 1976, two years before Marcuse's death.

RK *As a Marxist thinker of international renown and inspirational mentor of student revolutions in both the United States and Europe in the sixties, you have puzzled many by the turn to primarily aesthetic questions in your recent works. How would you explain or justify this turn?*

HM It seems to have become quite evident that the advanced industrial countries have long since reached the stage of wealth and productivity which Marx projected for the construction of a socialist society. Consequently, a quantitative increase in material productivity is now seen to be insufficient in itself, and a qualitative change in society as a whole is seen to be necessary. Such a qualitative change presupposes, of course, new and unalienating conditions of labour, distribution and living, but that *alone* is not enough. The qualitative change necessary to build a truly socialist society, something we haven't yet seen, depends on other values – not so much economic (quantitative) as aesthetic (qualitative) in character. This change in turn requires more than just a gratification of needs; it requires, in addition, a change in the nature of these needs themselves. This is why the Marxian revolution in our age must look to art also, if it is to succeed.

RK *If art, then, is to play such a central role in the revolutionary transition to a new society, why didn't Marx himself say that?*

HM Marx did not say that because Marx lived over a hundred years ago and so did not write in an age when, as I have just maintained, the problems of the material culture could in fact be resolved by the establishment of genuinely socialist institutions and relationships. Consequently, he did not fully realise that a purely economic resolution of the problem can never be enough, and so lacked the insight that a twentieth-century revolution would require a different type of human being and that such a revolution would have to aim at, and, if successful, implement, an entirely new set of personal and sexual relationships, a new morality, a new sensibility and a total reconstruction of the environment. These are, to a great extent, aesthetic values (aesthetic to be understood in the larger sense of our sensory and imaginative culture which I outlined in *Eros and Civilization*, following Kant and Schiller), and that is why I think that one viewing the possibility of struggle and change in our time recognises the decisive role which art must play.

RK *You spoke there, rather dangerously it seems to me, about the possible necessity of 'implementing' these new personal relationships, etc., which would characterise the qualitatively new society. How can art or culture be instrumental in this implementation without becoming the tool of some dictatorial elite (which would see it as its role to determine what should be 'implemented') and without, consequently, degenerating into propaganda?*

HM Art can never and never should become *directly* and immediately a factor of political praxis. It can only have effect *indirectly*, by its impact on the consciousness and on the subconsciousness of human beings.

RK *You are saying therefore that art must always maintain a critical and* negative *detachment from the realm of everyday political practice?*

HM Yes, I would claim that all authentic art is *negative*, in the sense that it refuses to obey the established reality, its language, its order, its conventions and its images. As such, it can be negative in two ways: *either* in so far as it serves to give asylum or refuge to defamed humanity and thus preserves in another form an alternative to the 'affirmed' reality of the establishment; *or* in so far as it serves to negate this 'affirmed' reality by denouncing both it and the defamers of humanity who have affirmed it in the first place.

RK *Is it not true, however, that in many of your writings (I think particularly of* An Essay on Liberation *and* Eros and Civilization*) you suggest that art can play a more directly political and indeed* positive *role, by helping to point the way to a socialist utopia?*

HM Art can give you the 'images' of a freer society and of more human relationships but beyond that it cannot go. In this sense, the difference between aesthetic and political theory remains unbridgeable: Art can say what it wants to say only in terms of the complete and formal fate of individuals in their struggle with their society in the medium of *sensibility*; its images are felt and imagined rather than intellectually formulated or propounded, whereas political theory is necessarily *conceptual*.

RK *How then would you view the role of reason in art – I refer not to* Verstand *(reason in the narrow Enlightenment sense of strictly logical, mathematical and empirico-metric calculation) but to the Kantian and Hegelian concept of* Vernunft *(reason in the larger sense of a critical and regulative faculty) concerned primarily with those realms of human perception, intuition, evaluation and ethical deliberation so central, it would seem, to the concerns of any cultural aesthetic?*

HM I believe that you cannot have the liberation of human sensitivity and sensibility without a corresponding liberation of our rational faculty (*Vernunft*). Any liberation effected by art signifies therefore, a liberation of both the senses and reason from their present servitude.

RK *Would you be opposed then to the emotionally euphoric and Dionysian character of much of contemporary popular culture – rock music, for example?*

HM I am wary of all exhibitions of free-wheeling emotionalism and as I explained in *Counter-revolution and Revolt*, I think that both the 'living' theatre movement (the attempt to bring theatre out into the street and make it 'immediate' by 'tuning in' to the language and sentiments of the working class) and the 'rock' cult are prone to this error. The former, despite its noble struggle, is ultimately self-defeating. It tries to blend the theatre and the revolution, but ends up blending a contrived immediacy with a clever brand of mystical humanism. The latter, the 'rock-group' cult, seems open to the danger of a form of commercial totalitarianism which absorbs the individual into an uninhibited mass where the power of a collective unconscious is mobilised but left without any radical or critical awareness. It could, at times, prove a dangerous outburst of irrationalism.

RK *Accepting the fact, then, that a revolutionary liberation of the senses requires also a liberation of reason, the question still remains as to who is to decide what is rational, what criteria, in turn, are to be deployed in such a decision and also, who is consequently to endorse and implement this rational liberation? In other words, how do you obviate the unsavoury prospect of a benevolent, 'rational' dictator or elite imposing their criteria on the manipulated and 'irrational' masses?*

HM The aesthetic liberation of the rational and sensible faculties (at present repressed) will have to begin with individuals and small groups, trying, as it were, such an experiment in unalienated living. How it then gradually becomes effective in terms of the society at large and makes for a different construction of social relationships in general, we cannot say. Such premature programming could only lead to yet another example of ideological tyranny.

RK *Would you then disagree with your former colleague, Walter Benjamin, when he urges that popular culture, and particularly the cinema (which he held enables the critical and receptive attitudes of the public to coincide) be used in a politically committed fashion to aid and abet the socialist revolution?*

HM Yes, I would have to disagree with Benjamin there. Any attempt to use art to effect a 'mass' conversion of sensibility and consciousness is inevitably an abuse of its true functions.

RK *Its true functions being . . .?*

HM Its true functions being (1) to negate our present society, (2) to anticipate the trends of future society, (3) to criticise destructive or alienating trends, and (4) to suggest 'images' of creative and unalienating zones.

RK *And this fourfold function of* negation, anticipation, critique *and* suggestion *would presumably be aimed at the individual or small group?*

HM Yes, that is correct.

RK *Would you wish to retract your allegiance to the Frankfurt School's Marxist aesthetic as expressed in the following formulation: 'We interpret art as a kind of a code language for processes taking place within society which must be deciphered by means of critical analysis'?*

HM Yes, that seems to me to be too reductive. Art is more than a code or puzzle which would 'reflect' the world in terms of a second-order aesthetic structure. Art is not just a mirror. It can never only imitate reality. Photography does that much better. Art has to transform reality so that it appears in the light (1) of what it does to human beings, and (2) of the possible images of freedom and happiness, which it might provide for these same human beings; and this is something photography cannot do. Art, therefore, does not just mirror the present, it leads beyond it. It preserves, and thus allows us to remember, values which are no longer to be found in our world; and it points to another possible society in which these values may be realised. Art is a code only to the extent that it acts as a mediated critique of society. But it cannot as such be a direct or immediate indictment of society – that is the work of theory and politics.

RK *Would you not say that the works of Orwell, Dickens, or the French Surrealists, for example, were directly an indictment of their society?*

HM Well, the Surrealists were never, it seems to me, *directly* political. Orwell was not a great writer; and Dickens, like all great writers, was far more than a political theorist; reading him gives us positive pleasure and thereby ensures that there is a reader for the book in the first place. This is one of the central dilemmas of art conceived as an agent of revolution. Even the most radical art cannot, in its denunciation of the evils of society, dispense with the element of entertainment. That is why Bertolt Brecht always maintained that even the work which most brutally depicts what is going on in the world must also please. And one additional point to be remembered here is that even when certain works of art *appear* directly social or political in *content*, e.g. Orwell and Dickens, but also Zola, Ibsen, Büchner, Delacroix, Picasso, they are never so in *form*, for the work always remains committed to the structure of art, to the form of the novel, drama, poem and painting, etc. and thereby testifies to a distance from reality.

RK *What is your opinion then of the notion of a 'proletarian' art?*

HM I think it is false for several reasons. Its attempt to transcend the distancing forms of classical and Romantic art and to unite art and reality by providing in their stead a 'living art' or 'anti-art' rooted in the actions, slang and spontaneous sensations of the oppressed folk, seems to me to be doomed to failure, as I have argued in *Counter-revolution and Revolt*. Although in earlier works I stressed the political potential of the linguistic rebellion of the blacks witnessed in their folk music, dance and particularly language (whose very obscenity I interpreted as a legitimate protest against their misery and repressed cultural tradition), I now believe that such a potential is ultimately ineffective, for it has become standardised and can no longer be identified as the expression of frustrated radicals, but all too often as the futile gratification of aggressiveness which too easily turns against sexuality itself. (For instance, the 'obligatory' verbalisation of the genital sphere in 'radical' speech has not been a political threat to the Establishment so much as a debasement of sexuality, e.g. if some radical exclaims, 'Fuck Nixon', he is associating the term for the highest gratification with the highest member of the oppressive Establishment!)

RK *What is your view of 'living' or 'natural' music, which has always been associated with the oppressed classes in the West and particularly with the black culture?*

HM Well, it seems to me that here again one finds the same thing occurring. What originally started out as an authentic cry and song of the oppressed black community has since been transformed and commercialised into 'white' rock, which, by means of contrived 'performances', serves as an orgiastic group therapy which removes all the frustrations and inhibitions of the audiences, but only *temporarily* and without any socio-political foundation.

RK *I take it then that you would not support the idea of an art of the masses, an art devoted to the working-class struggle?*

HM No, it seems to me that rather than being a particular code of the struggle of the proletariat or working class, art can transcend any *particular* class interest without eliminating such an interest. It is always concerned with history but history is the history of *all* classes. And it is this generality which accounts for that universal validity and objectivity of art which Marx called the quality of 'pre-history' and which Hegel called the 'continuity of substance' from the beginning of art to the end – the truth which links the modern novel and the medieval epic, the facts and possibilities of human existence, conflict and reconciliation between man and man, man and nature. A work of art will obviously contain a class content (to the extent to which it reflects the values, situations and sentiments of a feudal, bourgeois or proletarian world view) but it becomes transparent as the condition of the universal dreams of humanity. Authentic art never *merely* acts as a mirror of a class or as an 'automatic', spontaneous outburst of its frustrations and desires. The very 'sensuous immediacy' which art expresses, presupposes, however surreptitiously (and this is something which most of our popular culture has forgotten), a complex, disciplined and formal synthesis of experience according to certain universal principles which alone can lend to the work more than a purely private significance. It is because of this 'universal' dimension of art that some of the greatest political radicals have displayed the most apolitical stances and tastes in art (e.g. the famous sympathisers of the Paris Commune of 1871, or even Marx himself). Many of the apparently *formless* works of modern art (those of Cage, Stockhausen, Beckett or Ginsberg) are in fact highly intellectual, constructivist and *formal*. And indeed this fact hints, I believe, at the passing of anti-art and the return to *form*. It is because of this 'universal' significance of art as form that we may find the meaning of revolution better expressed in Bertolt

Brecht's most perfect lyrics than in his explicitly political polemics; or in Bob Dylan's most 'soulful' and deeply personal songs rather than in his propagandist manifestos. Both Brecht and Dylan have one message: to make an end with things as they are. Even in the event of a total absence of political content, their works can invoke, for a vanishing moment, the image of a liberated world and the pain of an alienated one. Thus, the aesthetic dimension assumes a political and revolutionary value, but without becoming the mouthpiece of any particular class interest.

RK *A certain detachment from the political reality would seem then almost prerequisite for a genuinely revolutionary art, would it not?*

HM Yes, art must always remain alienated to some extent and this precludes an identification of art with revolutionary praxis. As I argued in *Counter-revolution and Revolt*, art cannot represent the revolution, it can only invoke it in another medium, in an aesthetic structure in which the political content becomes *meta*political, governed by the formal necessity of art. And so the goal of all revolution – a world of tranquillity and freedom – can appear in a totally unpolitical medium under the aesthetic laws of beauty and harmony.

RK *Would it be fair to conclude, therefore, that you reject the various attempts by Lenin, Lukács and other Marxist dialecticians to formulate the possibility of* progressive art *as a weapon of class war?*

HM The belief that only a 'proletarian' literature can fulfil the progressive function of art and develop a revolutionary consciousness seems to me a mistaken one in our age. Today the working class shares the same world view and values as those of a large part of other classes, especially the middle class. The conditions and goals of a revolution against global monopoly capitalism today cannot therefore be adequately articulated in terms of a proletarian revolution; and so if this revolution is to be present in some way as a goal in art, such art could not be typically proletarian. Indeed, it seems to me more than a matter of personal preference that both Lenin and Trotsky were critical of the notion of a 'proletarian culture'. But even if you could argue for a 'proletarian culture', you would still be left asking whether there is such a thing as a proletariat (as Marx described it) in our age. In the United States, for example, one finds that the working people are often apathetic if not totally hostile to socialism, while in Italy and France, strongholds of the Marxist tradition of labour, the workers seem to be ruled by a Communist Party and trade unionism manipulated very often by the USSR and committed to the minimum strategy of compromise or tolerance. In both situations, that is, in the US and in Europe, it would seem that a large part of the working class has become a class of bourgeois society, and their 'proletarian' socialism, if it exists at all, no longer appears as a definitive negation of capitalism. Consequently, the attempt to turn the emotions of the working class into a standard for authentic radical and socialist art is a regressive step and can only result in a superficial adjustment of the established order, and a perpetuation of the prevailing 'atmosphere' of oppression and alienation. For instance, authentic 'black literature' is revolutionary but it is not a 'class' literature as such, and its *particular* content is at the same time a *universal* one. One finds here in the particular situation of an alienated radical minority the most 'universal' of all needs: the need of the individual and his group to exist as *human* beings.

RK *We seem to have returned again to the notion of 'aesthetic' revolution as something centred around individuals and small groups in its advocation of, and experimentation with, unalienated living. Are you in fact suggesting that it might be possible for certain individuals and small groups to live in a non-alienated manner in an alienated world? (I think here in particular of certain dissenting artists, intellectuals, ecologists, anti-nuclear pacifists, or the advocates of alternative modes of co-operative community existence.)*

HM No. One cannot actually *live* in a non-alienated manner in an alienated world. You can *experiment* with it, you can *remember* it; you can in your own little circle try your best to develop it, but beyond that you cannot go.

RK *Would you agree that it is by means of the aesthetic imagination that one can transcend one's alienated world, in order to 'experiment' with and 'remember' alternative forms of life as you suggest?*

HM Yes, that is correct, and imaginative remembrance is particularly important, for it is by remembering the values and desires which, unable over the ages to express themselves in a politically corrupt world, took refuge in art and thus preserved themselves, that we shall be able to find hints of a direction out of our present alienation.

RK *This notion of art as hinting at a new direction would seem to me to be a* positive *one; but have you not already on many occasions, and even in this interview, confirmed the view, held by Brecht, Beckett and Kafka, to name but a few, that art must be* negative *('estranged') and 'alienating' if it is to remain authentic?*

HM Yes, indeed, I did and still do support that view. Art must never lose its negative and alienating power, for it is there that its most radical potential lies. To lose this 'negating' power is, in effect, to eliminate the tension between art and reality, and so also the very real distinctions between subject and object, quantity and quality, freedom and servitude, beauty and ugliness, good and evil, future and present, justice and injustice. Such a claim to a final synthesis of these historical oppositions in the here and now would be the materialist version of absolute idealism. It would signal a state of perfect barbarism at the height of civilisation. In other words, to do away with these distinctions between value and fact is to deny present reality and forestall our search for another more human one. Indeed, the common negative force of a piece of music by Verdi and Bob Dylan, a piece of writing by Flaubert and Joyce or a painting by Ingres and Picasso is precisely that hint of beauty which acts as refusal of the commodity world and of the performances, attitudes, looks and sounds required by it.

RK *So the artistic imagination, you would say, can in no way be revolutionary in a 'positive' sense?*

HM Art, as we know it, cannot transform reality and cannot, therefore, submit to the actual requirements of the revolution without denying itself. It is only as a negative and alienating power that it can in fact negate, dialectically, the alienation of the political reality. And, as such, as the negation of the negation, to use Hegel's term, it is indeed revolutionary. That is why in *Counter-revolution and Revolt* and elsewhere I described the relation between art and politics as a unity of opposites, an antagonistic unity which must always remain antagonistic.

RK *In* An Essay on Liberation, *you speak at one point about technology being used by the revolutionary in the same way as the painter uses his canvas and brush. Does not this analogy suggest a direct and positive relationship to the socio-political reality?*

HM In some limited sense I suppose it does. It is true, I believe, that technology should, ideally, be used creatively and imaginatively to reconstruct nature and the environment.

RK *But according to what criteria?*

HM According to the criterion of beauty.

RK *But who decides this criterion? Is it universal for all men and women? And if so, in what way does it, as an 'aesthetic' criterion, differ from a theological or ontological system of value?*

HM I think that the striving for beauty is simply an essential part of human sensibility.

RK *But surely, if our world is to undergo a revolutionary reconstruction in the name of and for the sake of beauty, one must be quite sure in advance what this 'beauty' is – whether it is in fact the universal and absolute goal of all human striving, or merely the subjective and particular goal of one revolutionary leader/artist or an elite of revolutionary leaders/artists? If the latter, then how does one deny the charge of totalitarian imposition, manipulation and tyranny?*

HM A revolution cannot be waged for the sake of beauty. Beauty is but one criterion which plays a leading role in one element of the revolution, i.e. the restoration and reconstruction of the environment. It cannot be used to 'reconstruct' men without, as you correctly infer, running the risk of totalitarianism. It simply cannot presume to go that far.

RK *In* Eros and Civilization *it certainly seems, however, as if you are suggesting that 'beauty' is no less than the ultimate end or* telos *of all human struggle; and that this teleological struggle is itself synonymous with Freud's 'meta-psychological' interpretation of 'eros' or Kant's view that 'all aesthetic endeavour seeks beauty as its final purpose'.*

HM No. Beauty is only one amongst other goals.

RK *You would not wish then, in any sense, to ascribe an absolute character to beauty?*

HM No, beauty can never be absolute. Nevertheless, I think that certain evaluative criteria can be established in relation to it.

RK *How then would you react to Martin Jay's assertion in his book on the Frankfurt School,* The Dialectical Imagination, *that your repeated attempts to describe human desire for an ideal utopia are rooted in the latent Judaeo-Messianic optimism of the Frankfurt School, which, in fact, consisted almost exclusively of German Jewish intellectuals, e.g. Adorno, Fromm, Horkheimer, Benjamin and, of course, yourself, who wished to synthesise the intuitions of two other Jews, Marx and Freud?*

HM I do not recall on any occasion having described or even attempted to describe such a thing as utopia. The relationships which I indicate as essential for qualitative change are certainly 'aesthetic', but they are not utopian.

RK *So you would deny any link between your political optimism about a new society and the Messianic optimism of Judaism?*

HM Absolutely.

RK *Another current interpretation of the striving for universal and objective value-criteria in your writings on the 'aesthetic revolution' is that you are in fact returning, albeit surreptitiously, to the 'fundamental ontology' of your original mentor, Martin Heidegger – seeking a new kind of 'poetic dwelling on earth'. Do you see your later works as a return to your early attempts in the thirties to reconcile a Heideggerean phenomenology of subjective historicity with a Marxist dialectics of collective history?*

HM That Heidegger had a profound influence on me is without any doubt, and I have never denied it. He taught me a great deal about what real phenomenological 'thinking' is, about how thinking is not just a logical function of 'representing' what *is*, here and now in the present, but operates at deeper levels in its 'recalling' of what has been forgotten and its 'projecting' what might yet come to pass in the future. That appreciation of the temporal and intentional nature of phenomena has been extremely important for me, but that is as far as it goes.

RK *Evidently art has, in your opinion, a radical role to play in detaching individuals from their mindless slavery to the present conditions of work, competition, performance, advertising, mass media, etc., and thereby educating them in their own reality. Indeed, you have spoken very often of late about* art as education. *Would you like to comment on this relationship?*

HM Such an education in the reality of one's repressed faculties – sensory, imaginative and rational – and in our repressive environmental and working conditions would have to be based not on a mass education plan (that again would be to abuse art by turning it into propaganda) but in small communal projects of *auto-critique*. Such auto-critique would not, of course, replace a general education. It could not be a question of substituting one for the other, of abandoning the traditional tools of education altogether; not so much a question of *deschooling* as *reschooling*.

RK *Such an 'aesthetic' reschooling, which as you say would not be alternative, but supplementary to a general basic education, would presumably be concerned with those ethical and existential areas of human relations which constitute the locus of a* qualitative *leap to another society, would it not?*

HM Yes it would.

RK *And presumably you would like to be able to base such an aesthetic education on certain universal principles whose objectivity would preclude the danger of an ideological indoctrination of the 'ignorant' and 'gullible' masses by some 'enlightened' elite, an abuse of education which is directly conducive to totalitarianism and fascism.*

HM Yes, that is certainly a very real danger. And in order to be as objective as possible, one must try to determine objectively what are the seats of power today and how they influence what they have established as reality. This objectivity would then be based on what is the reality of our present society and not on ideological constructions.

RK *But I suspect that in your projection of the 'images' of a new society you tend to go behind an objectivity founded in* what is, *to an objectivity founded in* what ought to be*; and so we return to the old question: what is this 'ought' which would govern the aesthetic transformation of human beings and their relations with one another?*

HM There is no such thing as an absolute prescriptive criterion for change. If a man is happy in the society in which he presently finds himself, then he has condemned himself. This problem has never bothered me. A human being who today still thinks that the world ought not to be changed is below the level of discussion. I have no problems about the 'is' and the 'ought'; it is a problem invented by philosophers.

RK *But if the question is so unproblematical, what is it that separates human desire for a freer and unalienated society from the animal's? I mean, why doesn't an animal feel the imperative need to change its world into a qualitatively better one?*

HM It cannot, but it does at least have enough instinct to realise that when its environment is lacking in food, warmth and a mate it must migrate to another.

RK *How then would you account for the difference between the human desire to change his world and the animal's?*

HM An animal has no reason whereas a human being has and so can outline, indirectly by means of art and directly by means of political theory, *possible* directions for future improvement.

RK *Humans, therefore, would seem by virtue of their reason (*Vernunft*) to possess some universal orientation towards a future society – something which you frequently spoke of in your early writings – which the animal does not possess. But by viewing our rational imagination in this way, as a power capable of transcending the immediate continuum of history, and of projecting alternative possibilities for a future society, you would seem once again, would you not, to have moved beyond the strictly empirical realm of the 'is'? How would you account then for this exigency, so manifest in the passion of artists and intellectuals, to transcend the given mores and conventions of our present society in search of new and better ones?*

HM Everyone searches for something better. Everyone searches for a society in which there is no more alienated labour. There is no need for a guiding principle or goal; it is simply a matter of common sense.

RK *Would you wish to equate the striving for beauty and the ideal society with the abolition of alienated labour?*

HM Of course not. Once the problem of alienated labour is solved there will be many others which remain. The creative and imaginative faculties of man will never be redundant. If art is something which among other things can point to the 'images' of a political utopia, it is inevitably something which can never cease to be. Art and politics will never finally coalesce because the ideal society which art strives for in its negation of all alienated societies presupposes an ideal reconciliation of opposites, which can never be achieved in any absolute or Hegelian sense. The relationship between art and political praxis is therefore dialectical. As soon as one problem is solved in a synthesis, new problems are born and so the process continues without end. The day when men try to identify opposites in an ultimate sense, thus ignoring the inevitable rupture between art and revolutionary praxis, will sound the death-knell for art. Man must never cease to be an artist, to criticise and negate his present self and society and to project by means of his creative imagination alternative 'images' of existence. He can never cease to imagine for he can never cease to change.

(San Diego, 1976)

Select bibliography

Hegels Ontologie und die Grundlegung einer Theorie der Geschichtlichkeit, V. Klostermann, Frankfurt, 1932.

Reason and Revolution: Hegel and the Rise of Social Theory, Oxford University Press, New York, 1941.

Eros and Civilization: A Philosophical Inquiry into Freud, Beacon Press, Boston, 1955.

Soviet Marxism: A Critical Analysis, Columbia University Press, New York, 1958.

One-Dimensional Man: Studies in the Ideology of Advanced Industrial Society, Beacon Press, Boston, 1964.

Kultur und Gesellschaft, Suhrkamp, Frankfurt, 1965.

Das Ende der Utopie, Maikowski, West Berlin, 1967.

Psychoanalyse und Politik, Europäische, Frankfurt, 1968.

An Essay on Liberation, Beacon Press, Boston, 1969.

Ideen zu einer kritischen Theorie der Gesellschaft, Suhrkamp, Frankfurt, 1969.

Five Lectures, Beacon Press, Boston, 1970.

Counter-revolution and Revolt, Beacon Press, Boston, 1972.

Studies in Critical Philosophy, Beacon Press, Boston, 1973.
Revolution or Reform? A Confrontation, Afterword by Franz Stark, New University Press, Chicago, 1976.
Gespräche mit Herbert Marcuse, Suhrkamp, Frankfurt, 1978.
The Aesthetic Dimension: Toward a Critique of Marxist Aesthetics, Beacon Press, Boston, 1978.
Schriften, I: Der deutsche Künstlerroman/Frühe Aufsätze, Suhrkamp, Frankfurt, 1978.
Schriften, 3: Aufsätze aus der Zeitschrift für Sozialforschung, 1934–1941. Suhrkamp, Frankfurt, 1979.
Schriften, 5: Triebstruktur und Gesellschaft: Ein philosophischer Beitrag zu Sigmund Freud, trans. Marianne von Eckhardt-Jaffe, Suhrkamp, Frankfurt, 1979. This volume is a translation of *Eros and Civilization: A Philosophical Inquiry into Freud* (see above).

PAUL RICOEUR

The creativity of language

Prefatory note

PAUL RICOEUR was born in Valence, France, in 1913. During his captivity in Germany during the war, Ricoeur taught philosophy to his fellow prisoners and familiarised himself with German phenomenology and existentialism. On his return to France, he pursued his interest in the philosophy of subjectivity and existence, publishing works on *Gabriel Marcel and Karl Jaspers* in 1948; on *Karl Jaspers and the Philosophy of Existence* (with Mikel Dufrenne) in 1947; and on Husserl's *Ideas*, together with a translation, in 1950. In 1948, Ricoeur was appointed Professor of the History of Philosophy at the University of Strasbourg, where he remained until 1956 when he moved to Paris, serving as Professor of Metaphysics at both the Sorbonne (1956–66) and Nanterre (1966–80). He also held a post as John Nuveen Professor at the University of Chicago.

Ricoeur's first major contribution to contemporary thinking was his three volume *Philosophy of Will – The Voluntary and the Involuntary* (1950), *Fallible Man* (1960) and *The Symbolism of Evil* (1960). In these works of his middle period, Ricoeur argues that the ideal of a self-transparent, autonomous subjectivity, promoted by Descartes' *cogito* and Husserl's transcendental ego, is ultimately impossible. The human will, he claims, is always confronted by the 'involuntary' limits of finitude which defy or exceed its subjective powers. The subject can never lay claim, therefore, to pure, immediate self-reflection; it is always traversed by meanings other than its own; it is a decentred, split, fallible *cogito* which finds itself in a world whose meaning largely precedes its own voluntary initiatives. And so Ricoeur points to the necessity to move from a pure phenomenology of reflective consciousness to a hermeneutic phenomenology which recognises that the subject's retrieval of itself and of meaning requires a 'detour' through the 'objective' structures of culture, religion, society and language. He defines hermeneutics accordingly as 'the art of deciphering indirect meanings'. Only by clearly acknowledging the existence of such trans-subjective barriers to our subjective projects can we finally hope to interpret these 'mediations' in the light of the ultimate goals of freedom and understanding (what Ricoeur refers to as a 'teleology' or 'eschatology' of the subject).

It is just such a hermeneutic detour through the alienating and mediating structures of meaning which Ricoeur undertakes in *The Symbolism of Evil* and in the later more explicitly hermeneutic works, *Freud and Philosophy: An Essay on Interpretation* (1965), *The Conflict of Interpretations* (1969); *The Rule of Metaphor* (1975); *Time and Narrative* (1983–86) and *Oneself as Another* (1992). The primary aim of these hermeneutic studies is to show how the ideal of absolute knowledge is always deferred or displaced by an endless series of expropriations and reappropriations of meaning (via the notion of the 'unconscious' in psychoanalysis, of anonymous linguistic 'codes' in structuralism or of the impersonal 'facticity' of time and circumstance in the political philosophies of history).

A modern philosophy of consciousness, insists Ricoeur, must enter into dialogue with the human sciences – politics, sociology, linguistics, psychology, history, economics, etc. Only by recognising the various obstacles and opacities which the project of self-understanding encounters, and by thus resisting the facile solution of some 'absolute synthesis' of knowledge which would contrive to resolve prematurely the conflict of interpretations, can we achieve an authentic grasp of the role of human creativity and imagination in spite of all the odds. In other words, it is only if we take seriously the 'hermeneutics of suspicion', which in Freud, Marx, Nietzsche and elsewhere seeks to expose the idealist fallacy of self-transparent consciousness, that we may work towards a 'hermeneutics of affirmation' which continues to believe in the recovery of lost meanings and the creation of new ones – the opening up of 'possible worlds'.

The first part of the dialogues that follow was recorded in Paris in 1981 and the second in Paris in 1978.

The creativity of language

RK *How do your later works on metaphor (*La Métaphore vive, *1975) and* *narrativity (*Temps et récit*, 1983) fit into your overall programme of philosophical hermeneutics?*

PR In *La Métaphore vive* (*The Rule of the Metaphor*) I tried to show how language could extend itself to its very limits forever discovering new resonances within itself. The term *vive* (living) in the title of this work is all important, for it was my purpose to demonstrate that there is not just an epistemological and political imagination, but also, and perhaps more fundamentally, a *linguistic* imagination which generates and regenerates meaning through the living power of metaphoricity. *La Métaphore vive* investigated the resources of rhetoric to show how language undergoes creative mutations and transformations. My work on narrativity, *Temps et récit*, develops this inquiry into the inventive power of language. Here, the analysis of narrative operations in a literary text, for instance, can teach us how we formulate a new structure of 'time' by creating new modes of plot and characterisation. My chief concern in this analysis is to discover how the act of *raconter*, of telling a story, can transmute *natural* time into a specifically *human* time, irreducible to mathematical, chronological 'clock time'. How is narrativity, as the construction or deconstruction of paradigms of story-telling, a perpetual search for new ways of expressing human time, a production or creation of meaning? That is my question.

RK *How would you relate this hermeneutics of narrativity to your former phenomenology of existence?*

PR I would say, borrowing Wittgenstein's term, that the 'language-game' of narration ultimately reveals that the meaning of human existence is itself narrative. The implications of narration as a retelling of history are considerable. For history is not only the story (*histoire*) of triumphant kings and heroes, of the powerful; it is also the story of the powerless and dispossessed. The history of the vanquished dead crying out for justice demands to be told. As Hannah Arendt points out, the meaning of human existence is not just the power to change or master the world, but also the ability to be remembered and recollected in narrative discourse, to be *memorable*. These existential and historical implications of narrativity are very far-reaching, for they determine what is to be 'preserved' and rendered 'permanent' in a culture's sense of its past, of its own 'identity'.

RK *Could you outline some such implications for a political rereading of the past? How, for example, would it relate to a Marxist interpretation?*

PR Just as novelists choose a certain plot (*intrigue*) to order the material of their fiction into a narrative sequence, so too historians order the events of the past according to certain choices of narrative structure or plot. While history has traditionally concerned itself with the plot of kings, battles, treaties and the rise and fall of empires, one finds alternative readings emerging from the nineteenth century onwards whose narrative selection focuses on the story of the victims – the plot of suffering rather than that of power and glory. Michelet's romantic historiography of the 'people' was a case in point. And a more obvious and influential example is the Marxist rereading of history according to the model of the class struggle which champions the cause of the oppressed workers. In such ways, the normal narrative ordering of history is reversed and the hero is now the 'slave' rather than the 'master' as before; a new set of events and facts are deemed to be relevant and claim our attention; the relations of labour and production take precedence over the relations between kings and queens. But here again one must remain critical lest the new heroes of history become abstractions in their turn, thus reducing an alternative 'liberating' plot to another reified version of events which might only deepen the illusion that history somehow unfolds of its own accord independently of the creative powers of the labouring human subject. After such a manner, Marxism as an ideology of liberation, of the powerless, can easily become – as happened with the German Social Democrats or with Stalin – an ideology which imposes a new kind of oppressive power: the proletariat thus ceases to be a living human community of subjects and becomes instead an impersonal, abstracted concept in a new system of scientific determinism.

RK *Is narrative language primarily an intentionality of subjective consciousness, as phenomenology argued; or is it an objective and impersonal structure which predetermines the subjective operations of consciousness, as structuralism maintained?*

PR It is both at once. The invaluable contribution made by structuralism was to offer an exact scientific description of the codes and paradigms of language. But I do not believe that this excludes the creative expression of consciousness. The creation of meaning in language comes from the specifically *human* production of new ways of expressing the objective paradigms and codes made available by language. With the same grammar, for example, we can utter many novel and different sentences. Creativity is always governed by objective linguistic codes which it continually brings to their limit in order to invent something new. Whereas I drew from the objective codes of rhetoric in my analysis of the creative power of metaphor, in my study of narrativity I refer to the linguistic structures disclosed by the Russian Formalists, the Prague school and more recently by the structualism of Lévi-Strauss and Genette. My philosophical project is to show how human language is *inventive* despite the objective limits and codes which govern it, to reveal the diversity and potentiality of language which the erosion of the everyday, conditioned by technocratic and political interests, never ceases to obscure. To become aware of the metaphorical and narrative resources of language is to recognise that its flattened or diminished powers can always be rejuvenated for the benefit of all forms of language usage.

RK *Can your research on narrativity also be considered as a search for a shared meaning beyond the multiplicity of discourses? In other words, does the act of narrating history render it universal and common to all?*

PR This problem of unity and diversity is central to narrativity and can be summarised in terms of the two following, conflicting interpretations. In the *Confessions* Augustine tells us that the 'human body is undone', that human existence is in discord in so far as it is a temporal rupturing and exploding of the present in contrast to the eternal presence of God. To this Augustinian reading of human existence as *dispersion*, I would oppose Aristotle's theory of tragedy in *The Poetics* as a way of *unifying* existence by retelling it. Narrativity can be seen in terms of this opposition: the discordance of time (*temps*) and the concordance of the tale (*récit*). This is a problem which faces all historians, for example. Is history a narrative tale which orders and constructs the fragmentary, empirical facts offered by sociology? Can history divorce itself from the narrative structure of the tale, in its *rapprochement* to sociology, without ceasing to be history? It is interesting that even Fernand Braudel, who champions the sociological approach to history in his preface to *The Mediterranean in the Time of Philippe II*, still retains the notion of history as temporal duration; he stops short of espousing atemporal paradigms, *à la* Lévi-Strauss, for that would spell the demise of history. Lévi-Strauss's social anthropology can afford to dispense with history since it is only concerned with 'cold societies': societies without historical or diachronic development, whose customs and norms – the incest taboo, for example – are largely unaffected by temporal change. History begins and ends with the reciting of a tale (*récit*); and its intelligibility and coherence rest upon this recital. My task is to show how the narrative structures of history and of the story (i.e. of the novel or fiction) operate in a parallel fashion to create new forms of human time, and therefore new forms of human community, for creativity is also a social and cultural act; it is not confined to the individual.

RK *What exactly do you mean by 'human' time?*

PR I mean the formulation of two opposing forms of time: public time and private time. Private time is mortal time, for, as Heidegger says, to exist is to be a being-towards-death (*Sein-zum-Tode*), a being whose future is closed off by death. As soon as we understand our existence as this mortal time, we are already involved in a form of private narrativity or history; as soon as the individual comes up against the finite limits of its own existence, it is obliged to recollect itself and to make time its *own*. On the other hand, there exists public time. Now I do not mean public in the sense of physical or natural time (clock time), but the time of language itself, which continues on after the individual's death. To live in human time is to live between the private time of our mortality and the public time of language. Even Chénu, who tends towards a quantitative assessment of history, acknowledges that the kernel of history is demography, that is, the regeneration of generations, the story (*histoire*) of the living and the dead. Precisely as this recollection of the living and the dead, history – as public narrativity – produces human time. To summarise, I would say that my analysis of narrativity is concerned with three interrelated problems: (i) narration as history; (ii) narration as fiction; and (iii) narration as human time.

RK *What can this analysis contribute to your study of the biblical patterns of narration in* La Symbolique du mal*?*

PR The hermeneutics of narration is crucial to our understanding of the Bible. Why is it, for example, that Judaeo-Christianity is founded on narrative episodes or stories? And how is it that these succeed in becoming *exemplary*, co-ordinated into laws, prophecies and psalms, etc.? I think that the biblical co-ordination of narratives can perhaps best be understood in terms of Kristeva's notion of *intertextuality*: the idea that every text functions in terms of another. Biblical narratives operate in terms of other prescriptive texts. The kernel of biblical hermeneutics is this conjunction of narrativity and prescription.

RK *What is the rapport between your earlier analysis of the 'creative imagination' as an 'eschatological hope' for the 'not yet' of history, and your more recent analysis of narrativity as the production of human time and history?*

PR Whereas the analysis of creative imagination dealt with creativity in its prospective or futural aspect, the analysis of narrativity deals with it in a retrospective fashion. Fiction has a strong relation to the past. Camus' *L'Etranger*, like most other novels, is written in the past tense. The narrative voice of a novel generally retells something that has taken place in a fictional past. One could almost say that fictional narration tends to suspend the eschatological in order to inscribe us in a meaningful past. And I believe that we must have a sense of the meaningfulness of the past if our projections into the future are to be more than empty utopias. Heidegger argues in *Being and Time* that it is because we are turned towards the future that we can possess and repossess a past, both our personal past and our cultural heritage. The structure of narrativity demonstrates that it is by trying to put order on our past, by retelling and recounting what has been, that we acquire an identity. These two orientations – towards the future and towards the past – are not, however, incompatible. As Heidegger himself points out, the notion of 'repeating' (*Wiederholung*) the past is inseparable from the existential projection of ourselves towards our possibilities. To 'repeat' our story, to retell our history, is to re-collect our horizon of possibilities in a resolute and responsible manner. In this respect, one can see how the retrospective character of narration is closely linked to the prospective horizon of the future. To say that narration is a recital which orders the past is not to imply that it is a conservative closure to what is new. On the contrary, narration preserves the meaning that is behind us so that we can have meaning before us. There is always *more* order in what we narrate than in what we have actually already lived; and this narrative excess (*surcroît*) of order, coherence and unity, is a prime example of the creative power of narration.

RK *What about the modernist texts of Joyce and Beckett, etc., where the narrative seems to disperse and dislocate meaning?*

PR These texts break up the habitual paradigms of narrative in order to leave the ordering task of creation to the reader himself. And ultimately it is true that the reader composes the text. All narrative, however, even Joyce's, is a certain call to order. Joyce does not invite us to embrace chaos but an infinitely more complex order. Narrative carries us beyond the oppressive order of our existence to a more liberating and refined order. The question of narrativity, no matter how modernist or avant-garde, cannot be separated from the problem of order.

RK *What compelled you to abandon the Husserlian phenomenology of consciousness, with its claim to a direct and immediate apprehension of meaning, and to adopt a hermeneutic phenomenology where the meaning of existence is approached indirectly through myth, metaphor or narrativity, that is, through the detour of mediation?*

PR I think that it is always through the mediation of structuring operations that one apprehends the fundamental meaning of existence, what Merleau-Ponty called *l'être sauvage*. Merleau-Ponty sought this *être sauvage* throughout his philosophical career and consistently criticised its deformation and obfuscation in science. I for my part have always attempted to identify those mediations of language which are not reducible to the dissimulations of scientific objectivity, but which continue to bear witness to creative linguistic potentialities. Language possesses deep resources which are not immediately reducible to knowledge (particularly the intellectualist and behaviourist forms of knowledge which Merleau-Ponty rejected). And my interest in hermeneutics, and its interpretation of language which extends to the limits of logic and the mathematical sciences, has always been an attempt to detect and describe these resources. I am convinced that all figurative language is potentially conceptualisable and that the conceptual order can possess a form of creativity. This is why I insisted, at the end of *La Métaphore vive*, upon the essential connection or intersection between speculative and poetic discourse – evidenced, for example, in the whole question of analogy. It is simplistic to suggest that conceptualisation is *per se* antagonistic to the meaning of life and experience; concepts can also be open, creative and living, though they can never constitute a knowledge which would be immediately accessible to some self-transparent *cogito*. Conceptualisation cannot reach meaning directly or create meaning out of itself *ex nihilo*; it cannot dispense with the detour of mediation through figurative structures. This detour is intrinsic to the very working of concepts.

RK *In study 8 of* La Métaphore vive *you raised the complex philosophical problem of 'reference' in language. How does narrativity relate to this problem of reference?*

PR This question brings us to the intersection between history, which claims to deal with what actually happens, and the novel, which is of the order of fiction. Reference entails a conjunction of history and fiction. And I reckon that my chances of demonstrating the validity of reference are better in an analysis of narrativity than in one of metaphoricity. Whereas it is always difficult to identify the referent of poetic or metaphorical discourse, the referent of narrative discourse is obvious – the order of human action. Now of course human action itself is charged with fictional entities such as stories, symbols, rites, etc. As Marx pointed out in *The German Ideology*, when men produce their existence in the form of *praxis* they represent it to themselves in terms of fiction, even at the limit in terms of religion (which for Marx is the model of ideology). There can be no praxis which is not already symbolically structured in some way. Human action is always figured in signs, interpreted in terms of cultural traditions and norms. Our narrative fictions are then added to this primary interpretation or figuration of human action; so that narrative is a redefining of what is already defined, a reinterpretation of what is already interpreted. The referent of narration, namely human action, is never raw or immediate reality but an action which has been symbolised and re-symbolised over and over again. Thus narration serves to displace anterior symbolisations on to a new plane, integrating or exploding them as the case may be. If this were not so, if literary narrative, for example, were closed off from the world of human action, it would be entirely harmless and inoffensive. But literature never ceases to challenge our way of reading human history and praxis. In this respect, literary narrative involves a creative use of language often ignored by science or by our everyday existence. Literary language has the capacity to put our quotidian existence into question; it is *dangerous* in the best sense of the word.

RK *But is not the hermeneutic search for mediated and symbolised meaning a way of escaping from the harsh, empirical reality of things? Is it not always working at one remove from life?*

PR Proust said that if play was cloistered off in books, it would cease to be formidable. Play is formidable precisely because it is loose in the world, planting its mediations everywhere, shattering the illusion of the immediacy of the real. The problem for a hermeneutics of language is not to rediscover some pristine immediacy but to mediate again and again in a new and more creative fashion. The mediating role of imagination is forever at work in lived reality (*le vécu*). There is no lived reality, no human or social reality, which is not already *represented* in some sense. This imaginative and creative dimension of the social, this *imaginaire social*, has been brilliantly analysed by Castoriadis in his book, *L'Institution imaginaire de la société*. Literature supplements this primary representation of the social with its own narrative representation, a process which Dagonier calls 'iconographic augmentation'. But literature is not the only way in which fiction can iconographically mediate human reality. There is also the mediating role of models in science or of utopias in political ideologies. These three modes of fictional mediation – literary, scientific and political – effectuate a metaphorisation of the real, a creation of new meaning.

RK *Which returns us to your original question: what is the meaning of creativity in language and how does it relate to the codes, structures or laws imposed by language?*

PR Linguistic creativity constantly strains and stretches the laws and codes of language that regulate it. Roland Barthes described these regulating laws as 'fascist' and urged the writer and critic to work at the limits of language, subverting its constraining laws, in order to make way for the free movement of *desire*, to make language festive. But if the narrative order of language is replete with codes, it is also capable of creatively violating them. Human creativity is always in some sense a response to a regulating order. The imagination is always working on the basis of already established laws and it is its task to make them function creatively, either by applying them in an original way or by subverting them; or indeed both – what Malraux calls 'regulated deformation'. There is no function of imagination, no *imaginaire*, that is not structuring or structured, that is not said or about-to-be-said in language. The task of hermeneutics is to charter the unexplored resources of the to-be-said on the basis of the already-said. Imagination never resides in the unsaid.

RK *How would you respond to Lévi-Strauss's conclusion, in* L'Homme nu, *that the structures and symbols of society originate in 'nothing'* (rien)*?*

PR I am not very interested in Lévi-Strauss's metaphysics of nothingness. The great contribution made by Lévi-Strauss was to identify the existence of enduring symbolic structures in what he called 'cold societies', that is, societies (mainly South American Indian) resistant to historical change. The Greek and Hebraic societies which combined to make up our Western culture are, by contrast, 'hot societies'; they are societies whose symbolic systems change and evolve over time, carrying within themselves different layers of interpretation and reinterpretation. In other words, in 'hot' societies the work of interpretation is not – as in 'cold' societies – something which is introduced from without, but an internal component of the symbolic system itself. It is precisely this diachronic process of reinterpretation that we call 'tradition'. In the Greek *Iliad*, for example, we discover a myth that is already reinterpreted, a piece of history that is already reworked into a narrative order. Neither Homer nor Aeschylus invented their stories; what they did invent were new narrative meanings, new forms of retelling the same story. The author of the *Iliad* has the entire story of the Trojan War at his disposal, but chooses to isolate the exemplary story of Achilles' wrath. He develops this exemplary narrative to the point where the wrath expires in the cathartic reconciliation – occasioned by Hector's death – with King Priam. The story produces and exemplifies a particular meaning: how the vain and meaningless wrath of one hero (Achilles) can be overcome when this hero becomes reconciled with his victim's father (Priam) at the funeral banquet. Here we have a powerful example of what it means to create meaning from a common mythic heritage, to receive a tradition and re-create it poetically to signify something new.

RK *And of course Chaucer and Shakespeare produced different 'exemplary' reinterpretations of the* Iliad *myth in their respective versions of Troilus and Cressida; as did Joyce once again in* Ulysses. *Such reinterpretation would seem to typify the cultural history of our Hellenic heritage. Is this kind of historical reinterpretation also to be found in the biblical or Hebraic tradition?*

PR Yes, the biblical narratives of the Hebraic tradition also operate in this *exemplary* or exemplifying fashion. This is evident in the fact that the biblical stories or episodes are not simply added to each other, or juxtaposed with each other, but constitute a cumulative and organic development. For example, the promise made to Abraham that his people would have a salvific relation with God is an inexhaustible promise (unlike certain legal promises which can be immediately realised); as such it opens up a history in which this promise can be repeated and reinterpreted over and over again – with Moses, then with David, and so on. So that the biblical narrative of this 'not yet realised' promise creates a cumulative history of repetition. The Christian message of crucifixion and resurrection then inserts itself into this biblical history, as a double rapport of reinterpretation and rupture. Christianity plays both a subversive and preservative role *vis-à-vis* the Judaic tradition. Saint Paul talks about the overcoming of the Law; and yet we find the synoptic authors continually affirming that the Christian event is a response to the prophetic promise, 'according to the Scriptures'. The Judaic and Christian reinterpretations of biblical history are in 'loving combat', to borrow Jaspers' phrase. The important point is that the biblical experience of faith is founded on stories and narratives – the story of the exodus, the crucifixion and resurrection, etc. – *before* it expresses itself in abstract theologies which interpret these foundational narratives and provide religious tradition with its sense of enduring identity. The *future* projects of every religion are intimately related to the ways in which it remembers itself.

RK *Your work in hermeneutics always displays a particular sensitivity to this 'conflict of interpretations' – even to the point of providing one of the titles of your books. Your hermeneutics has consistently refused the idea of an 'absolute knowledge' which might reductively* totalise *the multiplicity of interpretations – phenomenological, theological, psychoanalytic, structuralist, scientific, literary, etc. Is there any sense in which this open-ended intellectual itinerary can be construed as a sort of odyssey which might ultimately return to a unifying centre where the conflicting interpretations of human discourse could be gathered together and reconciled?*

PR When Odysseus completes the circle and returns to his island of Ithaca there is slaughter and destruction. For me the philosophical task is not to close the circle, to centralise or totalise knowledge, but to keep open the irreducible plurality of discourse. It is essential to show how the different discourses may interrelate or intersect but one must resist the temptation to make them identical, the same. My departure from Husserlian phenomenology was largely due to my disagreement with its theory of a controlling transcendental *cogito*. I advanced the notion of a wounded or split *cogito*, in opposition to the idealist claims for an inviolate absolute subjectivity. It was in fact Karl Barth who first taught me that the subject is not a centralising master but rather a disciple or auditor of a language larger than itself. At a broader cultural level, we must also be wary of attending exclusively to *Western* traditions of thought, of becoming *Europocentric*. In emphasising the importance of the Greek or Judaeo-Christian traditions, we often overlook the radically heterogeneous discourses of the Far East for example. One of my American colleagues recently suggested to me that Derrida's deconstruction of logocentrism bears striking resemblances to the Buddhist notion of nothingness. I think that there is a certain 'degree zero' or emptiness which we may have to traverse in order to abandon our pretension to be the centre, our tendency to reduce all other discourses to our own totalising schemas of thought. If there is an ultimate unity, it resides elsewhere, in a sort of eschatological hope. But this is my 'secret', if you wish, my personal wager, and not something that can be translated into a centralising philosophical discourse.

RK *It appears that our modern secularised society has abandoned the symbolic representations or* imaginaire *of tradition. Can the creative process of reinterpretation operate if the narrative continuity with the past is broken?*

PR A society where narrative is dead is one where men are no longer capable of exchanging their experiences, of sharing a common experience. The contemporary search for some narrative continuity with the past is not just nostalgic escapism but a contestation of the legislative and planificatory discourse which tends to predominate in bureaucratic societies. To give people back a *memory* is also to give them back a *future*, to put them back in time and thus release them from the 'instantaneous mind' (*mens instans*), to borrow a term from Leibniz. The past is not *passé*, for our future is guaranteed precisely by our ability to possess a narrative identity, to recollect the past in historical or fictive form. This problem of narrative identity is particularly acute, for instance, in a country like France, where the Revolution represented a rupture with the patrimony of legend and folklore, etc. (I have always been struck, for example, by the fact that most of the so-called 'traditional' songs the French still possess are drinking songs.) Today the French are largely bereft of a shared *imaginaire*, a common symbolic heritage. Our task then is to reappropriate those resources of language which have resisted contamination and destruction. To rework language is to rediscover what we are. What is lost in experience is often salvaged in language, sedimented as a deposit of traces, as a thesaurus. There can be no pure or perfectly transparent model of language, as Wittgenstein reminds us in his *Philosophical Investigations*; and if there were it would be no more than a universalised *vide*. To rediscover meaning we must return to the multilayered sedimentations of language, to the complex plurality of its instances, which can preserve what is said from the destruction of oblivion.

RK *In* History and Truth *you praise Emmanuel Mounier as someone who refused to separate the search for philosophical truth from a political pedagogy. What are the political implications, if any, of your own philosophical thinking?*

PR My work to date has been a hermeneutic reflection upon the mediation of meaning in language, and particularly in poetic or narrative language. What, you ask, can such hermeneutics contribute to our understanding of the rapport between the mediations of such symbolic discourses and the immediacy of political praxis? The fact that language is disclosed by hermeneutics (and also by the analytic philosophy of Wittgenstein) as a non-totalisable plurality of interpretations or 'language-games' means that the rhetorical discourse of politics, which serves as a justification or critique of power, is but one among many other 'language-games' and so cannot pretend to the status of a universal science. Some recent exchanges I had with Czech philosophers and students in the Tomin seminar in Prague taught me that the problem of totalitarianism resides in the lie that there can be a universally true and scientific discourse of politics (in this instance, the Communist discourse). Once one recognises that political language is basically a rhetoric of persuasion and opinion, one can tolerate free discussion. An 'open society', to use Popper's term, is one which acknowledges that political debate is infinitely open and is thus prepared to take the critical step back in order to continually interrogate and reconstitute the conditions of an authentic language.

RK *Can there be a positive rapport between language, as political ideology, and utopia?*

PR Every society, as I mentioned earlier, possesses, or is part of, a socio-political *imaginaire*, that is, an ensemble of symbolic discourses. This *imaginaire* can function as a rupture or a reaffirmation. As reaffirmation, the *imaginaire* operates as an '*ideology*' which can positively repeat and represent the founding discourse of a society, what I call its 'foundational symbols', thus preserving its sense of identity. After all, cultures create themselves by telling stories of their own past. The danger is of course that this reaffirmation can be perverted, usually by monopolistic elites, into a mystificatory discourse which serves to uncritically vindicate or glorify the established political powers. In such instances, the symbols of a community become fixed and fetishised; they serve as lies. Over against this, there exists the *imaginaire* of rupture, a discourse of *utopia* which remains critical of the powers that be out of fidelity to an 'elsewhere', to a society that is 'not yet'. But this utopian discourse is not always positive either. For besides the authentic utopia of critical rupture there can also exist a dangerously schizophrenic utopian discourse which projects a static future without ever producing the conditions of its realisation. This can happen with the Marxist–Leninist notion of utopia if one projects the final 'withering away of the State' without undertaking genuine measures to ever achieve such a goal. Here utopia becomes a future cut off from the present and the past, a mere alibi for the consolidation of the repressive powers that be. The utopian discourse functions as a mystificatory ideology as soon as it justifies the oppression of today in the name of the liberation of tomorrow. In short, *ideology* as a symbolic confirmation of the past and *utopia* as a symbolic opening towards the future are complementary; if cut off from each other they can lead to a form of political pathology.

RK *Would you consider the Liberation Theology of Latin America to be an example of a positive utopian discourse in so far as it combines a Marxist utopianism with the political transformation of* present *reality?*

PR It also combines it with the *past*, with the memory of the archetypes of exodus and resurrection. This memorial dimension of Liberation Theology is essential, for it gives direction and continuity to the utopian projection of the future, thus functioning as a *garde-fou* against irresponsible or uncritical Futurism. Here the political project of the future is inseparable from a continuous horizon of liberation, reaching back to the biblical notions of exile and promise. The promise remains unfulfilled until the utopia is historically realised; and it is precisely the not-yet-realised horizon of this promise which binds men together as a community, which prevents utopia detaching itself as an empty dream.

RK *How exactly does utopia relate to history?*

PR In his *History of the Concept of History*, Reinhart Kosselek argues that until the eighteenth century, the concept of history, in the West at any rate, was a plural one; one referred to 'histories' not History with a capital H. Our current notion of a single or unique history only emerged with the modern idea of progress. As soon as history is thus constituted as a single concept, the gap between our 'horizon of expectancy' and our 'field of experience' never ceases to widen. The unity of history is founded on the constitution of a common horizon of expectancy; but the projection of such a horizon into a distantly abstract future means that our present 'field of experience' can become pathologically deprived of meaning and articulation. The universal ceases to be concrete. This dissociation of *expectancy* from *experience* enters a crisis as soon as we lack the intermediaries to pass from the one to the other. Up to the sixteenth century, the utopian horizon of expectancy was the eschatological notion of the Last Judgment, which had as mediating or intermediating factors the whole experience of the millennium of the Holy Roman and Germanic Empires. There was always some sort of articulated path leading from what one had to what one expected to have. The liberal ideology of Kant and Locke produced a certain discourse of democracy which served as a path for the citizen towards a better humanity; and Marxism also promoted mediating stages leading from capitalism through socialism to Communism. But we don't seem to believe in these intermediaries any more. The problem today is the apparent impossibility of unifying world politics, of mediating between the polycentricity of our everyday political practice and the utopian horizon of a universally liberated humanity. It is not that we are without utopia, but that we are without *paths* to utopia. And without a path towards it, without concrete and practical mediation in our field of experience, utopia becomes a sickness. Perhaps the deflation of utopian expectancies is not entirely a bad thing. Politics can so easily be injected with too much utopia; perhaps it should become more modest and realistic in its claims, more committed to our practical and immediate needs.

RK *Is there any place in contemporary politics for a genuine utopian discourse?*

PR Maybe not in politics itself but rather at the junction between politics and other cultural discourses. Our present disillusionment with the political stems from the fact that we invested it with the totality of our expectancies – until it became a bloated imposture of utopia. We have tended to forget that beside the public realm of politics, there also exists a more private cultural realm (which includes literature, philosophy and religion, etc.) where the utopian horizon can express itself. Modern society seems hostile to this domain of private experience, but the suppression of the private entails the destruction of the public. The vanquishing of the private by the public is a pyrrhic victory.

RK *Are you advocating a return to the bourgeois romantic notion of private subjectivity removed from all political responsibility?*

PR Not at all. In my recent discussions with the Prague philosophers I spoke about the crisis of the subject in contemporary Continental philosophy, particularly structuralism. I pointed out that if one does away with the idea of a subject who is responsible for his or her words, we are no longer in a position to talk of the freedom or the rights of man. To dispense with the classical notion of the subject as a transparent *cogito* does not mean that we have to dispense with all forms of subjectivity. My hermeneutical philosophy has attempted to demonstrate the existence of an opaque subjectivity which expresses itself through the detour of countless mediations – signs, symbols, texts and human praxis itself. This hermeneutical idea of subjectivity as a dialectic between the self and mediated social meanings has deep moral and political implications. It shows that there is an *ethic of the word*, that language is not just the abstract concern of logic or semiotics, but entails the fundamental moral duty that people be responsible for what they say. A society which no longer possesses subjects ethically responsible for their words is a society which no longer possesses citizens. For the dissident philosophers in Prague the primary philosophical question is the integrity and truthfulness of language. And this question becomes a moral and political act of resistance in a system based on lies and perversion. The Marxism of Eastern Europe has degenerated from dialectics to positivism. It has abandoned the Hegelian inspiration which preserved Marxism as a realisation of the universal subject in history, and has become instead a positivistic technology of mass manipulation.

RK *So the hermeneutical interrogation of the creation of meaning in language can have a political content?*

PR Perhaps the most promising example of a political hermeneutics is to be found in the Frankfurt School synthesis between Marxist dialectics and Heideggerean hermeneutics – best expressed in Habermas's critique of ideologies. But here again one must be careful to resist the temptation to engage in an unmediated politics. It is necessary for hermeneutics to keep a certain distance so as to critically disclose the underlying mediating structures at work in political discourse. This hermeneutic distance is particularly important today with the post-1968 disillusionment, the demise of the Maoist ideology and the exposure of Soviet totalitarianism by Solzhenitsyn and others.

RK *Is this disillusionment a world-wide phenomenon?*

PR It exists in varying degrees, but is most conspicuous in countries like France where the essential distinction between state and society has been largely occluded. The French Revolution apportioned political sovereignty to all levels of the community, from the government at the top to the individuals at the bottom. But in this process, the state became omnipresent, the citizen being reduced to a mere fragment of the state. What was so striking in the Solidarity movement in Poland was their use of the term 'society' in opposition to the term 'state'. Even in the Anglo-Saxon countries one finds certain national institutions – such as the media or universities – which are relatively independent of state politics. (It is difficult to find examples of this in France.) The weak ideologisation of politics in America, for instance, means that it can at least serve as a sprawling laboratory where a multiplicity of discourses can be tried and tested. This phenomenon of the 'melting-pot' is an example of what Montesquieu called the 'separation of powers'. It is interesting to remember that the state was originally conceived by the liberal thinkers as an agency of toleration, a way of protecting the plurality of beliefs and practices. The liberal state was to be a safeguard against religious and other forms of fanaticism. The fundamental perversion of the liberal state is that it came to function as a totalising rather than a de-totalising agency. That is why it is urgent for us today to discover a political discourse which would not be governed by states, a new form of society guaranteeing universal rights yet dispensing with totalising constraints. This is the enormous task of reconstituting a form of sociality not determined by the state.

RK *How does one go about discovering this new discourse of society?*

PR One of the first steps would be to analyse what exactly happened in the eighteenth century when the Judaeo-Christian horizon of eschatology was replaced by the Enlightenment horizon of humanism with its liberal notions of autonomy, freedom and human rights. We must see how this Enlightenment humanism developed through the Kantian notion of the autonomous will, the Hegelian notion of the universal class (of civil servants) to the Marxist universal class of workers, etc., until we reached a secularised version of utopia which frequently degenerated into scientific positivism. We must ask: can there be any sort of continuity between the religious-eschatological projection of utopia and the modern humanist projection of a secularised utopia? The challenge today is to find alternative forms of social rationality beyond the positivistic extremes of both state socialism and utilitarian–liberal capitalism. Habermas's distinction between three forms of rationality is essential here: (i) *calculative rationality*, which operates as positivistic control and manipulation; (ii) *interpretative rationality*, which tries to represent the cultural codes and norms in a creative way; (iii) *critical rationality*, which opens up the utopian horizon of liberation. For a genuine social rationality to exist we must refuse to allow the critical and interpretative functions to be reduced to the calculative. Habermas is here developing Adorno's and Horkheimer's critique of *positivist rationality*, which exists in both state Communism and in the argument of liberal capitalism that once the society of abundance has been achieved all can be distributed equally (the problem being, of course, that liberalism employs the means of an hierarchical and unequal society to achieve such an end of abundance – an end which never seems to be realised). So our task remains that of preserving a utopian horizon of liberty and equality – by means of interpretative and critical rationality – without resorting to a positivistic ideology of bad faith. I agree here with Raymond Aron's contention that we have not yet succeeded in developing a political model which could accommodate the simultaneous advancement of liberty and equality. Societies which have advocated liberty have generally suppressed equality and vice versa.

RK *Do you think that the critique of political power carried out by left-wing political philosophers in France, such as Castoriadis and Lefort, contributes to the hermeneutic search for a new discourse of sociality?*

PR Their contribution has been absolutely decisive. This critique has attempted to show that the error of Marxism resides not so much in its lack of a political horizon as in its reduction of the critique of power to the economic transfer of work to capital (that is, the critique of surplus value). Thus the Marxist critique tends to ignore that there can be more pernicious forms of power than capital – for example, the totalisation of all the resources of a society (the resources of the work-force, of the means of discussion and information, education, research, etc.) by the central committee of the party or state. In this manner the handing over of the private ownership of the means of production to the state can often mean a replacement of the alienation of society by the alienation of the state. The power of the totalitarian party is perhaps more nefarious than the dehumanising power of capital in so far as it controls not only the economic means of production but also the political means of communications. Maybe the economic analysis of class struggle is but one of the many plots that make up the complex of history. Hence the need for a hermeneutics of sociality that could unravel the plurality of power plots which enmesh to form our history.

RK *In 'Non-violent Man and his Presence in History' (*History and Truth*) you asked: 'Can the prophet or non-violent man have an historical task which would obviate both the extreme inefficacity of the Yogi and the extreme efficacity of the Commissar?' In other words, can one commit oneself to the efficacious transformation of political reality and still preserve the critical distance of transcendence?*

PR This idea of transcendence is essential for any sort of non-violent discourse. The pacifist ideal resists violence by attesting to values which transcend the arena of political efficacity, without becoming irrelevant dreams. Non-violence is a form of genuine utopian vigil or hope, a way of refuting the system of violence and oppression in which we live.

RK *Is it possible to reconcile the exigency of an authentic social rationality with the eschatological hope of religion?*

PR This has never struck me as an insoluble problem for the basic cultural reason that our Western religiosity of Judaeo-Christianity has always functioned in the philosophical climate of Greek and Latin rationality. I have always objected to the simplistic opposition of Jerusalem and Athens, to those thinkers who declare that true spirituality can only be found in monotheism; or try to drive a wedge between Greek and Hebraic culture, defining the former as a thought of the cosmos and the latter as a thought of transcendence, etc. From the eleventh century onwards we find models for reconciling reason and religion – in Anselm, for example – and the Renaissance confirms this primary synthesis of rationality and spirituality. If it is true that the rationality of scientific positivism has divorced itself from spirituality, there are many signs today that we are searching for new forms of connection.

(Paris, 1981)

Myth as the bearer of possible worlds

RK *One of your first attempts at hermeneutic analysis concentrated on the way in which human consciousness was mediated by mythic and symbolic expressions from the earliest times. In* The Symbolism of Evil *(1960) you demonstrated how mythic symbols played an important ideological and political role in the ancient cultures of the Babylonians, Hebrews and Greeks. And in this same work you declared that 'myth relates to events that happened at the beginning of time which have the purpose of providing grounds for the ritual actions of men of today'. Are you suggesting that mythic symbols can play a relevant role in contemporary culture? And if so, could you elaborate on how it might do so?*

PR I don't think that we can approach this question directly, that is, in terms of a direct relationship between myth and action. We must first return to an analysis of what constitutes the *imaginary nucleus* of any culture. It is my conviction that one cannot reduce any culture to its explicit functions – political, economic and legal, etc. No culture is wholly transparent in this way. There is invariably a hidden nucleus which determines and rules the *distribution* of these transparent functions and institutions. It is this matrix of distribution which assigns them different roles in relation to (1) each other, (2) other societies, (3) the individuals who participate in them, and (4) nature, which stands over against them.

RK *Does this ratio of distribution differ from one society to another?*

PR It certainly does. The particular relationship between political institutions, nature and the individual is rarely if ever the same in any two cultures. The ratio of distribution between these different functions of a given society is determined by some *hidden* nucleus, and it is here that we must situate the specific identity of culture. Beyond or beneath the self-understanding of a society there is an opaque kernel which cannot be reduced to empirical norms or laws. This kernel cannot be explained in terms of some transparent model because it is constitutive of a culture *before* it can be expressed and reflected in specific representations or ideas. It is only if we try to grasp this kernel that we may discover the *foundational mytho-poetic* nucleus of a society. By analysing itself in terms of such a foundational nucleus, a society comes to a truer understanding of itself; it begins to critically acknowledge its own symbolising identity.

RK *How are we to recognise this mythical nucleus?*

PR The mythical nucleus of a society is only *indirectly* recognisable. But it is indirectly recognisable not only by what is said (discourse), but also by what and how one lives (praxis), and thirdly, as I suggested, by the distribution between different functional levels of a society. We cannot, for example, say that in all countries the economic layer is determining. This is true for our Western society. But as Lévi-Strauss has shown in his analysis of many primitive societies, this is not universally true. In several cultures the significance of economic and historical considerations would seem to be minor. In our culture the economic factor is indeed determining; but that does not mean that the predominance of economics is itself explicable purely in terms of economic science. This predominance is perhaps more correctly understood as but one constituent of the overall evaluation of what is primary and what is secondary. And it is only by the analysis of the hierarchical structuring and evaluation of the different constituents of a society (i.e. the role of politics, nature, art, religion, etc.) that we may penetrate to its hidden *mytho-poetic nucleus*.

RK *You mentioned Lévi-Strauss. How would you situate your own hermeneutical analyses of symbol and myth in relation to his work in this area?*

PR I don't think that Lévi-Strauss makes any claim to speak of societies in general. He has focused on certain primitive and stable societies, leaving aside considerations of history. This is important to realise so as not to draw hasty conclusions from his analyses. Lévi-Strauss has deliberately chosen to speak of societies *without history*, whereas I think that there is something specifically historical about the societies to which we in the West belong, depending on the extent to which they are affected by Hebraic, Hellenic, Germanic or Celtic cultures. The development of a society is both synchronic and diachronic. This means that the distribution of power-functions in any given society contains a definite *historical* dimension. We have to think of societies in terms of both a set of simultaneous institutions (synchronism) and a process of historical transformation (diachronism). Thus we arrive at the panchronic approach to societies, i.e. both synchronic and diachronic, which characterises the hermeneutical method. And we must also realise that the kinds of myth on which our societies are founded have themselves this twofold characteristic: on the one hand, they constitute a certain system of simultaneous symbols which can be approached through structuralist analysis; but, on the other hand, they have a history, because it is always through a process of interpretation and reinterpretation that they are kept alive. Myths have a historicity of their own. This difference of history typifies, for example, the development of the Semitic, pre-Hellenistic and Celtic mythical nuclei. Therefore, just as societies are both structural and historical, so also are the mythical nuclei which ground them.

RK *In the conclusion to* The Symbolism of Evil *you state that 'a philosophy instructed by myths arises at a certain moment in reflection and wishes to answer to a certain situation in modern culture'. What precisely do you mean by this 'certain situation'? And how does myth answer to this problematic?*

PR I was thinking there of Jaspers' philosophy of 'boundary situations', which influenced me so strongly just after the Second World War. There are certain boundary situations such as war, suffering, guilt, death, etc., in which the individual or community experiences a fundamental existential crisis. At such moments the whole community is put into question. For it is only when it is threatened with destruction from without or from within that a society is compelled to return to the very roots of its identity; to that mythical nucleus which ultimately grounds and determines it. The solution to the immediate crisis is no longer a purely political or technical matter but demands that we ask ourselves the ultimate questions concerning our origins and ends: Where do we come from? Where do we go? In this way, we become aware of our basic capacities and reasons for surviving, for being and continuing to be what we are.

RK *I am reminded here of Mircea Eliade's statement in* Myths, Dreams, Mysteries *that myth is something which always operates in a society regardless of whether this society reflectively acknowledges its existence. Eliade maintains that because modern man has lost his awareness of the important role that myth plays in his life, it often manifests itself in* deviant *ways. He gives as an example the emergence of fascist movements in Europe characterised by a mythic glorification of blood sacrifice and the hero-saviour together with the equally mythical revival of certain ancient rituals, symbols and insignia. The suggestion is that if we do not explicitly recognise and reappropriate the mythic import of our existence it will emerge in distorted and pernicious ways. Do you think this is a valid point?*

PR You have hit here on a very important and difficult problem: the possibilities of a perversion of myth. This means that we can no longer approach myth *at the level of naiveté*. We must rather always view it from a critical perspective. It is only by means of a selective reappropriation that we can become aware of myth. We are no longer primitive beings, living at the immediate level of myth. Myth for us is always mediated and opaque. This is so not only because it expresses itself primarily through a particular apportioning of power-functions, as mentioned earlier, but also because several of its recurrent forms have become deviant and dangerous, e.g. the myth of absolute power (fascism) and the myth of the sacrificial scapegoat (anti-Semitism and racism). We are no longer justified in speaking of 'myth in general'. We must critically assess the content of each myth and the basic intentions which animate it. Modern man can neither get rid of myth nor take it at its face value. Myth will always be with us, but we must always approach it *critically*.

RK *It was with a similar scruple in mind that I tried to show in* Myth and Terror *(1978) that there are certain mythic structures operative in extreme Irish Republicanism – recurrence of blood sacrifice, apocalypse/renewal, etc. – which can become deviant manifestations of an original mythical nucleus. And I feel accordingly that any approach to myth should be as much a demythologisation of deviant expressions as a resuscitation of genuine ones.*

PR Yes. And I think it is here that we could speak of the essential connection between the 'critical instance' and the 'mythical foundation'. Only those myths are genuine which can be reinterpreted in terms of *liberation*. And I mean liberation as both a personal and collective phenomenon. We should perhaps sharpen this critical criterion to include only those myths which have as their horizon the liberation of humanity *as a whole*. Liberation cannot be exclusive. Here I think we come to recognise a fundamental convergence between the claims of myth and reason. In genuine reason as in genuine myth we find a concern for the *universal* liberation of all. To the extent that myth is seen as the foundation of a particular community to the absolute exclusion of all others, the possibilities of perversion – chauvinistic nationalism, racism, etc. – are already present.

RK *So in fact you suggest that the foundational power of myth should always be in some sense chaperoned by critical reason?*

PR In our Western culture the myth-making of man has often been linked with the critical instance of reason. And this is because it has had to be constantly interpreted and reinterpreted in different historical epochs. In other words, it is because the survival of myth calls for perpetual historical interpretation that it involves a critical component. Myths are not unchanging and unchanged antiques which are simply delivered out of the past in some naked, original state. Their specific identity depends on the way in which each generation receives or interprets them according to their needs, conventions and ideological motivations. Hence the necessity of critical discrimination between liberating and destructive modes of reinterpretation.

RK *Could you give an example of such reinterpretation?*

PR Well, if we take the relation of *mythos* and *logos* in the Greek experience, we could say that myth had been absorbed by the *logos*, but never completely so; for the claim of the *logos* to rule over *mythos* is itself a mythical claim. Myth is thereby reinjected into the *logos* and gives a mythical dimension to reason itself. Thus the rational appropriation of myth becomes also a revival of myth. Another example would be the reinterpretative overlap between the mythical paradigms of the Hebraic exodus and the prophetic dimension in Hebrew literature. And then at a second level, this Hebraic *mythos* came down to us through a Hellenisation of its whole history. Even for us today, this Hellenisation is an important mediation because it was through the conjunction of the Jewish *Torah* and Greek *logos* that the notion of law could be incorporated into our culture.

RK *You would not agree then with those modern theologians, such as Moltmann and Bultmann, who suggest that the Hellenisation of the Judaeo-Christian culture is a perversion of its original richness?*

PR No. The tension between the Greek *logos* and the Semitic nucleus of exodus and revelation is fundamentally and positively constitutive of our culture.

RK *Several critics have described your hermeneutical approach to myth and symbol as an attempt, almost in the manner of psychoanalysis, to reduce myth to some hidden rational message. In* The Symbolism of Evil *you say that the aim of your philosophy is to disclose through reflection and speculation the* rationality *of symbols. And again in* On Interpretation *you state that 'every* mythos *harbours a* logos *which requires to be exhibited'. But is it possible to extract the* logos *and yet leave the* mythos *intact? Or is myth something essentially enigmatic and therefore irreducible to rational content?*

PR This criticism must be understood in the following way. There are two uses of the concept of myth. One is myth as the *extension* of a symbolic structure. In this sense it is pointless to speak of a demythologisation for that would be tantamount to desymbolisation – and this I deny completely. But there is a second sense in which myth serves as an *alienation* of this symbolic structure; here it becomes reified and is misconstrued as an actual materialistic explanation of the world. If we interpret myth *literally*, we misinterpret it. For myth is essentially *symbolic*. It is only in instances of such misinterpretation that we may legitimately speak of demythologisation; not concerning its symbolic content but concerning the hardening of its symbolic structures into dogmatic or reified ideologies.

RK *Do you think that Bultmann's use of the term demythologisation had something to do with this confusion between two different types of myth (as creative symbol or reductive ideology)?*

PR Yes I do. Bultmann seems to ignore the complexity of myth. And so when he speaks, for example, of the necessity to demythologise the myth of the threefold division of the cosmos into Heaven, Earth and Hell, he is treating this myth only in terms of its literal interpretation or rather misinterpretation. But Bultmann does not realise that there is a symbolic as well as a pseudosymbolic or literal dimension in myth, and that demythologisation is only valid in relation to this second dimension.

RK *Are myths* universal, *in terms of their original symbolic structures, or do they originate from* particular *national cultures?*

PR This is a very difficult problem. We are caught here between the claims of two equally valid dimensions of myth. And it is the delicate balance between them that is difficult to find. On the one hand, we must say that mythical structures are not simply universal any more than are languages. Just as man is fragmented between different languages, so also he is fragmented between mythical cycles, each of which is typical of a living culture. We must acknowledge, then, that one of the primary functions of any myth is to found the specific identity of a community. On the other hand, however, we must say that just as languages are in principle translatable one into the other, so too myths have a horizon of universality which allows them to be understood by other cultures. The history of Western culture is made up of a confluence of different myths which have been expatriated from their original community, i.e. Hebrew, Greek, Germanic, Celtic. The horizon of any genuine myth always exceeds the political and geographical boundaries of a specific national or tribal community. Even if we may say that mythical structures *founded* political institutions, they always go beyond the territorial limitations imposed by politics. Nothing travels more extensively and effectively than myth. Therefore we must conclude that while mythic symbols are rooted in a particular culture, they also have the capacity to emigrate and develop within new cultural frameworks.

RK *Is there not a sense in which perhaps the* source *and not only the historical* transmission *of symbols may be responsible for their universal dimension?*

PR It is quite possible that the supranational quality of myth or symbol may be ultimately traced back to a prehistorical layer from which all particular 'mythical nuclei' might be said to emerge. But it is difficult to determine the nature of this prehistory, for all myths as we know them come down to us through history. Each particular myth has its own history of reinterpretation and emigration. But another possible explanation of the universally common dimension of myth might be that because the myth-making powers of the human imagination are finite, they ensure the frequent recurrence of similar archetypes and motifs.

RK *Certainly the myth of the fall as you analyse it in* The Symbolism of Evil *would seem to be common to many different cultures.*

PR Yes. We could say that genuine myth goes beyond its claim to found a particular community and speaks to man as such. Several exegetes of Jewish literature, for example, have made a distinction between different layers of myth: those which are foundational for the Jewish culture – the 'chronicle dimension'; and those which make up a body of truths valid for all mankind – the 'wisdom dimension'. This seems to me an important distinction and one applicable to other cultures.

RK *In Irish literature over the last 80 years or so one finds a similar distinction between these dimensions. In the Fenian literature of the nineteenth century or the Celtic Twilight literature of Yeats, Lady Gregory and others, myth seems to have been approached as a 'chronicle' of the spiritual origins of the race. For this reason it often strikes one as suffering from a certain hazy occultism and introversion. Joyce, on the other hand, used myth, and particularly the myth of Finn, in its 'wisdom dimension'; that is, as an Irish archetype open to, and capable of assimilating, the rich resources of entirely different cultures.* Finnegans Wake *or* Ulysses *seem to represent an exemplary synthesis of the particular and universal claims of myth.*

PR The important point here is that the original potential of any genuine myth will always transcend the confines of a particular community or nation. The *mythos* of any community is the bearer of something which exceeds its own frontiers; it is the bearer of other *possible* worlds. And I think it is in this horizon of the 'possible' that we discover the *universal* dimensions of symbolic and poetic language.

RK *You have stated that what animates your philosophical research on symbolism and myth is not 'regret for some sunken Atlantis' but 'hope for a re-creation of language' (*The Symbolism of Evil*). What precisely do you mean by this?*

PR Language has lost is original unity. Today it is fragmented not only geographically into different communities but functionally into different disciplines – mathematical, historical, scientific, legal, psychoanalytic, etc. It is the function of a philosophy of language to recognise the specific nature of these disciplines and thereby assign each 'language-game' its due (as Wittgenstein would have it), limiting and correcting their mutual claims. Thus one of the main purposes of hermeneutics is to refer the different uses of language to different regions of being – natural, scientific, fictional, etc. But this is not all. Hermeneutics is also concerned with the permanent spirit of language. By the spirit of language we intend not just some decorative excess or effusion of subjectivity, but *the capacity of language to open up new worlds*. Poetry and myth are not just nostalgia for some forgotten world. They constitute a disclosure of unprecedented worlds, an opening on to other *possible* worlds which transcend the established limits of our *actual* world.

RK *How then would you situate your philosophy of language in relation to analytic philosophy?*

PR I certainly share at least one common concern of analytic philosophy: the concern with ordinary language in contradistinction to the scientific language of documentation and verification.

Scientific language has no real function of communication or interpersonal dialogue. It is important therefore that we preserve the rights of ordinary language where the communication of experience is of primary significance. But my criticism of ordinary language philosophy is that it does not take into account the fact that language itself is a place of prejudice and bias. Therefore, we need a third dimension of language, a critical and creative dimension, which is directed towards neither scientific verification nor ordinary communication but towards the disclosure of possible worlds. This third dimension of language I call the poetic. The adequate self-understanding of man is dependent on this third dimension of language as a *disclosure of possibility*.

RK *Is not this philosophy of language profoundly phenomenological in character?*

PR Yes it is. Because phenomenology as it emerged in the philosophies of Husserl and Heidegger raised the central question of 'meaning'. And it is here that we find the main dividing line between the structuralist analysis and phenomenological hermeneutics. Whereas the former is concerned with the immanent arrangement of texts and textual codes, hermeneutics looks to the 'meaning' produced by these codes. It is my conviction that the decisive feature of hermeneutics is the capacity of world-disclosure yielded by texts. Hermeneutics is not confined to the *objective* structural analysis of texts nor to the *subjective* existential analysis of the authors of texts; its primary concern is with the *worlds* which these authors and texts open up. It is by an understanding of the worlds, actual and possible, opened by language that we may arrive at a better understanding of ourselves.

(Paris, 1978)

Select bibliography in English

Fallible Man, trans. C. A. Kelbley, H. Regnery, Chicago, 1965.

History and Truth, trans. C. A. Kelbley, Northwestern University Press, Evanston, 1965.

Freedom and Nature: The Voluntary and the Involuntary, trans. E. V. Kohák, Northwestern University Press, Evanston, 1966.

Husserl: An Analysis of his Phenomenology, Northwestern University Press, Evanston, 1967.

The Symbolism of Evil, trans. E. Buchanan, Harper & Row, New York, 1967.

Freud and Philosophy: An Essay on Interpretation, trans. D. Savage, Yale University Press, New Haven, 1970.

Political and Social Essays, eds D. Stewart and J. Bien, trans. D. Siewert *et al.*, Ohio University Press, Athens, Ohio, 1974.

The Conflict of Interpretations: Essays in Hermeneutics, ed. D. Ihde, trans. W. Domingo *et al.*, Northwestern University Press, Evanston, 1974.

Interpretation Theory: Discourse and the Surplus of Meaning, Texas Christian University Press, Forth Worth, 1976.

The Philosophy of Paul Ricoeur: An Anthology of His Work, eds C. E. Regan and D. Stewart, Beacon Press, Boston, 1978.

The Rule of Metaphor: Multi-disciplinary Studies in the Creation of Meaning in Language, trans. R. Czerny, Routledge and Kegan Paul, London, 1978.

Main Trends in Philosophy, Holmes and Meier Publishers, Inc., New York, London, 1979.

Hermeneutics and the Human Sciences, ed. and trans. J. B. Thompson, Cambridge University Press and Editions de la Maisons des Sciences de l'Homme, 1981.

Time and Narrative (3 vols.), trans. K. McLaughlin and D. Pellauer, University of Chicago Press, Chicago, 1984–88.

From Text to Action: Essays in Hermeneutics II, trans. K. Blamey and J. B. Thompson, Athlone University Press, London, 1991.

Oneself as Another, trans. K. Blamey. The University of Chicago Press, Chicago and London, 1992.

STANISLAS BRETON

Being, God and the poetics of relation

Prefatory note

STANISLAS BRETON was born in Gironde, France, in 1912. While still in his teens, he joined the Passionist order of Catholic priests. Accordingly, his early philosophical schooling was deeply influenced by the Thomistic and scholastic traditions, as well, he insists, as by his childhood experiences of nature in rural France. This formative dual fidelity to the immanence of finite being and the transcendence of an infinite God expressed itself in his first published work in 1951, *L'Esse 'in' et l'esse 'ad' dans la métaphysique de la relation.* Moreover, this central relationship between the claims of immanence and transcendence, appropriation and disappropriation, habitation and exodus also profoundly determined his interpretation of phenomenology, which he discovered after the war, and particularly the key notion of 'intentionality' as a dynamic movement of consciousness beyond the self towards what is *other* (*Approches phénoménologiques de l'idée d'être*, 1959, and *Etre, monde, imaginaire*, 1976).

The main body of Breton's writings has focused on contemporary philosophy, and especially on the ways in which the contemporary theories of phenomenology, logic and mathematics help us to reinterpret the ontologies of Neoplatonism and Thomism (see *Essence et existence*, 1962; *Situation de la philosophie contemporaine*, 1959; *Saint Thomas d'Aquin*, 1965; *Philosophie et mathématiques chez Proclus*, 1969; *Du principe*, 1971). In addition to these philosophical studies, however, Breton has published a number of influential works on more specifically religious and mystical subjects, such as *La Passion du Christ et les philosophies* (1954), *Mystique de la Passion* (1962), *Foi et raison logique* (1971) and *Théorie des idéologies* (1976). A further dimension of his thought has been a pioneering attempt to build bridges not only between the rival traditions of Greek ontology and Judaeo–Christian theology, but also between the modern movement of religious philosophy and political theory – in particular that of Marxism.

Common to Breton's three major intellectual concerns – ontology, religion and politics – is his insistence on the indispensable necessity of a critical disposition, what he calls *'l'opérateur de transcendance'*. This critical operation serves to expose the limitations of every form of established power, every pretence at a fixed or absolute determination, forever redirecting us towards the possibility of an elsewhere; it consists, writes Breton in *Théorie des idéologies*, in 'imagining another space in which another indeterminate possibility freely unfolds, and which demands to be *thought* even if it is impossible to be *known*'.

Having taught at the Pontifical University in Rome during the fifties, Breton returned to France to become Professor of Philosophy, first at the University of Lyons and later at the *Institut Catholique* in Paris. In 1970, he was appointed *Maître de Conférence* at *l'Ecole Normale Supérieure*, an honour shared with Jacques Derrida and Louis Althusser, the Marxist theoretician who proposed his nomination. Breton was the first 'Catholic' philosopher to obtain this post, an indication, it would seem, of the high esteem in which he is regarded by the new generation of intellectuals on the continent. Though few of his works have as yet been translated into English, Breton remains the most eminent Catholic thinker living in France today.

This dialogue took place at Clamart, France, in 1982.

RK *Your philosophical journey has been wide ranging. You have published works on such diverse topics as Neoplatonism, Thomism, Marxism, phenomenology, logic and poetics. What would you consider to be the unifying threads in this tapestry of intellectual interests?*

SB First, I would say that my philosophical journey is related to my biographical one. My early upbringing and education in a rural community in La Vendée certainly had a significant impact on my subsequent thinking; it determined my later leanings towards a certain philosophical *realism*. This perhaps accounts somewhat for the fact that in the doctorate I presented to the Sorbonne, *Approches phénoménologiques de l'idée d'être*, I tended to see the key metaphysical concept, 'Being as Being', in terms of the four elements of the concretely experienced, real world – earth, fire, water, air. Strange as it may sound, the monastic experience of my early years in a Passionist seminary, which I entered at the age of fifteen, also corresponded in some way to my conceptualisation of *Being as Being*: this decisive concept thus emerged as both a monastic desert and an all-englobing shelter of the four elements of nature. Philosophy begins, I believe, in the lifeworld. So it is not very surprising that our understanding of Being should be coloured by our lived experience, by the formative *images* of our being in the world. This conviction predisposed me, of course, to a *phenomenological* approach to philosophy; it also confirmed my belief that a poetics of imagination is an indispensable dimension of genuine thinking.

RK *I think that your conviction would be shared by many of the phenomenologists. Sartre, Camus and Merleau-Ponty all spoke of the decisive way in which their concretely* lived experience *affected their subsequent understanding of Being, which they saw as a 'universal' reflection on their 'particular', prereflective existence. But what philosophical or intellectual influences on your thinking would you consider to be of primary importance?*

SB The earliest intellectual influence I can recall was the Latin language – the way in which it was used in the seminary with a scholastic emphasis on professorial rigour and prepositional distinctions: *ex, in, ad, de* and so on. This language of *relations*, which Lévinas calls 'transitive language', greatly influenced my doctorate in Rome entitled *L'Esse 'in' et l'esse 'ad' dans la métaphysique de la relation*. This scholastic logic of relations was the second major influence on my philosophical imagination for it raised the fundamental question of how man can be *in* being (immanence) and still be said to be moving *towards* it (transcendence). Once applied to the work of St Thomas, it opened up the whole problematic of the 'operations' of ontological immanence with its crucial theological implications for our understanding of the Trinity: How does the Son belong to the Father and the Father to the Son through the agency of the Spirit? I would almost say that my mature interest in philosophy sprang from theological questions which theology itself could not answer. For example, the *being-in* relation provided an explanation of the unity of the Three Persons of the Trinity, while the distinction and difference between the Three could be understood in terms of the intentional or transitive relation of the *being-towards*. The Spirit could thus be interpreted as a twofold relation: (i) the perpetual attraction between the Father and the Son; and (ii) the power of movement and carrying-beyond (*meta-pherein*), which refuses the finite limits of proprietal possession and makes the Trinity an *infinite relation*.

This theology of operations also has important implications for our understanding of the Incarnation. The 'substantialist' theology of the Councils, which spoke of the two natures in one, seemed to me insufficient in so far as it privileged the notion of *substance* over that of *function* or *relation*. The dynamic relation of the being-towards category struck me as being closer to the biblical language of transitivity. God as a being-in-itself, as an identical substance, cannot be thought by us; we can only know or speak about God in terms of His relation to us, or ours to Him.

My interest in the theology of operations soon led to an interest in the philosophy of mathematical relations. When I was captured by the Germans during the war, I had three books in my bag: Bochenski's *Elements of Mathematical Logic*, Brunschvicg's *Modality of Judgment* and Hamelin's *The Principal Elements of Representation*. Another work which deeply fascinated me at the time was Bertrand Russell's *Introduction à la philosophie mathématique*, where he outlined a sophisticated philosophy of descriptive relations. In short, what I appreciated most in these thinkers was their analysis of the operative terms of relation – prepositions such as *in*, *towards*, and the conjunctions *as*, *as-if*, which I called 'those little servants of the Lord'. I believe they are not only the indispensable accompaniment of all thought but also the secret messengers of the philosophical future.

RK *Could you elaborate on your philosophical transition from the initial question of* being as being *(an ontology of the four elements of nature) to the correlative question of* being-in *and* being-towards *(a metaphysics of relation)?*

SB I was drawn towards the metaphysical problematic of relations in order to try to understand not just what being is as such, but how it relates to man or accounts for the way in which the Three Divine Persons relate to each other. The relation of being-towards constitutes the element of metaphor or metamorphosis, that which assures the infinite movement of existence as a passing over from one phase to the next; it is that which compels us to continually alter our concepts, making each one of us a 'being in transit'.

The relation of being-in, by contrast, is that *élément neutre* which draws together and unifies existence; it is that which founds our notion of ontological self-identity. In the *Metaphysics*, Aristotle refers to this principle when he states that the addition of being or the One to something changes nothing. Being added to man adds nothing. For being is not a predicate but the most essential, necessary and universal function of existence: the function which allows each thing to be itself, to be one and the same. The principle of being-in is that which freely grants each thing the permission to *be*, to rest and recollect itself from the movement of becoming.

RK *Do you see this Greek metaphysics of relation as radicalising our understanding of the Judaeo-Christian tradition?*

SB I believe that both metaphysical relations – the being-towards and the being-in – are equally essential for an understanding of Judaeo-Christian theology. At this level, I see no great opposition between Greek and biblical thought. What we call the historical 'meaning' of Christianity or Judaism is the tradition of interpretations that have been historically ascribed to them; and in the history of Western thinking these interpretations are inextricably related to Hellenic concepts of ontology. Between the two traditions – the Greek and the biblical – there is a creative tension which ensures that we are never fully at our intellectual ease in either. We are inevitably committed to this philosophical exodus, this vacillation between two 'homes' of thought. We have left the home of Israel just as we have left the home of Greece. We remain homesick for both. We cannot renounce the intellectual nostalgia of this double allegiance. The Western thinker is divided from *within*.

RK *Do you see Thomism as an attempt to bridge these two traditions in your own thought?*

SB I consider Thomism to be the paleoancephalus of my philosophical formation. There were three areas in the work of St Thomas which particularly preoccupied me: (1) the attempt to think God and being together; (2) the theory of intentionality and formal objects – which I rediscovered later in Brentano and Husserl (I was especially impressed by Thomas' statement that relation consists of a certain transit or transitivity; this implies that being is transitive and that our entire existence is a series of transitions towards the other, the loving potency which forever searches for its fulfilment in act); (3) the Thomistic definition of freedom or the free being as the being that is 'cause of itself' (*causa sui*). This third concept occupied a very important place in my thought. For something to be free thus meant that, as cause of itself, it can create something new, almost from nothing. For the thinker it offers the free possibility to open up new paths of enquiry not already charted or inscribed in the map of the world.

RK *How did you find your way from Thomism to phenomenology?*

SB Like most philosophers of my generation I was deeply influenced by the phenomenological movement inaugurated by Husserl and his disciples, Ingarden, Häring, Heidegger and so on. I saw the phenomenological emphasis on intentionality – the methodological investigation of how our consciousness is always intentionally directed towards something *beyond* itself – as a means of extending three of my primary intellectual concerns: (1) the logic of relations governing the activity of the human mind; (2) the dynamic teleological aspect of Thomistic metaphysics expressed in the notion of the *esse ad*; and (3) the biblical concept of exodus. Of course, the original contribution of Husserlian phenomenology was to delineate and describe the relation of intentionality in terms of concrete experience – our everyday being-in-the-world, to ground our logical and metaphysical concepts in the lived experience of consciousness. Later, particularly in a work like *Etre, monde, imaginaire*, I tried to combine these Husserlian insights into a philosophy of intentional relations invoking a more poetic language of metaphor and metamorphosis. My aim here was to suggest how our being-in-the-world, and our understanding of this being, unfolds as a creative interplay between the *logos* of reason, which unifies, regulates, structures, and the *mythos* of poetry, symbol and myth, which is forever transcending and revising the order of *logos*. Both of these directions of consciousness – the positing power of *logos* and the differentiating power of *mythos* – are founded on an *imaginaire-rien* which I define as the universal principle of language, a superabundant play which engenders all meanings.

RK *What would you describe as the specifically phenomenological characteristics of your work, given your early fascination for the Husserlian notion of intentionality?*

SB First, I would say it was through my interest in the 'metaphysics of relation' that I became interested (via Brentano, on whom I was working in my Rome lectures) in Husserlian phenomenology. In fact, the relation of intentionality, which Brentano had retrieved from medieval scholasticism and 'reactivated' for contemporary philosophical purposes, struck me as offering a very liberating understanding of meaning, irreducible both to the strictly 'logical' notion of relations current in the forties and fifties, and to the traditional ontological notion of the 'transcendental' rapports between matter and form, essence and existence, and more generally between potency and act (rapports which I preferred to call 'structural' and which were typically articulated in Hamelin's *Eléments principaux de la représentation*). In my early work *Conscience et intentionalité*, I had already projected an enlarged notion of intentionality and I well remember a discussion with Jean Beaufret (one of the first advocates of existentialist and Heideggerian phenomenology in France) in which I engaged him on the crucial question of the transition from intentionality to 'existence': a question which, it seemed to me, represented a new and deeper understanding of the concept of the *esse ad* which was to pursue me all of my life. My initial interest in phenomenology, which corresponded therefore to my keenest philosophical preoccupations, also extended to my later works, in particular *Approches phénoménologiques de l'idée d'être* and *Etre, monde, imaginaire*. Overall I would say that the most inspiring aspect of phenomenology for me was its emphasis on the *prepredicative* and prereflective dimensions of experience. Indeed it was with this precise emphasis in mind that I distinguished in *Conscience et intentionalité* between several stratifications of consciousness: intentionality as a psychological act; intentionality as a 'potency/power' (*puissance*) relating to formal objects; and a transcendental intentionality representing the opening of the soul to *being as being*. It is along similar lines that, in the first part of *Etre, monde, imaginaire*, I proposed an analysis of what is meant by the 'language of being' in a less rudimentary way than that proposed by scholasticism or Thomism. I must admit, however, that in my early studies in phenomenology I paid little attention to the celebrated phenomenological reduction which, in the fifties, tormented those philosophers of my generation inspired by the Husserlian 'discovery'. (It was only later, by means of my reflections on freedom, that I came to appreciate somewhat what was involved in the reduction.) In summary, I would say that for me phenomenology was an extraordinary stimulant to my thinking, serving to crystallise some of my most formative philosophical concerns and ultimately providing me with an effective method of analysing the key notions of 'passage' and 'transit' which the metaphysics of relation first impressed upon me.

RK *Another of your recent works,* Théorie des idéologies, *also seems to be a variation on this theme of creative intentionality or transcendence. I'm thinking particularly of the key term of this work – the 'operator of transcendence'.*

SB This recent critique of ideology sprang from my fundamental preoccupation with the question of the 'zero'. The zero is a conceptual or mathematical way of formulating the metaphysical idea of the quasi-nothing (*rien*), or the Christian notion of the Cross – the emptiness of the crypt where Christian thinking as a critical thinking takes its source. A genuine questioning of ideology requires such a critical distance or dis-position. Without it, one can easily be misled by dogmatic ideologies – be they political or philosophical, or ecclesiastical.

The Neoplatonists also taught the importance of keeping a distance from all categories of facile objectivisation. Their very definition of being as *Eidos* or Form expresses this critical reserve. They realised that our philosophical categories are really *figures* of thought, and are thus capable of being critically altered or transcended towards the truth of the One which is beyond all the forms and figures of established ontology. So that when the Neoplatonists spoke of the One or God, they spoke of it in terms of critical reserve or qualification: *hos* or *oion*, *quasi* or *quatenus* – God *as* this or that ontological form. In short, since the Divine One was considered to be 'beyond being', He could only be thought of *as* being, or *as if* He were being. One could not say: God *is* being. The critical notion of the quasi-nothing, functioning as the 'operator of transcendence', thus prevented God from being reduced to a simplified or idolatrous ontology.

This Neoplatonic notion of critical distance is confirmed by the Christian notion of mystery – and particularly the practice of mystical speculation advanced by Eckhart and other Christian mystics who remained very suspicious of all ontological objectivisations of God. The model of reason demanded by metaphysical thinking must, I believe, be accompanied by a mystical appreciation for that which remains beyond the reach of this metaphysical model. This is why I always felt the need to balance the Greek fidelity to being with a biblical fidelity to the exodus – particularly as expressed in the Christian theology of the Passion and the Cross.

RK *Could you explain in more detail how your theological interpretation of the Passion as dispossession/disposition relates to the critique of contemporary ideologies? I think this is a crucial transition in your thinking and perhaps accounts for your occasional leanings towards the Marxist critique.*

SB I believe that the Christian doctrine of dispossession can be translated into modern 'socio-political' terms as a critique of power. There is a certain correspondence between the mystical-Neoplatonic critique of the Divine attributes – as an attempt to *possess* God in terms of ontological properties which would reduce His transcendence to the immanence of Being – and the Marxist critique of private property. Christianity and authentic Marxism share a common call to dispossession and a critical detachment from the prevailing order. I was always struck by the similarities between the Christian doctrine of eschatological justice where Jesus identified with the poor – 'I was naked. I was hungry. I was thirsty. I was imprisoned' (Matthew, 10:9) – and the Marxist ideal of universal justice for the dispossessed. I think that this universal 'I' of Christ – not to be confused with a transcendental or absolute Ego – which is enigmatically present in every poor or outcast person who has not yet been allowed the full humanity of justice, can find common cause with what is best in genuine Marxism. I am not saying that the two are the same. For while Christianity sponsors a categorical imperative for human justice and liberation (which certain brands of Marxism also endorse), it is not simply reducible to this imperative. While both share what Ernst Bloch called a common 'principle of hope' (*principe-espérance*), pointing towards a utopian horizon in the future, Christianity transcends the limits of historical materialism in the name of a prophetic eschatology (i.e. the Coming of the Kingdom).

The term 'Christian-Marxist' is a loaded and ambiguous one: it may serve as a *question* – with all the creative, thought-provoking tensions that genuine questioning implies – but not as a *solution*. We should remain cautious about invoking such terms uncritically as yet another ideological authority.

RK *How would you react to those who construe your recent work as a 'Christian atheism?'*

SB This is a dangerous term and I would not like to be thus characterised. To refuse the attempts to possess God by reducing Him to an ontological substance or political power – that is, an ideological weapon – is not to disbelieve in God; on the contrary, I would argue that it is a way of remaining faithful to one's belief. The critical refusal of ideological theism is not a refusal of God. It implies rather that the secondary definitions of God in terms of proposition (I believe *that* God exists) or predication (God *is* this or that) must be continually brought back to their primary origin in existential belief (I believe *in* God). This existential belief involves the believer in an intentional relation with God which is perhaps best described in terms of trust and transition. The move to institutionalise this belief in an invariant corpus of dogmas, doctrines and propositions was natural, perhaps even inevitable if Christianity was to survive the vagaries and contingencies of history. But this movement of *conservatism* must always be accompanied by a *critical* counter-movement which reminds us that God cannot ultimately be objectified or immobilised in ontological or institutional (i.e. anthropomorphic) structures. In a recent study entitled *Théorie des idéologies et la réponse de la foi* I tried to reflect on this problem by discussing the central implications of the term *credo* in relation to the three major movements of belief – existential, propositional and predicative – mentioned above. Religious faith begins with belief-in-God which expresses itself as an intentional being-towards-God. It involves the primary existential idioms of desire, enchantment and hope, etc. It is only subsequently that we return upon the existential level to appropriate the riches encountered in the immediacy of this original experience. Thus the second movement of faith takes place as an attempt to define and order the content and form of one's existential belief. It is as if one thus draws a golden circle around one's religious experience which one calls 'tradition' or 'heritage' or 'doctrine' and affirms *that* God exists and *that* God is good and almighty, etc. In this way the vertical arrow of our primary intentional belief becomes a reflective or recollective circle – with those on the inside calling themselves Christian and those on the outside non-Christian. I think that this second move is indispensable in that every religion requires the form of a 'society', and every society requires a specific identity and foundation. A religion that is content to be 'anything at all' very easily becomes 'nothing at all' – as indeterminate and all-inconclusive as the category of being-as-being. In the third movement, reflection goes beyond both the modalities of 'I believe *in*' and 'I believe *that*' to the definition of God as a *proposition in itself*: 'God *is* this or that'. Hence the intentional distance or commitment implied by the first two movements of '*I* believe' is transcended and dogmatic theology instantiates itself as an historical institution or organisation. It is the duty of the religious or theistic thinker to serve such institutional belief by reminding it that its doctrines are not autonomous or eternally guaranteed but intellectual sedimentations of the original 'I believe' wherein God reveals Himself to man. This critical exigency of faithfulness to the irreducible mystery and radicality of Divine revelation is beautifully expressed in a passage in Kings 1:2, where Elijah goes in search of God but discovers him not in the rocks, in the storm, in the shaking earth, nor in the fire, but in the voice of a gentle breeze as it passes through the mountain cave. God is passage not possession.

RK *Can this critique of theistic ideology also be applied to political ideologies which constitute the objectified or impersonalised institutions of contemporary society?*

SB I think so. But we must remember the natural and almost inevitable reasons for the emergence of ideologies. Ideology springs from the fact that there is an ontological rupture between existence and consciousness. We do not coincide with ourselves. We exist before we are conscious of our existence; and this means that our reflective consciousness is always to some extent out of joint with the existential conditions that fostered it. Freud realised this when he spoke about the gap between the conscious and the unconscious. I would say that every form of *thought* is ideology to the extent that it does not and cannot fully coincide with the *being* of which it is the thought. The existence of ideologies reminds us that there is a margin of obscurity which we can never completely recuperate or remove. The pure identification of being and thought – i.e. the thought that thinks itself as being/being as the self-thinking-thought – is the Aristotelian-Thomistic definition of Divine self-understanding that no ideology can legitimately pretend to emulate. Human thought can never be perfectly transparent or adequate to itself. It is the role of the philosopher to challenge all ideological claims to such absolute knowledge and, by implication, to absolute power.

RK *You once stated: 'The cross of my faith, will it not remain this interrogation mark which ancient legend tells us is the firstborn of all creation? If your philosophy does remain this critical interrogation mark, can it ever serve as a creative affirmation? Is it not inevitably condemned to a* via negativa*?*

SB The two aspects of philosophy – as negation and affirmation – are for me by no means incompatible. Though the critical aspect is more in evidence in contemporary thinking, including my own, I would insist that the first step in philosophy – and therefore its *sine qua non* – is a fundamental experience of wonder, curiosity, or enchantment: in short *affirmation*. My enthusiasm for philosophy began in the same way as my enthusiasm for poetry or the Bible, by *responding* to texts that sang to me. Writing retraces those paths that sing to us (*chantent*) and thus enchant (*enchantent*) us. In this sense, I see a close relationship between philosophy, theology and poetics. Philosophy never speaks to us in the abstract with a capital P, but in the engaging terms of certain chosen texts (*morceaux choisis*) – in my own case, certain texts of the pre-Socratics, Aristotle, Plato, the Neoplatonists or St Thomas, Schelling, Husserl and Heidegger. The desire to know philosophy as a totality – the Hegelian temptation to absolute knowledge – is not only dangerous but impossible; one can never reduce the infinite richness of our existential experience to the totalising limits of reason.

RK *But would you not acknowledge essential differences between philosophy and poetry as modes of this* affirmation enchantée*?*

SB The main difference between philosophy and poetry as I see it is that while both originate in an experience of enchantment which draws us and commits us to the world, philosophy is obliged, in a second movement, to critically transcend and interrogate the world, both as life-experience and poetic-experience. Philosophy thus leads a double life of residing within and without the world. Perhaps one of the greatest enigmas of philosophy is that a thinking being can serve as a chain in the historical world and yet also break free from this chain, rise above it (partially at least) in order to question its ultimate origin and meaning. Poetry celebrates *that* the world exists; philosophy asks *why* the world exists. Schelling and Husserl implicitly acknowledged this distinction when they spoke of the philosophical need to go beyond or suspend the natural attitude (which would include our primary poetic experience), in which all thinking begins, to a transcendental or questioning attitude: to be *in* the world and yet not *of* the world, to be *inside* and *outside* at once.

RK *How do you see this double fidelity to the philosophical and poetic attitudes operating in your own work?*

SB My work operates on the basis of two overriding impulses or passions. On the one hand, it strives for scientific rigour and form – a striving epitomised by my preoccupation with the mathematical logic of religions and the search for the principle of reason. On the other hand, I began to wonder if this search for rigour and reason might not ultimately lead to the sterile tautologies of a *mathesis universalis*: the pretentious claim to possess an absolutely certain Principle-foundation through a synthesis of Aristotelian logic, Euclidean geometry and the Scholastic doctrine of Transcendentals. And this doubt provided a space for the emergence of a second fundamental passion – what I might call my 'poetic inclination'. This second poetic passion challenged the speculative claim to absolute identity or totality and revived an attentiveness to the vibrant multiplicity of the lifeworld. I suppose this poetic inclination can be witnessed, in its modernist guise, in Mallarmé's notion of 'dissemination'. I chose the terms 'metaphor' and 'metamorphosis' to express this reality of movement, alteration and diversification. And Derrida, Lyotard, Deleuze and Lévinas have developed their respective philosophies of 'difference', repudiating the principle of identity for either the subject or the object. It is my own conviction that the classical metaphysics of identity and the modernist poetics of difference need each other, for both correspond to fundamental impulses in human thinking. This is what I tried to express in *Etre, monde, imaginaire* when I analysed how the speculative principle of the *logos* and the poetic principle of the *mythos* are committed to each other in a creative conflict which unfolds in the free space of the *imaginaire*. This act of faith in the 'imaginary', in the open horizon of the possible where oppositions confront and recreate each other, is where my initial reflections on the *esse-in* and the *esse-ad* have led me.

I might summarise this dual allegiance of my work as follows. To consider philosophy as an exclusively critical or speculative movement is to condemn it to an endless contestation which can easily slip into the nihilism of a *reductio ad absurdum*. Philosophy must continually remind itself of its origins in the bedrock of real experience. Only when one has experienced the opaque profundity of existential or religious reality can one legitimately take one's critical distance in order to question or reflect upon it. Similarly, it is only when one has been immersed in the social lifeworld that one can begin to interrogate the ideological structures which regulate it. Philosophy always presupposes the ability to say: *this* is what a tree is, *this* is how authority works, *this* is what a tribunal consists of, etc. The speculative instance is inextricably dependent upon the concrete immediacy of the person's lived experience. It cannot afford to ignore the existential conditions which precede it. I have always been struck by Suarez's principle of identity, which states that 'every being has an essence which constitutes and determines it'. Philosophy begins with a commitment to the determining world and only in an ulterior, reflexive moment proceeds to 'objectify' or 'formalise'. Philosophy does not begin with Kant – though the 'critical' turn is a crucial stage in its development. I think we should be grateful to Marx for having turned idealism on its head and for making it more humble towards reality; only by being engaged to the living body of history can critical thinking avoid becoming a corpse of solipsistic introspection. It is because philosophy is both *critique* and *commitment* that it can distance itself from the world precisely in order to transform it.

RK *This summary analysis of your philosophy reminds me of your theological interpretation of the ecumenical dialectic between Catholic, Protestant and Orthodox thinking in* La Foi et raison logique.

SB In this work I tried to rethink ecumenism in terms of a group of metaphysical operations. In this schema, the Catholic tradition privileged the operation of transitivity and transformation, functioning as a process of historical realism bound to the preservation of Revelation in the temporal world. The Protestant Reform privileged the operation of a critical conversion (turning around) which returned to the fundamental origins of Christianity. And thirdly, the Orthodox church of oriental Christianity privileged the operation of 'manence' (*esse-in*) or in-dwelling. I argued that all three movements – of historical transformation, critical return and spiritual dwelling – are essential to the Christian reality, ensuring that it remains transitive and intransitive, transcendent and immanent. The history of Christianity is the drama of this divergence and belonging-together of Catholicism, Protestantism and Orthodoxy as a fecund tension between complementary differences. I think that ecumenism is facile if it ignores the importance of this creative tension. It is only when one assumes the specificity of one's own religious tradition (in my case Catholic) that one can fully appreciate the *other* – the essential contribution which the other traditions make to one's own.

RK *France produced a considerable number of 'Christian philosophers' in the first half of this century, including Marcel, Mounier, Maritain and Gilson. Would you consider yourself a Christian philosopher?*

SB I am a Christian philosopher to the extent that the primary experience that fostered and coloured much of my philosophical thinking was, as I explained at the outset, specifically Christian in certain respects – particularly as it determined my reflections on the Passion and the Cross. Such Christian reflection frequently dovetailed with my preoccupation with Greek and Neoplatonic thought. For example, my description of the Cross as the 'seed of non-being' (*germen nihili*) bears an intimate correspondence to Proclus's notion of the *sperma meontos*. The Neoplatonic attempts to critically radicalise the Platonic philosophy of being (*On*) find common ground here with the theology of the Cross. If the theology of Glory – with its splendid doctrine of the superabundance of grace – is divorced from the critical theology of the Cross, it can degenerate into triumphalism. Grace is not power but dispossession because it is given under the interrogative sign of the Cross. To the extent, therefore, that the theology of the Cross deeply affected my whole attitude to thought, I would be prepared to consider myself a 'Christian' philosopher. But I would insist that philosophy and theology are separate, if equally valid, disciplines of thought. Whereas the theologian can presuppose the Christian tradition as a series of Revealed doctrines, the philosopher – even the Christian philosopher – cannot. The theologian believes truth is given, the philosopher goes in search of it.

(Clamart, France, 1982)

Select bibliography

L'Esse 'in' et l'esse 'ad' dans la métaphysique de la relation, Rome, 1951.
La Passion du Christ et les philosophies, Eco, Teramo, 1954.
Conscience et intentionalité, Vitte, Paris-Lyon, 1956.
Approches phénoménologiques de l'idée d'être, Vitte, Paris-Lyon, 1959.
Situation de la philosophie contemporaine, Vitte, Paris-Lyon, 1959.
Essence et existence, PUF, Paris, 1962.
Le Problème de l'être spirituel dans la philosophie de N. Hartmann, Vitte, Paris-Lyon, 1962.
Mystique de la Passion, Desclée, Tournai, 1962.
Saint Thomas d'Aquin, Seghers, Paris, 1965.
Philosophie et mathématique chez Proclus, Beauchesne, Paris, 1969.

Du principe, coéd. Aubier, Cerf, Desclée, Delachaux, Paris, 1971.
La Foi et raison logique, Le Seuil, Paris, 1971.
Etre, monde, imaginaire, Le Seuil, Paris, 1976.
Théorie des idéologies, Desclée, Paris, 1976.
Spinoza, Théologie et politique, Desclée, Paris, 1977.
Unicité et monothéisme, Cerf, Paris, 1981.
La Poétique du sensible, Les Editiors du Cerf, Paris, 1988.
Le Rien ou quelque chose, Flammarion, Paris, 1987.
La Philosophie buissonière, Jérôme Millon, Grenoble, 1989.
La Pensée du Rien, Kok, Hollande, 1992.
Matière et disposition, J. Millon, Grenoble, 1993
L'autre et l'ailleurs, Descartes, Paris, 1995.

HANS-GEORG GADAMER

Text matters

Prefatory note

HANS-GEORG GADAMER was born in Marburg, Germany, in 1900. He remained in Marburg to pursue his education in philosophy and classical philology, studying with such renowned thinkers as Paul Natorp, Martin Heidegger and Paul Friedländer. Gadamer finished his doctorate on Plato in 1922, and held university posts in Marburg (1929–37), Leipzig (1938–47), Frankfurt (1947–49), and Heidelberg (1949–68) until his retirement. Many of the essays written on philosophical hermeneutics and language throughout his fruitful academic life were first gathered together as *Kleine Schriften* (4 vols., Tübingen, Mohr, 1967–79), and later translated for numerous anthologies in English, as cited in our select bibliography. At present, Gadamer's collected works in German are projected to fill ten volumes, nine of which have already appeared.

We shall see that a main theme reverberating throughout Gadamer's hermeneutic philosophy is that 'understanding' (*Verstehen*) must be historically and linguistically mediated. There is always some pre-understanding or 'prejudice' that makes our encounter with history possible at all. In other words, both the tradition and those who attempt to interpret it constitute part of a historical continuum that cannot be artificially separated or segregated. According to Gadamer, the error of the Enlightenment was its 'prejudice against prejudice', i.e. the refusal to recognise the significance of our own insertion in a tradition that, at some level, we already understand. Thus, he emphasises the importance of what he calls the 'effective history' that underlies any potential 'fusion of horizons' that we could hope to achieve.

Equally dangerous, in Gadamer's view, is the Romantic or psychologistic approach of nineteenth-century hermeneutics, particularly

Schleiermacher, who sought to collapse historical distance by fostering 'empathy' with the mental attitude, dispositions, and worlds of those who created the traditional texts we interpret. For Gadamer, this merely presents the mirror-image of the Enlightenment's ideal of a detached and privileged 'reason', by substituting the Romantic ideal of an ancient, primeval wisdom that could somehow be recuperated. While less critical, in this regard, of a hermeneutic predecessor such as Dilthey, Gadamer also rejects Dilthey's suggestion that the historical or human sciences can be studied by applying the same methodology as that applied to the natural sciences. The transmission of culture, as well as the understanding of ourselves as human beings, can never be reduced to what Gadamer considered the often positivistic methodologies of natural scientists. Gadamer examined these and related issues in great detail in his influential work *Truth and Method* (*Wahrheit und Methode*, 1960).

In his attempt to broaden the significance of a truly 'philosophical hermeneutics', Gadamer stresses the dominant role of language (*Sprachlichkeit*) and the linguistic resources that mediate both our encounters with tradition and with each other. We are always partners in dialogue, whether it be with 'eminent texts' or with one another in conversation. Thus, the path to understanding can only be traversed through language, as he emphasises repeatedly in the conversation which follows. This exchange between Hans-Georg Gadamer, John Cleary and Richard Kearney took place in 1994, and was translated by Mara Rainwater.

RK *What were the milestones on your own way to hermeneutics?*

H-GG My way to hermeneutics describes my initial experiences with the study of language as a young philologist in Marburg. I had already completed a dissertation on Plato for my first philosophical studies with Hönigswald, Natorp, and Nicolai Hartmann, and I had also met Heidegger. Only then did I actually begin my course of studies as a classical philologist with Paul Friedländer. It was at that point I had the opportunity to recognise the vital importance of a *literary genre* itself, especially when we are trying to correctly understand the *product* of such a genre. For example, in a debate I had with Werner Jaeger at that time, I took issue with his use of Aristotle's *Protreptikos* as a significant measure of early Aristotelian thought. The genre of the '*protreptikos*' among the Greeks offered essentially nothing more than an advertisement for competing schools of rhetoric and philosophy seeking patronage. To expect that controversial questions in philosophy could be settled by appealing to such a genre, as Jaeger apparently did, seemed quite erroneous to me.

Or to take another example, I realised that the meaning of Plato's *Republic* could only be correctly understood after noting that we are dealing here with the literary genre of 'utopia'. To write in the utopian genre, especially under the political conditions of a Greek polis that afforded no separation of powers, was the only possible way to criticise the degeneration of a democracy through corruption, nepotism, etc., without suffering political consequences. The comedies of Aristophanes had a similar function. In more recent times, we also know what political censorship can mean for literary production. Goethe actually attributed the increase of the linguistic art of expression to this kind of censorship, and, in this respect, paid tribute to it. Leo Strauss pointed to Spinoza as an example of the difficult situation of 'thinking' in the era of the European Enlightenment, and he showed how the worry about censorship influenced Spinzoa's *Ethics*. Strauss also indicated that similar concerns could be applied to Arabian repression in the case of the medieval Jewish thinker Moses Maimonides.

RK *What did you learn from these early observations?*

H-GG I learnt to attend more fully to the addressees of philosophical texts – to those for whom the writer writes. I thus encountered the twofold hermeneutic problem: 1) how we make ourselves understood to others through language, and 2) how we have to deal with writing to avoid misunderstanding, misuse and distortion – as Plato had already warned us. In order to appreciate this, we have to acknowledge the central importance of *rhetoric*, which achieved its highest development in the blossoming of Greek culture in the city-state. At the time of the decline of the Greek polis, rhetoric turned into a literary genre that subsequently dominated the entire academic culture, only losing its leading role as a transmitter of culture in our era of modern science. I therefore constructed my studies with ancient rhetoric in mind, and, above all, on Plato's critique of rhetoric and his qualified recognition of rhetoric.

RK *Why did you choose hermeneutics as the best means of developing the phenomenology of Husserl and Heidegger?*

H-GG One doesn't really 'choose' things like that. We always find ourselves in a tradition that is speaking to us. Therefore, there is an easy answer to your question. Philosophy only works by means of linguistic formulation, and for this to carry conviction it must include rhetoric. It is an error to think that mathematical formalism – whose clarity certainly constitutes its advantage – can be everywhere substituted for the use of natural language. In the mathematical and natural sciences, where it is a question of exact measurable results, the apparatus of mathematics plays a decisive role. But in those sciences where one is *not* dealing with quantitatively measurable objects of research, the research is conducted and communicated to others by means of human language. In the course of time, philosophy has increasingly found that the elaborate conceptual language of Latin scholastics, a language that has penetrated into modern national languages, often introduces unrecognised and invisible prejudices. Even the philosophical reform movement, heralded by phenomenology and philosophical research at the beginning of our century, had to trust more and more in the power of living language to awaken insight. In particular, Husserl was a master of a highly discriminating art of description, exposing thoughtless professional constructions and jargon, through the powerful language of phenomena.

RK *Was Husserl alone in this?*

H-GG By no means. The great thinkers in the history of this new philosophy, above all Kant and the German Idealists, had modelled their conceptual art on the linguistic power of the German language. They used models like Meister Eckhart and Martin Luther, and finally, through the return to the Graeco-Roman ancients, entered again into the teaching of their linguistic culture. Ever since the German Romantic period, this attention to language also marks the work of those thinkers who came later, including such great thinkers as Bergson in France, as well as thinkers of the historical school in Germany, whose philosophical interpreter was Dilthey. Dilthey had a decisive influence on the continued growth of phenomenology, extending from Martin Heidegger to other newer tendencies in the phenomenological school. Since Schleiermacher's modern development of hermeneutics, much of its older history has remained concealed in the background.

JC But many people assume as self-evident that hermeneutics first begins with Schleiermacher.

H-GG One ought not to present the case in quite that way, as if something like hermeneutics first appeared with German Romanticism. 'Hermeneutics' is actually a Greek term, and the conditions under which the art of understanding 'the other' places its special demands are not first derived from the age of modern science. The genesis of the word 'hermeneutics' itself shows an original connection with the god Hermes, the divine mediator between the will of the gods and the acts of mortals. It is clear that such a concept of hermeneutics comes very near to the concept of translation. The role played by the Delphic oracle in Greek history – namely, the interpretation of prophecies – rests especially on this concept of hermeneutics. The art of interpreting these prophecies through the committee of the Delphic priesthood truly made history in the political sense. One has to realise that the Greeks were the brilliant disciples of the high culture of the Near East. They were the first to develop a rational energy and thirst for knowledge that led them into inevitable tension with their own religious tradition, which, thanks to their poetic representation in the epics of Homer and Hesiod, deeply determined their own way of thinking. That goes right through the Greek educational movement in the narrow sense of the Sophists, and still distinguishes the lasting foundation of Greek philosophy for the history of the West going back to Plato and Aristotle.

RK *Could you say more about these 'beginnings' with Plato and Aristotle?*

H-GG In Plato we find a complex artistic incorporation of mythic-religious traditions into mathematical research and cosmological knowledge, and in the end, into the constant question about 'the good' posed by Socrates. In general, the expression 'hermeneutics' is not used for this. Actually, the term 'hermeneutics' is given a thematic treatment for the first time by Aristotle, but only in a very special and narrow sense. As the founder of ancient logic, Aristotle called 'hermeneutics' the teaching of propositions of judgment, and it is upon this teaching that the secret of logical inference is based. Everyone recognised the importance of syllogistics – that is, the form of reaching valid logical conclusions – because Aristotle developed it with an eye towards supporting the new mathematical science, as well as defending rational thought against the rhetorical tricks of the Sophists.

JC But isn't philosophy always afflicted with the art of understanding the unintelligible, if only in an unnamed way?

H-GG Yes, indeed. We would like to know once-and-for-all what the Socratic question of the good really *is*, and it has in this way dominated all of Western thought. Particularly in late antiquity, this question proved to be the preparation for the debate with the Judaeo-Christian religious heritage. In this respect, it is not surprising that Christian theology and especially Augustine, the great Latin scholar among the church fathers, developed the fundamental teaching of ancient and Graeco-Christian hermeneutics in his *De Doctrina Christiana.*

JC Wasn't it necessary for theology to go its own way under the changing signs of the new secular science in the age of the Renaissance?

H-GG That goes without saying. Especially Luther and the great Aristotelian Melanchton played a decisive role amongst the Reformers. Luther's textbook of interpretation has become one of the most important hermeneutic documents in world literature. And to Melanchton goes the unique merit of having defended the already-mentioned great heritage of ancient rhetoric, a heritage which he defended as the transmitter of cultural values of the entire ancient and medieval educational system, as opposed to the iconoclastic radicalism in the Protestant movement. Melanchton also deserves credit for having established it as hermeneutics. In his Latin lecture on rhetoric, Melanchton deals with the theory of rhetoric of the Greeks and Romans and the Latin Middle Ages, first as the art of making a speech or writing a speech. In truth, though, he diverted this ancient heritage of rhetoric into the art of *reading* speeches or texts. Ever since Melanchthon made such a lasting imprint on the Central European educational system and on the entire academic culture of his era, an integrated line of hermeneutics runs through this culture, mainly due to the central place of the Holy Scriptures within the Protestant church system. Since the empirical sciences of the modern world challenge philosophy and metaphysics, hermeneutics directs itself to the task of seeking a scientific-theoretical way towards a universal art of interpretation based on the special domains of theology and jurisprudence. This task gained importance with the end of the age of metaphysics, or more precisely in the Age of Romanticism.

RK *Could you spell out the seminal relation of philosophical hermeneutics to theology and law?*

H-GG It was vital to implement a methodology of hermeneutics-as-philosophy in the theological and jurisprudential spheres that had already been cultivated. And that is what Schleiermacher achieved in his *Hermeneutics*, but even more so in his *Dialectic*. The spread of hermeneutic methodology into other content-areas lies not so much in this direction, but in the direction of common foundational questions (as in theology, in religious research, in historical research, in art, music, etc.), which call for philosophical work, as we see today particularly in the work of Paul Ricoeur. However, the most important step taken by hermeneutics-as-philosophy was a new focus on the '*lifeworld*' as the major field of phenomenological research. Philosophy was no longer limited to the narrow programme dictated by the 'fact of science', as Neo-Kantians or Logical Positivists would have maintained.

RK *Are you saying that the concept of method in modern science is not applicable to hermeneutics-as-philosophy?*

H-GG Philosophical hermeneutics *doesn't* mean a scientific method. All scientific methods are good only under the condition of their reasonable and judicious application. Here lies the boundary of all method and hypostasisation. This state of affairs has been acknowledged since the development of historical consciousness, and it became increasingly important as scientific methods spread to the languages of modern civilisation, which set the stage through their mutual influence on one another. Anyone who has used a translation where he himself knows and commands the original language, has the undeniable experience that the translation is very much harder to understand than the original. The natural use of language is less a question of texts than the 'matter' of experience itself.

Hermeneutics and the Greeks

RK *In what sense do you believe that the origins of hermeneutics are to be found in the Greek philosophers?*

H-GG Do you mean, why must Greek philosophy still be the actual point of departure for hermeneutic questioning?

RK *Yes.*

H-GG In the intellectual culture of Europe, the Greeks were the people who first developed science and the logic of proof. And for this they used their own living language, which the citizens of their cities spoke and their poets had elevated to literary language. They didn't have to struggle with a technical language of philosophy, which would have been for them a second and strange language, as it was for the Romans when the upper classes absorbed Greek culture.

The problem of moulding the Greek language into Latin became more noticeable in late antiquity when the emerging Christian church began to formulate its teachings of faith in Latin, with the help of Greek philosophy. In the end, this led to the 'forced' logical culture of the medieval Scholastics. Their language of concepts, in more or less refined or alienated forms, has informed the conceptual language of modern philosophy. Since then, the task has been to re-learn what the Greeks showed us, namely, to summon up the imaginative power of living language for conceptual thinking. This doesn't mean that we should adopt Greek philosophy, but it does mean that we should learn from it how to think in concepts with the help of our own spoken language. Luther became a great translator because he paid attention to the language of the people.

JC In this connection, can you explain to us what is involved in the idea of 'eminent texts'?

H-GG These are texts that we may refer to as literary or poetic texts, and the same distinction is also applicable to other art forms. The question that I especially pose to Derrida, is the distinctive role which this kind of text plays. I call these 'eminent texts' because in them the true nature of 'textura', that is, the indissoluble inter-weaving of threads, is the appropriate description. We cannot extract information from literary works if we allow them to speak to us merely *as* literary works. But that's exactly it; they speak to us, and they are even tireless, with questions as well as answers, so that we don't simply consult them once and then know everything about them. Rather, we find ourselves questioned again and again, receiving answers that are always new. And this experience *stays* with us, so that we recognise ourselves when allowing ourselves to be affected by the great portrayals of human destiny and suffering in tragedies, novels or poems.

It is no exaggeration to claim that a poetical text is a partner in conversation. Furthermore, the literary text speaks to us only so long as it is and remains such a partner, and not merely an object of objectifying research. These are things that we misunderstand and cover over if we speak of 'fiction' only in order to emphasise a contrast with scientific knowledge. In that instance, a scientific concept of truth functions in an improper context.

JC What are philosophical texts?

H-GG These are naturally not 'eminent texts', which is to say that they are not linguistic works of art. But what the 'eminent text' is for the partner-in-dialogue, the 'problem' is for the philosophical thinkers. We make it too easy for ourselves if a 'problem' is seen simply as a 'question' to which there is an answer. Rather, a problem is precisely that which is thrown into our path and which cannot easily be avoided. Certainly we cannot get around it by alternative questions that require a mere 'Yes' or 'No' in response. Here I believe that the close intertwining of philosophy with literary language, which I have often described in this context, receives its own crucial priority. In philosophy, as in art, it's a matter of coaxing prereflective knowledge out of its depths. It is almost as if everybody basically knows it. Everybody who can think and speak a language lives in the totality of a world-orientation which is always already on-the-way-towards-understanding.

Faced with a question that we don't completely understand, it remains an open question. This invites the process of recognition that Plato called '*anamnesis*'. He demonstrated it with mathematics, but we would do well to take the concept of *anamnesis* so that it broadly corresponds to its original Pythagorean idea of salvation from the circle of rebirth. Foreknowledge guides that which we ask – ourselves or another – and our answer is recognised as true. This confirms the religious tradition of *anamnesis*. We ourselves only truly 'know' when we re-cognise or encounter something again. And we are sure that another has understood us when he or she has responded. This is the only, albeit relative, criterion of truth.

Hermeneutics and dialogue

RK *Is it the concept of 'dialogue' in particular that marks the difference between your philosophy and that of other hermeneutic thinkers in our century such as Heidegger, Habermas, or Ricoeur?*

H-GG It is well known that philosophy always had a basis in spoken language, which, prior to all science, constituted a guide in the unfolding of vocabulary, grammar and syntax for human thought – a guide which helps to determine conceptual formation. Admittedly, with the advent of reading culture in the Gutenberg era and the rise of the mathematical sciences, this is not always as evident as it should be. The foundational concepts of philosophy originally stem from the Greek tradition, but at present these concepts just seem to exercise a purely instrumental function of ordering experience, which has become dominated by the language of mathematical symbols. As the reference to the original proximity of language to the philosophical thought of the Greeks has indicated, the concepts of philosophy were not a mere working tool for them. These concepts were rather formed in *spoken* language, drawing on all the raw materials that constituted the totality of world experience. Thus, Plato could say that all learning and knowledge is a remembering (*anamnesis*) which comes in the play between question and answer.

On this basis, the great turn of philosophical thought towards the primary concept of the 'subject' and the modern idea of methodology took place. This turn has dominated all of modern German philosophy, and this is true even for the transcendental self-interpretation of the later Husserl of *Ideas*. It is also true, to some degree, for the transcendental framework Heidegger used for presenting his masterpiece, *Being and Time*, a work which exhibited a residual Neo-Kantianism that eventually generated new critiques by thinkers like Martin Buber. Heidegger eliminated this transcendental framework in his search for the new way of the so-called 'turn' or '*Kehre*', by which he meant a path in the forest that makes a turn in ascending to the top. But what Heidegger described as a new way is, in fact, a return to his own beginnings in the reinterpretation of Aristotle.

In any case, whatever importance the hermeneutic approach has for philosophy only comes into general consciousness slowly. Otherwise Derrida would hardly complain about 'phonocentricity' in this regard. Phonocentricity is only another expression for the concept of presence-at-hand, introduced by Heidegger, or of *présence*, introduced by Derrida.

RK *How would you identify your own specific approach to hermeneutics on this issue?*

H-GG I think there is a decisive point here which distinguishes me from Habermas and Ricoeur and others who appeal to hermeneutics. The crucial step is indicated in the title of my book *Truth and Method*, which marks a gap between 'truth' and 'method'. Understanding, trying to comprehend others, seeking communication with others, all these are processes of the lifeworld. One should, of course, be able to take on tasks of communication where understanding is the issue, as it interacts with art and science. However, when human beings speak with one another and inhabit the communicative world, this complex interaction can't be fully captured by scientific method alone.

Since human experience goes far beyond the questioning attainable through knowledge of the quantitative sciences, it is pointless to create a false contrast between the objectivity of science and the alleged relativism of hermeneutic sciences – those sciences for which objectivity cannot be the final goal. It is a fatal error to assume that the incomplete nature of our world experience can ever be negotiated through the so-called empirical sciences. When we seek communication with others, we ourselves are no mere 'objects' of science. The natural sciences aim at universal 'knowledge', as Husserl correctly emphasised. That assures their success, but also marks their limit.

Incidentally, this difference between the natural and human sciences has nothing to do with the famous quarrel between the ancients and moderns. That was a literary dispute between the traditional humanists and modern poets that took place in France during the seventeenth and eighteenth centuries. One can extend the same quarrel to other areas, as Leo Strauss does in his Spinoza critique and his Maimonides studies, consciously taking the side of the ancients. But basically that is not a viable alternative. Ever since the work of C. P. Snow, we speak of science and the humanities as 'two worlds', yet we also desire to overcome this difference between the natural and human sciences. For the twentieth century and the future, this European debate, which exists even in philosophy, will ultimately appear far too provincial. The hermeneutic art of understanding others, in *spite* of the otherness of the 'other', will have to tackle harder tasks, when, as at present, the large world cultures meet each other more often as real partners in conversation.

RK *In this respect, how would you defend yourself against Derrida's charge that you subscribe to the phonocentrism of traditional metaphysics?*

H-GG I especially want to say that there are a *plurality* of traditions, out of which human questioning arises. It cannot be denied that philosophy too must give an account of itself to people coming from other traditions. However, I do not believe that Derrida's choice of 'writing' has achieved a higher universal validity, as he apparently believes. True, we can't deny the fact that the written evidence of human life in Chinese literature or Central African myths, Indian epics or the Koran certainly takes the form of written traditions. But while these texts derive from the most diverse origins and symbols, they all refer back to lived life and spoken language. In this respect, phonocentrism is a common *condition* for all human writing, and naturally also for the 'deconstruction' demanded by Derrida and his friends. To me, Derrida appears to be the victim of a curious metaphysical remnant in Husserl's thought. What Derrida means by 'phonocentrism' can be found in his debate with Husserl: the assumption that the 'voice' is something 'material'. One can only be amazed. Voice, this fleeting breath of air that passes and which first allows the 'written' to be conveyed as meaningful, is itself a text-to-be-understood. Whether as a text recited aloud or as a text read silently to myself, the articulation of meaning first fulfils itself by means of the sound formation. In any case, the one who speaks, hears; and the one who understands, answers – *not* to the particular voice that one recognises on the telephone, but rather to that of which the talk is about.

RK *So there are different concepts of 'voice'?*

H-GG Yes. Apparently, Derrida has in mind the narrow view of '*logos*' that he found in Husserl. However, this ancient concept was again put into a new light by Christianity as cited in the beginning of the Gospel According to St John: 'In the beginning was the Word . . .'. Thus, if we focus only on sentential propositions and those sciences founded on such 'true' propositions, we will indeed arrive at a very one-sided rendering of the meaning of '*logos*'. This is an artificial restriction, which Aristotle first made explicit when he talked about hermeneutics with logic in mind. I think that we must free ourselves from such theoretical burdens, precisely because the linguisticality of human beings doesn't produce structures made of propositions. It rather consists in a living exchange of question and answer, request and fulfilment, command and obedience, etc. To whatever degree one extends reciprocity, that alone allows communication to take place.

JC Are hermeneutics and deconstruction capable of communicating with each other?

H-GG I cannot accept that there is a *single* hermeneutic position that ought to agree with the position of deconstruction. But neither is the hermeneutic position at all a counter-position. Hermeneutics doesn't rely on *one* point of view; rather, it refers to *mutual* praxis. We both seek in dialogue to convince the other, or at least to share with the other what we mean. Both partners have the experience that this is only possible by going beyond what has been said *literally* to me, and by the other seeking to understand me. We may not succeed on the first or second attempt, especially when it is a question of partners speaking different languages. But, by the same token, it is certainly not being claimed that the hermeneutic effort of communicating with the other is always crowned with success. That's how I think matters stand between myself and Derrida, in so far as we could learn to understand one another, and then neither of us would remain the same as we were before our conversation. In short, we learn from one another.

Let me illustrate this with another example. I refer to the well-known debate between Habermas and myself. That debate was, at the time, a publicly argued, written dialogue that raised a great deal of interest. Now people want us to engage in such a conversation again, but conversations are not the kind of thing that one can programme. This 'written conversation' that occurred was an especially fortunate constellation, consisting of comprehensive common elements shared by many others, elements that could be brought into the written conversation from both sides. The conversation with Derrida in Paris didn't achieve such a fortunate literary organisation of form, and what is more, was subjected to the mutilations that translation brings about between two foreign languages.

RK *What do you mean exactly?*

H-GG I mean that we hold no 'opposed' positions, rather that we are all 'on the way', even when we resort to writing. When one reads something written – whether it is something like a poem by Goethe, or lines of verse scribbled down in the moonlight or found in a book – the reader is not the one first addressed. Only personal correspondence in a private letter names and means *its* addressee, and nobody else. When we are dealing with texts, the reader is involved and he or she is the 'Other'. Similarly, in a conversation we need attention and co-operation to reach some understanding. I can see how someone could be overwhelmed by the silent stillness in which a sudden insight dawns and definite preconceptions collapse. But we should be able to agree that writing must be read, and that writing is only read when it is read-with-understanding. Only reading-with-understanding makes the signs of writing speak. Whether it is an inner voice or an audible voice that speaks makes no *différence* to the *différance*.

RK *How does this relate to your understanding of Derrida's critique of metaphysics?*

H-GG It isn't really clear to me that what I've been discussing ought to have something *necessarily* to do with 'metaphysical thinking'. This always seemed to me a weak point in Derrida's book on Husserl, *Speech and Phenomena*. I can't understand what metaphysical thinking is supposed to be. Certainly, I can imagine a *language* of metaphysics which has been marked by Aristotle's ontology of substance. And I can also imagine the role played in this context by the concept of 'presence' – a role which, at least since the analysis of time in Aristotle's *Physics*, leads to the dead-end described by Augustine. On the other hand, I don't see how the issue of understanding is seriously affected by whether a text appears in the continuity and coherence or a book of in the discontinuity of aphorisms *à la* Schlegel or Nietzsche. I find it quite incomprehensible to interrogate this discontinuity under the guise of a critical scrutiny of the 'unconscious' hiding in a text. Naturally, we *can* do this at any time. But in my eyes, that's not conversation at all: the partner is merely 'objectively' observed and doesn't sit there willing or able to respond.

Derrida loves to speak of a 'break' in such a context. However, we know that Freud himself was able to make the ruptures of dream-events fruitful, and eventually even cure patients through interpretation and understanding. It should thus apply all the more to aphorisms or to the ambiguity of words that we are left with *something*, a significant remainder. It is not true that we simply play a game. Certainly, there are differences in the weight of interpretation, in the pregnancy, the amazement, the evidence, the thoughtfulness with which we move in conversation. But all these are 'modes' of understanding. It is no different in actual conversation or in handling a text, especially when genuine communication doesn't occur. We may initially talk past the other, and then return to the other with clarification. Even if both partners in dialogue finally have something as a result of conversation, it may only be a superficial 'harmony of agreement' that never quite escapes 'distorted communication'. Merely 'understanding' the viewpoint of the other isn't enough. Understanding may be where the conversation actually stopped, and perhaps the other has already changed his or her standpoint in the process of presenting it. Nobody who takes the hermeneutic problem seriously imagines that we can ever *entirely* understand the other or know what the other is thinking. More important is the fact that we *seek* to understand one another at all, and that this is a thoughtful path.

RK *So you would repudiate Derrida's critique of metaphysics as logocentric?*

H-GG What the metaphysical concept of 'presence' has to do with such a context is a complete mystery to me. A conversation worthy of the name remains with one over time and is not simply about the 'presence' of a voice speaking to a listener. Again I cannot understand how Derrida thinks that one can listen to one's own voice. We all have the experience of being startled by our own voice, for example on radio, as if by something entirely strange. Hearing our own voice is one of the strangest things that self-knowledge can experience. Perhaps it is exactly in this shock that unconscious familiarity is concealed. Derrida has himself developed the concept of *différance*, a concept that has an exact parallel in Heidegger's treatment, or whatever one may call the '*Da*' ('there') of being (*Da-Sein*). This is a 'being-there' which is like a reverse electrical current. In any case, Heidegger's '*Da*' is not '*Präsenz*' like the presence that dominates the Greek worldview and that is fixed by Derrida as the concept of *présence*.

RK *What do you believe Derrida actually means by deconstruction?*

H-GG When Derrida speaks of deconstruction, I understand it precisely in its concrete execution, specifically as a surprising radical upheaval that sheds new light. I won't venture to exemplify his French concept in quite this way, because connotations intrude in a foreign language. I prefer to look at Derrida's reflection, say, on Heidegger's 'Nietzsche' and the quotation marks surrounding it. I understand that reflection very well, and would even maintain that Derrida understands Heidegger very well. The quotation marks indicate that Heidegger was here suggesting an 'interpretation-unit' which he himself disagreed with. In Heidegger's view, for the will-to-power and eternal recurrence to be the same only means that both present a dwindling stage of a being that has sunk into the foregetfulness-of-Being. And Heidegger did not think that this forgetfulness-of-Being can ever be definitive.

To look at another example, in *What Is Thinking*? Heidegger is playing with a double meaning. We may say that deconstruction alerts us to the fact that behind the apparent 'meaning', there is a secret call that suddenly breaks through. Wherever one meets such examples in Derrida's own work, the reader seeks to understand and to enter new horizons through them. Why would he write otherwise? In any case, such a break is not a breaking-off, but rather a beginning, and this beginning represents a going beyond everything said. Such is the hermeneutic experience that we create with each other constantly. Each of us would become a comedy figure if we took the 'other' at his *literal* word, even though we have really understood him. I wouldn't want to say that deconstruction is incompatible with hermeneutics, rather the reverse. All of us rely firmly on hermeneutics, as soon as we open our mouths to speak.

JC What role does the concept of intersubjectivity play in hermeneutics?

H-GG If we describe conversation as an intersubjective 'play' with language, we are already deeply immersed in the language of metaphysics. This immersion is so deep that we no longer believe ourselves able to say what we mean by a 'conversation' without the concept of the 'subject'. The term 'intersubjective' has become fashionable ever since the beginning of our century. At that time, Buber, Haecker and others, stimulated by Kierkegaard, began the critique of transcendental idealism. With Husserl, we can understand how he arrives at a concept like 'intersubjectivity' because he is determined to remain in the Cartesian sphere of subjectivity. That leads to Husserl's tireless phenomenological investigations which now fill three thick volumes. It also leads to the utterly absurd consequence that we first intend the 'other' as an object of perception constituted by aspects, etc., and then in a higher-level act, confer on this 'other' the character of a 'subject' through transcendental empathy. We can admire the consistency with which Husserl holds fast to the primacy of his approach. However, we notice that the narrowness and one-sidedness of the ontology of presence cannot be avoided by such an approach.

RK *Was Heidegger captive to a similar one-sidedness?*

H-GG In my opinion, Heidegger did not succeed in jumping over Husserl's shadow with his concept of '*Mitsein*' (being-with) in *Being and Time*. Heidegger's analyses were so pioneering because he disclosed the hermeneutic structure of *Dasein* and explored the possibility of '*Mitsein*'. However, he diminished the truth of 'conversation' when he got lost in the critique of idle talk (*Gerede*). I don't say this merely to criticise, but rather to reveal the flaws whereby Heidegger's attempt to connect with Husserl by deploying a transcendental framework in *Being and Time* led to a dead-end. The absence of the projected second volume of *Being and Time* is evidence of this dead-end. I would also characterise Habermas's 'ideal-speech situation' in the same way. It is an 'ideal-type' construction which collapses under the burden of what Habermas seeks to build on it. He attacks rhetoric as a means of illegitimate and forced persuasion. Such a view indicates the narrowness of a lifeworld that seems like a 'detention pending trial', wherein an ongoing interrogation is artificially isolated and scientifically analysed. Sometimes it seems the same with Ricoeur, whose sensitive richness and attention to theoretical differences I certainly admire, in particular his teaching on metaphor. In a poem, it has been rightly said, every word is a metaphor. But I miss the fundamental ground of rhetoric - the art of wanting to convince others of what we are already convinced.

RK *In your opinion, what precise role does the language of rhetoric and metaphor play in hermeneutics?*

H-GG If we want to clarify the role of language in hermeneutics, we discover that Greek already gives us some indication – because it doesn't even have a specific word for 'language'! That shows how much language is unconscious of itself. But that doesn't mean that it remains entirely hidden and concealed. Quite the opposite! Language is wherever it is, where conversation takes place. It is so omnipresent that nothing else is really present, not the speaker and not the one spoken to. In the hermeneutic analysis of *Truth and Method*, I hit upon the insight that language isn't exclusively a matter of spoken expression. The diversity of languages does not present the problem here. Language as a hermeneutic phenomenon is not an example among different languages. I have used the artificial expression 'linguisticality' (*Sprachlichkeit*) to refer to interior speech. This concept is developed from the Stoics, and differs especially from the '*logos prophorikos*', in that it is in no way found in any *one* of the many spoken languages. *Sprachlichkeit* rather indicates the inexpressible capacity that underlies and is actualised in all particular linguistic expression. From my studies of Augustine I have drawn analyses of the process-character of internal speech, analyses which show how a happening-of-being manifests itself for him in the mystery of the Trinity – for which presence (*Präsenz*) or other models of time are not at all appropriate.

Even the 'while' or 'duration', with which Bergson contrives to avoid the time of the moment, is admittedly not yet radical enough to successfully stand against the ontology of substance and presence. Neither is the concept of communication adequate for that purpose, because here the particularity of '*Sprachlichkeit*' is not articulated along with it. Infectious laughter is perhaps one of the strongest forms of communication between human beings, but that is really not language, and even less écriture. Laughter also has nothing of the inner language which is put into words in the hundreds of different languages of mankind.

Hermeneutics and politics

RK *What are the ethical and political implications of your hermeneutics? Is there a conservative agenda, as some suggest, behind your respect for tradition?*

H-GG When such questions are put to me, I always sense an expectation that I must leave unfulfilled. Even if one grants me that hermeneutics is not a 'method', in our thinking the schema of means-and-ends takes such priority that the question of what hermeneutics actually is *meant for* always intrudes. One would at least like to be told whether or not it overlaps with practical philosophy, thereby legitimating itself by its usefulness.

But even the idea of practical philosophy resonates strongly with the misunderstanding of modern utilitarianism. A practical philosophy is, of course, supposed to be practical, applicable like an instruction manual. In reality, that is a misreading of the concepts of 'praxis' and 'practical'. These Greek ideas have no such petty connotation. One realises particularly in this concept of 'praxis' how, in much the same way, the concept of substance in Aristotle's ontology becomes misleading through its modern historical development.

RK *What precisely do you understand as 'praxis' in this context?*

H-GG 'Praxis' is not an 'action' (*Handeln*) – a word which is very often incorrectly substituted for it in German. The concept of action (*Handeln*) is imbued with voluntarism and resonates with the calculations of profit and cost; it has no place really in the linguistic field of 'praxis'. Praxis is a self-comportment, and we apply the word in entirely different domains: for example, the medical praxis of a doctor does not take place in his private apartment. And even when one uses the expression 'behaving' (*sich-verhalten*) for praxis, the concept of 'action' (*Handeln*) is still very much part of it. One is hardly able to overhear or discern that in all 'behaving' (*sich-verhalten*), there is also tucked away a 'containing-oneself' (*an-sich-halten*); or even a 'holding-oneself-back' (*sich-zurückhalten*) and a 'finding-oneself' (*sich-befinden*). We ought to remember that the standard phrase concluding a letter in Greek was '*eu prattein*', which in German would be '*Lass es dir gut gehen*' ('Let it go well with you'). In many regions in Germany one still says '*machs gut*' ('do good'), without asking oneself what it actually is that one will or should do.

It is helpful to remember this lexical domain if we want to understand practical philosophy. We mustn't understand it as applied science, for example, something like applied mathematics that differs from pure mathematics. Obviously, in the expression 'practical philosophy', we have before us a peculiar creation of Aristotle. In its more usual sense, philosophy is theory; indeed, it is the embodiment of a theoretical comportment. And now Aristotle asserts that there is also a 'practical philosophy'. We here find ourselves right in the middle of hermeneutic philosophy in our own day; and this demands something decisive from the return to Aristotle's concepts. This concerns the difference between theoretical and practical knowledge: the difference between the wisdom of the knower and the wakefulness of one who acts. The Aristotelian expression for the latter is '*phronesis*'.

By the way, this question presents itself independently of the linguistic observations we are making. The old Socratic pseudo-solution – that virtue is knowledge and lack of virtue is ignorance – tries to steer clear of the entire problem. Practical philosophy, which speaks of virtue, would then be akin to theoretical philosophy that speaks of nature. There is something unsatisfactory about that. Should one just talk about virtue in the same way that one speaks about mere occurrences? Should one neither lead nor educate towards virtue? Can the difference between the theoretical knowledge of celestial phenomena, on the one hand, and the foundations established in education, on the other hand, be dispensed with so easily? It becomes apparent that such a fusion of theoretical and practical philosophy is impossible, when one acknowledges that virtue or goodness (or whatever one calls it) has a political and social component. Practical philosophy doesn't just apply to the individual who acts in society: it applies to society itself, which can be constituted in its political condition for better or worse, and which can act for better or worse. Ethics and politics are both practical philosophies in their Greek genesis.

JC But what is philosophical ethics and what is political science in our own day?

H-GG To approach this question we have to return once again to Aristotle, the founder of practical philosophy. At the beginning of the *Nicomachean Ethics*, Aristotle considers practical philosophy in relation to both ethics and politics. The two are not independent of each other. Ethics concerns the life of the individual in society, while politics, by comparison, concerns the proper constitution of society itself. For both there is only one good – the life-happiness of the individual as well as the polis. However, the highest aim of politics is linked with the well-being of the individual. Politics concerns the legal regulation of our life-in-community (*Zusammenleben*) that in Greek was called 'legislation', and it also includes the education of the young. Therein lies the difficult question: what does philosophy as philosophy have in both instances for its legitimation?

Obviously, it's not always a case of purely theoretical interests, just rather the highest practical ideal of human happiness. Just as the individual, who in every case must make his or her choice in a unique situation, wishes to serve this highest goal, the same holds true for the political office-holder in the polis. Expertise will be indispensable for both, what the greeks called '*episteme*' or '*techne*'. In his dialogue *The Statesman*, Plato makes a specific distinction between that which can be taken possession of with precise measurement, and that which has its own measures within itself – for instance, the virtue of moderation. And he declares both necessary for politics. But the individual, like the politician, must also look towards the highest aim of all praxis – and this 'looking' the Greeks called '*nous*'. Both must internalise this highest goal. Useless beauty has priority over usefulness, unless necessity compels an insistence upon the useful.

RK *Is is misguided to look to philosophy for guidance in moral and political life?*

H-GG Philosophy itself is in no position to give an actual foundation for virtue or duty. That is what people have mistakenly sought in the Kantian approach to duty-ethics in Kant's *Foundations of the Metaphysics of Morals*. Philosophy can't give the foundation of right action for either the individual or society; rather, it helps keep us on course in the direction of the good (to which one is already open), and seeks to safeguard us from error. That is all. And it is already a great deal. This is the autonomy which Kant defends. One doesn't give oneself the law, but rather accepts the law, so that one will not sneak by it.

RK *Is hermeneutics 'neutral' then?*

H-GG It is senseless to want to designate any political orientation to hermeneutics. Admittedly, a certain expertise may be required to comment concretely on the situation of the individual as well as of society as a whole. But in every case we must remember to keep in mind the *well-being* of the individual and the *well-being* of the whole. This is true especially in democracy, whose essential features Aristotle was the first to outline. We have political parties, all of which claim to have the correct proposals for ordering social matters. Naturally, this holds true for every political aberration as well, whose cause lies in a lack of expertise that oversimplifies utopian ways of thinking. All of us, as individuals and citizens, are capable of such reductionist thinking, and this lack of expertise makes itself felt through all judgements in individual and political life. Above all, this tendency to oversimplify means that every human being has his weaknesses.

Our political world has its own problems. Even though a democracy need not be defined as a parliamentary democracy, it's still true that the formation of parties which repudiate the very foundation of political constitutions are not permitted. Whether one is more conservative or more innovative has nothing to do with it. Thus, we can already recognise, in the case of Heidegger, the portents of the terribly wrong decision of 1933, as well as a certain one-sidedness in his earlier development and thought. However, this doesn't at all affect the basic insight we owe him: that human *Dasein*, in all its domains, possesses a hermeneutic structure. Heidegger's error of political judgement regarding the 'Being' of the Führer, or his own unsuitability for politics, is not due to his characterisation of the hermeneutic structure of *Dasein* as understanding itself and things.

RK *Hermeneutics is not just a matter of interpreting texts therefore?*

H-GG For me hermeneutics is more than the interpretation of texts. Hermeneutics is not only a Being-towards-text. Whoever thinks this annihilates the decisive step of Husserl and Heidegger that led to the lifeworld. One can only recommend today a reading of the chapters of Aristotle's *Politics*. What was at that time to be criticised is still to be criticised today: namely, the priority of the useful *vis-à-vis* the beautiful.

RK *Are you suggesting that hermeneutic philosophy can guide or direct us from interpretation to social commitment?*

H-GG There is a natural demand latent in that question: what does hermeneutics as philosophy have to offer for the solution of our problems today or in the future? I don't believe that we would ask this question of theologians or prophets. We know that worldly wisdom is not to be gotten from them. Why expect advice and instruction from philosophers in such a situation? Surely, it must have something to do with our reflections on the vital problems of human *Dasein*, for example, on beginning and end, birth and death, evil and good, right and wrong. However, all of these milestones lie on a path that doesn't lead to a goal that can be reached quickly. We can't expect that the mere power of thought, concentration, and dedication to thinking can become another kind of trail-blazing.

My attempt to dampen this expectation, by specifically dealing with the paradox of practical philosophy, will hardly reach human beings who are oppressed by the worries of daily existence. But that is precisely what is so hard for human beings to grasp: that we all stand in such complicated life-circumstances that nobody is in a position to work out clear final goals that are agreeable to everyone. According to Socrates, the question of the good is actually unanswerable; and yet for everyone a knowledge of the good is indispensable if we are to remain directed toward the future in what we do and don't do. We must take the Socratic question seriously. We know then that we ourselves are responsible for our actions. We have to admit that for a long time we've been ready to overestimate the capabilities of experts in this world. But the true expert knows the limits of his competence. Why do we expect the philosopher not to recognise the boundaries of his competence? That is the true situation. I have only this answer: like everyone else, we philosophers are not excused from the question of the good, nor do we have privileged access to it. We are not experts. Everyone must pose this question for himself.

Even the conscientious expert will hesitate and carefully maintain his limits when giving advice, so that the road towards 'the good' won't be blocked by his advice. These are the inevitable features of our complicated delegation of knowledge to the expert, which apply to experts in politics as well. And yet it is not much different in every stage of human social development. We are never exempt from the question of whether we can justify what we do – or don't do – before ourselves or before God. The issue of human weakness can't be ignored, and we should, moreover, remain aware of the limits of our ever attaining mastery in our present and future existence. Hermeneutics insists that we recognise these limits, both in general and in particular cases. Only then can a real coexistence of cultures and societies on this planet become possible. Only then can we discover solidarity through the exchange of our limited experiences. Hermeneutics isn't the invention of any particular thinker; it names what we all have known since human beings have organised their lives together. At best, philosophy has eased some of the burdens on us through its expertise.

Hermeneutics and science

RK *Is hostility towards science implicit in your confrontation between truth and method, as it is in Heidegger?*

H-GG Let's change the formulation of the question a bit. It's not a case of a friendly or hostile relationship with science. This doesn't apply in the least to Heidegger. In his 'Examen Rigorosum' Heidegger elected to take mathematics and physics as examination subjects, in addition to philosophy. He did not confine his examinations to the historical sciences, for example, church history or religious scholarship, in which he was certainly competent. Philosophy is not concerned with the *methods* of science: it is concerned with the *foundations* of all science and all other experience. Hermeneutic philosophy doesn't exclude the sciences; therefore, it frees us from a superficial conception of subjective and objective in order to properly grasp the foundations of science.

RK *Does this entail a reorientation of our understanding of truth?*

H-GG It certainly requires an enlargement of our concept of 'truth' reaching beyond the ideal of precision in the quantitative sciences, an ideal which the natural sciences cannot completely fulfil. In the so-called human sciencies (*Geisteswissenschaften*), one operates for the most part in a sphere different from 'exactness'. One is not in the domain of precise measurement, but rather in the domain of things that have measures in themselves, such as the virtues of moderation, courage, etc. Fundamentally, this problem concerns the relationship between rules and regulations. With his emphasis on judgement, Kant correctly said that for the correct application of rules, there is *not* just another rule. One cannot learn judgement as if it were a science made up of true propositions. One must practise it and develop it out of one's own experience.

JC How can one reconcile the domains of understanding (Verstehen) and explanation (Erklärung)?

H-GG The much-discussed opposition of understanding and explanation lags far behind the universality of hermeneutic experience. It is understood as an opposition of a scientific-theoretical kind. The debate of the nineteenth century in Germany was totally dominated by this question. 'Value philosophy' was the theoretical expression of an alternate approach. As I have shown, however, judgement isn't a question of the correctness of rules, but rather a question of the appropriate application or non-application of rules. And so hermeneutics is that aspect of philosophy that includes the universal expanse of all problems of application, as well as of values and therefore of all technology. It can itself have no criteria. Take the example of a brain transplant or genetic cultivation of a robot. As these phenomena emerge, the first reaction of the public is strong and disturbed, pointing to a dimension that neither science as such, nor value philosophy, nor so-called 'ethics' could claim for themselves.

This may all sound general, especially when conversational dialogue is here again placed in the foreground, in contrast to our educational institutions and universities where the fundamental style of teaching is the lecture. Indeed, it is an astounding atavism that we still use the lecture as a method of teaching, since it is based on the mere transmission of a general body of recognised knowledge. Even Kant had to give his lectures based on previously written textbooks in philosophy, and from these he had to work out his own revolutionary way of thinking. Today the universities can no longer support such a one-sided transmission of an unquestioned canon. Nor can the professors of philosophy. However, we can demand what Kant demanded: to teach thinking, instead of passing on doctrine. This is what is called 'ability' (*Können*): to practise an ability-to-question and an ability-to-think. Naturally, one uses this in all sciences, but these sciences have only developed their *methods* with it. Are there corresponding rules and customs in the praxis of life? We return once again to the fact that we need judgement in science as well as in the lifeworld.

Hermeneutics and theology

RK *Is the hermeneutic question of Being compatible with the question of God?*

H-GG That sounds too much like a scientific-theoretical thematic! However, in formulating the question this way, we thereby underestimate both philosophy and theology. On the one hand, philosophy may have a universal hermeneutic basis, but it also deals with other problems. We likewise underestimate theology by treating theology as identicial with religion. This is simply not the case. We can think of the special place of so-called Greek 'orthodoxy' within Christianity which, despite its name, involved no theology at all, but rather the practical care and worship of the soul and its unassailable status in human life. However, we cannot ignore the fact that the idea of ecumenism in the present world situation concerns not only the Christian world, but the other great world religions as well, or perhaps even religious experiences that have almost no written tradition at all.

We can, of course, ask ourselves how philosophy stands *vis-à-vis* religion. Heidegger's well-known methodological verdict – that there cannot be a Christian philosophy because philosophy in the methodical sense is atheistic – obviously accentuates the difference between philosophy and theology. We might ask whether there can be 'theology' in other world religions or whether this is a specific development of the West. As we know, historically speaking, science itself has been a phenomenon of Western civilisation.

It is incorrect, however, to suggest a special affinity for hermeneutics with the theology of nineteenth-century Germany and its exponent, Schleiermacher. The whole history of theology speaks against it, in particular the pedagogical tradition of the Catholic Church. Unlike the Reformation, Catholicism insisted there be something like a philosophical theology, that is, a science based on reason. The question of God had to be open to examination by everyone without relying on revelation or faith. We can say, however, that with the advance of the Enlightenment in the modern era, the tension between philosophy and religion in the face of Luther's reformationist 'By faith alone' came into sharpened conflict with the scientific mind. In earlier centuries, a universal science based on reason contained the concept of all science. In this respect, it is naturally true that with the rising self-consciousness of the Age of Science, the appeal to absolute faith turned into a hermeneutic mysticism. The modern Enlightenment thinker speaks then of '*sacrificium intellectus*'; and on the other side, the Christian speaks of the paradox of faith, or about how the limits of understanding faith become manifest to the believer.

Certainly, we can ask if the question of God, which belongs to theology, has grown together with the philosophical question of Being. Heidegger's dictum that a Christian philosophy is absurd is directed against such harmonisations. We must, after all, ask if the question of Being, which Parmenides was the first to ask, isn't closely related to all the wonders of *Dasein*, and whether it leads to Leibniz's foundational question: 'Why is there something rather than nothing?' We call *that* the basic question of metaphysics. But is the 'religious' thought of the creation and the creator included in this question? Would that not include the Greek concept of Being which has dominated both Greek philosophy, and the thought of the Christian Middle Ages? In the church history of the West, this has issued in a lasting debate with Platonic heresies. On the other hand, it applies equally to the Gnostic heresies which maintained that, in the end, human reason needed no divine revelation but would unite the self with the One.

The future of hermeneutics

RK *What do you see as the future of hermeneutics?*

H-GG When we ask about the future of hermeneutics we mean not only its own internal process, but also the claim that in a world organised more and more through regulation, an awareness of the limits of our world-system is emerging. It is not easy to imagine a future in which the robot thrives supreme. We see ourselves referring back to the fact that our mother tongue is an inviolable endowment for the course of our lives. The German word [*Muttersprache*] reminds us of the mother and, by extension, thereby of birth. At the same time, it reminds us of the way human life articulates itself in different language communities and how secondary all interlingual possibilities of understanding between speech communities are. This is essentially the problem of translation, of its desirability and its questionability.

We cannot blind ourselves to the fact that the peaceful coexistence of human beings on this earth depends, to a large extent, on the cultivation of interlingual exchanges between nations. The breath-taking expansion of the world economy that today embraces humanity cannot deceive us about the fact that such a competitive economy, in which human capacities are developed, simultaneously creates new controversies and contains the temptation to resort to violence. Nevertheless, we cannot easily convince ourselves that the elementary drives of will-to-power that permeate everything should have the last word. With due respect to economic competition and performance, to the self-discipline of human beings and to their energy for work – it seems inevitable that there will always be some object of conflict, if only because nobody can possess it without others claiming a share in it too.

RK *So what does this augur for the future in practical terms?*

H-GG Certainly, humanity today is still far removed from a unified ideal of world culture in which all human beings could have a part. Such an ideal would encompass a higher moral value, in so far as more human beings could gain a share in it. Sometimes it seems as if the world of music might announce such a world culture beyond all differences of language and culture. But then we remember and know the kind of incomparable intimacy possessed for its part by the mother tongue, nativeness, the care of ancestral memory, and all the other unconscious characteristics that form us from an early age. These are traditions in which all human beings stand and from which we look forward. It strikes me as a bit ridiculous to regard these traditions and formative experiences – which are forms of self-understanding for human beings – as atavisms to be overcome. Hermeneutics as philosophy demands a special awareness of these differences and their reconciliation as a task which has founded community among humans since time immemorial. And in any conceivable future it must continue to do the same. Can we really believe that a 'correct speech' or analytically linguistic precision could replace the mother tongue and her world-disclosing power? We must think *with* language, not about it or against it.

(Paris–Heidelberg, 1994)

Select bibliography in English

Truth and Method, trans. and ed. G. Barden and J. Cumming, Seabury Press, New York, 1975.

Philosophical Hermeneutics, trans. and ed. D. E. Linge, University of California, Berkeley, 1976.

Dialogue and Dialectic: Eight Hermeneutical Studies on Plato, trans. P. Christopher Smith, Yale University Press, New Haven, 1980.

Reason in the Age of Science, trans. F. G. Laurence, MIT Press, Cambridge, 1981.

Hegel's Dialectic: Five Hermeneutical Studies, trans. P. Christopher Smith, Yale University Press, New Haven, 1982.

Philosophical Apprenticeship, trans. R. R. Sullivan, MIT Press, Cambridge, 1985.

The Idea of the Good in Platonic-Aristotelian Philosophy, trans. P. Christopher Smith, Yale University Press, New Haven, 1986.

The Relevance of the Beautiful and Other Essays, trans. N. Walker, ed. R. Bernasconi, Cambridge University Press, Cambridge, 1986.

'Reply to Jacques Derrida', in *Dialogue and Deconstruction: The Gadamer-Derrida Encounter*, trans. and ed. D. P. Michelfelder and R. E. Palmer, State University of New York Press, Albany, 1989.

Plato's Dialectical Ethics: Phenomenological Interpretations Relating to the Philebus, trans. R. M. Wallace, Yale University Press, New Haven, 1991.

Heidegger's Ways, State University of New York Press, Albany, 1994.

Literature and Philosophy in Dialogue, State University of New York Press, Albany, 1994.

JEAN-FRANÇOIS LYOTARD

What is just? (*Ou Justesse*)

Prefatory note

JEAN-FRANÇOIS LYOTARD was born in Versailles, France in 1924. Although he began his philosophical career with a study entitled *La Phénoménologie* (1954), devoted largely to the work of Merleau-Ponty, it was with the publication of *The Postmodern Condition* in 1979 that Lyotard's thought gained widespread currency in the English-speaking world. Lyotard's critical insights into contemporary connections between culture, science, technology and politics have exerted a radical impact not just on philosophy but on the human sciences generally. Indeed the innovative and interdisciplinary manner of his thinking has set the style for a distinctively 'postmodern' approach.

While Lyotard's thinking is deeply informed by phenomenological thinkers like Heidegger, Merleau-Ponty and Lévinas, it is also marked by other influences. During his association with the *Socialisme ou barbarie* group in the sixties, Marx and Adorno were frequent references. In the seventies Freud became a central figure as evidenced in such publications as *Dérive à partir de Marx et Freud* (1973), *Des dispositifs pulsionnels* (1973) and *Economie libidinale* (1974). In the eighties and nineties, Wittgenstein, Nietzsche and the Kant of the Third Critique were added to the list of critical influences, particularly the latter's thinking on 'reflective judgment' and the 'sublime'.

But Lyotard is far more than the sum of his intellectual mentors. His contributions to the 'postmodern' debate – in philosophy, art and politics – are singular in matter and style. They represent original reflections on language, time, desire, production and justice, summed up in his hallmark concept of the 'differend' – a difference between two parties which cannot be reduced to neutral categories of consensus, universality or symmetry. It is this sublime irreducibility of the 'thing' which, for Lyotard, marks the 'event' of ethics and aesthetics. The so-called Grand Narratives of Western culture – from Greek and Christian metaphysics to Enlightenment rationalism – stand rebuked by the singularity of events which refuse to be 'totalised' or explained away. Such events can only be represented, Lyotard believes, by 'little narratives' (*petits récits*) which testify to a lack of closure, an absence of final authority and, ultimately, a fundamental 'irrepresentability' of what matters. 'Justice', for Lyotard, is the mark of such vigilant testimony. It is the sign of a humility of thought and action which defies ideological and speculative systems.

Lyotard's trenchant critique of key categories of modernity – humanism, theory, capitalism, universality – has placed him in the 'deconstructive' and 'post-structuralist' camps of Continental thinking, alongside Derrida, Foucault and Deleuze. But Lyotard resists all easy categorisations, calling as he does for a 'new responsibility' capable of distinguishing genuine postmodern intelligence from the 'paranoia that gave rise to modernity'.

Lyotard taught philosophy at the University of Paris for many years and has been a Visiting Professor at the Universities of California, Wisconsin, Montreal, Stoneybrook, Minnesota, Emory, Yale and Johns Hopkins. He is a council member, and former President, of the Collège International de Philosophie.

This dialogue was completed in Atlanta, Georgia in April 1994 and translated by Richard Kearney.

RK *Today you are seen as the first philosopher of the 'postmodern' condition. Yet one of your earliest works was entitled* La phénoménologie *(1954). How would you describe the development of your own thinking – from phenomenology to postmodernism? Is there a continuity between the two?*

J-FL *La phénoménologie* was a homage to the thought of Merleau-Ponty: a meditation on the body, on sensible experience and, therefore – in contradistinction to Hegel, Husserl, Sartre – on the 'aesthetic' dimension which unfolds beneath the phenomena of consciousness. I was also reading at this time what was available of Heidegger's work. The little book on phenomenology was motivated by a concern to address the absence in Marxism of any genuine thinking about ideology. I felt it was important to establish how the possibility, and success, of the revolution depended on the 'consciousness' that workers could and should have of their situation and desire. The work done by both Tran-Duc-Thao and Claude Lefort in this direction was very useful. I was then a committed member of the *socialisme ou barbarie* project (from 1952 to 1966), whose main objects of critique were dogmatic Marxism, Stalinist politics, the class structure of 'Soviet' society, the inconsistencies of the Trotskyist position and post-war capitalism (quite the opposite of 'late' or declining capitalism). Our practical activities included co-operating with workers, wage-earners and students with a view to establishing self-management groups. I left this project in 1966 when I realised that the basis of both our practice and theory was lacking – the alternative figure of the proletariat (Marx's 'spectre') as a labouring class conscious of its goals. I only began to formulate the idea of the 'postmodern' in the late 1970s, after a long detour. The term, purposefully ambiguous, was borrowed from American criticism and Ihab Hassan. I used it to 'name' the transformation of bourgeois capitalism and its contradictions into a global 'system' ruling, for better or worse, its imbalances (including those in the 'ideological' field, henceforth entitled 'cultural') with the help of growth due to techno-scientific means. Several things were becoming clear: that a new dominant class – the managers – was replacing the private owners without capital, that the work-force was no longer of the nineteenth-century kind, that the redistribution of surplus value was done in a completely different way, and that a structural level of unemployment was emerging even though we were still in a period of full employment. In these changing circumstances, it was necessary to review radically the nature of history and politics.

RK *Given the multiple definitions of 'postmodernism' which circulate in contemporary debate, do you believe your initial formulations of this term – in* The Postmodern Condition *and* The Postmodern Explained *– have been misinterpreted or altered? Could you describe the basic meaning of 'postmodern' as something more than an historical 'period'?*

J-FL There have been many misunderstandings indeed, including my own. The notion of periodisation is one of them – a typically 'modern' mania. The essential features of the postmodern as it manifests itself today seem to me numerous. They include the generalisation of the constraint of exchangeability (the old 'exchange value' of Marx) which traditionally weighs on the objects and 'services' of capitalism, and its extension to include hitherto unexploited objects and activities: opinions, feelings, cultural pleasures, leisure, disease and death, sexuality, and so on. (Totalitarian systems took the lead here in a terrifying fashion and the message was heard and duly corrected.) One might also mention the constraint of 'complexification' with respect to the relations of work, consummation and communication, whose effect is to 'optimise' the performance of the system; the concomitant collapse of traditional values (labour, disinterested knowledge, virtue, the sense of life-debt) – the crisis of education in all the developed countries is a direct witness to this collapse. Then there are the current phenomena of latent nihilism (in Nietzsche's 'passive' sense) and 'discontent' (in Freud's sense), not to mention chronic anxiety due to absence of symbols – which camouflage themselves as individualism, cynicism, the cult of play, the almost compulsory sense of celebratory conviviality, the obsession with participation and interaction, the return to roots. This 'postmodern' situation discloses nothing new. On the contrary, in the name of the fulfillment of liberties, the Western will-to-knowledge (and by extension doubt) and will-to-power (and by extension mastery) has 'secreted' (*secrète*) nihilism from its beginnings: death of the gods, death of God, death of Man. The 'system' functions simply as a very improbable type of organisation – the living organism, and subsequently the human being and the brain already functioned in this way – which draws the energy it needs in the energetic chaos which formerly went by the name of nature or cosmos (the immense fall-out from an enigmatic explosion . . .). But in response to your question, I would situate the 'basic meaning' of the postmodern above all in the way the Western will discovers the 'nothingess' (*néant*) of its objects and projects, thereby finding itself inhabited by something which it neither comprehends nor masters. Some 'thing' crypted in itself, which resists us. Its name is irrelevant. It is 'unnameable' because too rapidly named.

RK *How then can we say anything about it? What evidence do we have of its existence? How does 'it' show itself?*

J-FL All the thinkers, writers and artists of the West, including the great 'rationalists', stumbled upon this 'thing', sought to name it, realised its inexpungeability, and recognised that no odyssey, no Grand Narrative could contain it.

RK *This brings us, of course, to your famous critique of the 'grand narratives' of the Western tradition (Marxism, Judaeo-Christianity, Enlightenment rationalism, etc). But is it possible, or even desirable, to do away with every kind of narrative model? Is there a way in which* des petits récits *might serve an ethical-political task? Is the commitment to a pluralistic paradigm of little narratives compatible, for example, with a basic defence of a charter of universal rights? What I'm really asking is: is it possible to avoid relativism in order to save what is best in the Enlightenment fidelity to shared human values that are non-culture-specific? In short, is it possible to reconcile your defence of the singularity of the event with a certain minimal* universality *of rights and duties – that is, of justice?*

J-FL I protest, first, against the expression 'Judaeo-Christian'. The hyphen signals the annexation of the Torah to the Good News of the Incarnation. This is a traditional usage, I know. But it is nevertheless unjust in the strongest sense of the term; and after the Shoah, it represents an insult to the 'people' who were victims of extermination (when one recalls the role of Vatican politics at the time). That said, I do not know whether the defence of universal valid human rights is 'compatible', as you say, with a proper attention to the event in its opacity (as mentioned above in relation to 'the thing'). To tell the truth, this question of compatibility doesn't really bother me, being neither Leibnizean nor Hegelian. On the one hand, it is evident that rights must be defended by every citizen against the 'cynical' effects of the efficiency demands of the system; and on the other hand, we are indebted to the 'thing' irremediably. Why seek to reconcile these? That kind of fraternisation is always to be feared.

RK *Why? Can you give me an example?*

J-FL A notorious example: Heidegger, the author of *Sein und Zeit*, construing the politics of *Mein Kampf* as pretext for the manifestation of *Dasein*'s dread.

RK *Are you saying that we cannot use 'little narratives' in the cause of universal rights?*

J-FL I am saying that it would be futile to consider using *des petits récits*. Always and everywhere, in Tibet, the Amazon or Livry-Gargan, they use us to tell themselves. They mock illusions of grandeur. The kitchens and stables of Shakespeare laugh at the tragedies of court, just as in Rabelais the bad boys mock the knowing and the powerful. What is little is almost invariably comic. To laugh is to acknowledge that the thing is unsayable – that its tragic dramatisation is pure vanity. Beckett is funny in this way also. But that doesn't make up a humanist party.

RK *Does your departure from the Enlightenment and Marxist projects necessarily condemn you to 'neo-conservatism' as Habermas and others claim? How do you now consider the political positions you adopted during the* Socialisme ou barbarie *period?*

J-FL It is logical to accuse 'postmodernism' (a term I never use to describe my work) of neo-conservatism if one holds to the modern project. Reciprocally, the modernist obstinacy could be taxed with 'archeo-progressivism' . . . I never used these kinds of terms to differentiate myself from Habermas and his disciples. This rhetoric of political tribunals had some sense when conflicts of thought were immediately transcribable into public tragedy: one was obliged to solemnly denounce the Enemy in the adversary. Habermas has obviously mistaken his epoch. I never viewed his discourse ethics as an ideology of the enemy.

RK *How would you identify the ethical and political motivation implicit in the arguments of* The Postmodern Condition, *and subsequent works such as* The Inhuman? *What are the implications of Apollinaire's claim that artists and intellectuals nowadays should make themselves 'inhuman'? Does this mean that postmodernism is incompatible with 'humanism'?*

J-FL I only use the term 'postmodernism', let me repeat, as a label of convenience for a certain movement or school (in literary criticism, in architecture). I personally prefer the expressions 'the postmodern' and 'postmodernity'. I quote Apollinaire's phrase – from the *Peintres Cubistes* and which applies to cubism as a whole – because it states that the inhuman in us is the unknown thing (*la chose méconnue*), the only genuine resource of art, of literature and of meditation. *Les Essais, L'Eloge de la folie, Le Neveu de Rameau*: humanism has always been inhumanism.

RK *I'm interested in the political implications of this position, particularly as outlined in your* Political Writings. *Could you elaborate on the distinction between 'specific intellectual' and 'organic intellectual' in this work? Does the intellectual still have a role to play in the project of emancipation? And what critical function, if any, remains for the philosopher once one has declared the death of the 'modern idea of a universal subject of knowledge'? Must the postmodern intellectual limit him/herself, as you suggest, to the 'resolution of questions posed to a citizen of a particular country at a particular moment'?*

J-FL The organic intellectual has a role to play in countries more or less relegated to the margins of development. Here his work is itself the proof of both his emancipation and his belonging, and the basic problem confronting these countries is emancipation without betrayal of local culture. (One would have to locate the phenomenon of fundamentalism here and its strategy of assassination.) In the privileged developed countries, by contrast – and one knows how scandalously exclusive this privilege can be – great prosecution witnesses like Voltaire, Zola, Gramsci, Horkheimer, Russell, no longer seem to play a role. Formerly emancipation was under threat in Europe itself, with absolutism and totalitarianism, and the work of these already famous figures was in itself a demand for liberties. Today we face a different scenario, where critical works are rarely read, sparsely distributed except when the media latch onto them and serve them to a consumer public hungry for cultural commodities. In fact, the person who speaks for liberties on radio or television doesn't need to possess an '*oeuvre*'; it is sufficient that his/her eloquence and 'presence' on the platform are better (more effective and credible) than those of other media professionals or even than other thinkers, writers or artists. The only exceptions here are the scientists, and that by reason of the fact that the system idolises techno-scientific performances.

RK *You speak in 'Tomb of the Intellectual' of a 'new responsibility' which renders intellectuals impossible – a 'responsibility to distinguish intelligence from the paranoia that gave rise to "modernity"'? What do you mean by this 'paranoia'? And how are we to differentiate between the new responsibility of postmodern 'intelligence' and the irresponsibility of irrationalism?*

J-FL Some rationalism is the paranoia of discourse: I will say everything, know everything, possess everything, be everything. Nothing will escape the concept. On the other hand, literature must plead guilty because it is *authorised* by nothing, as Georges Bataille said (following Kafka). The 'thing' that demands writing or art has no *right* to demand it. This 'irresponsibility' is the greatest responsibility, that of remaining attentive to an Other, who is neither an interlocutor nor a party to contractual closure. It is essential to guard over this 'secret existence', as Nina Berberova called it, to protect it against the *indiscretion* of the system which wants to see and know everything, have an answer for everything, exchange everything. We need to reread Orwell.

RK *What are the implications of your postmodern idea of 'inhumanity' for our understanding of the 'social bond'? Do you think traditional concepts of nation, state and civil society are adequate to the analysis of these implications? Have universalist notions of social progress been altered by the transition to postmodernity?*

J-FL The implosion of the big totalitarian regimes engendered by the modern dream provokes a nostalgia for 'natural' communities, defined by blood, land, language, custom. Fidelity to the *demos* takes priority here over respect for the republican ideal. The latter is nonetheless the only veneer of legitimacy for the system to require all countries in the world to remain open to the free circulation of goods, 'services' and communications. It is in fact essential for the Republic to become universal. In its name, the 'market' is permitted to assume world proportions. That is why, today, the privilege of sovereignty which nation states enjoyed for several centuries (at most), appears an obstacle to the furtherance of development in every domain: multinational transactions, immigrant populations, international security . . . It may even be the case, despite appearances, that the unification of Europe is more easily achievable through the federation of 'natural communities' ('regions' like Bavaria, Scotland, Flanders, Catalonia, etc.) than through sovereign states – with all the risks attendant upon the dominance of the *demos* in each of these communities.

RK *This scenario would seem to support your suggestion that the 'modern' category of 'universal thinker' will be replaced by the 'symptomatologist' who responds to singular phenomena of irreducible difference* (le différend). *But would this not imply the end of philosophy as an academic discipline? What do you believe is the function now of philosophy and the university generally?*

J-FL Philosophy, we should remember, has only recently – 1811, Berlin – been recognised as an academic discipline. The ancients and the medievals didn't teach philosophy, they taught how to philosophise. It was a question of 'learning' rather than 'teaching'. To learn to find one's way in thinking, as Kant put it. Or to borrow Wittgenstein's formula – 'I no longer know where I am' is the basic position of philosophical questioning. To philosophise is not to produce useful servants of the community, as Kant well knew, which is why philosophy faculties never have the same prestige as faculties of medicine, law, economics (not to mention the exact sciences). The philosopher always has a a fundamental difficulty in presenting himself as an expert. This is not a recent phenomenon; in fact, it goes back to Socrates' struggle with the 'experts'. One could tolerate the presence (inexpensive) in pedagogical institutions of an *inexpert* discipline for as long as this aimed at forming 'enlightened citizens', capable of coping with complex or unprecedented conjunctures. The contemporary system aims at forming the experts it requires. The capacity to meditate is not much use to it. Even less so when the system has managed to produce more sophisticated automatons than digital computers. A considerable part of the academic discipline of philosophy is already geared to research (direct or indirect) into 'artificial' languages. And an inevitable consequence of this is that those who continue to think about the unexploitable 'thing' find themselves half inside the institution, half out. I think, I hope, that philosophy will manage to limp along like this for a long time, in spite of its growing loss of credibility (which also affords some prestige).

RK *Much of your work has focused on the relationship between aesthetics and politics. Why has the notion of the 'sublime', particularly as enunciated by Kant in the Third Critique, come to occupy such a pivotal position in your thinking on this relationship?*

J-FL What, from Kant to Adorno, has often been called the 'aesthetic' is that region where rational thinking encounters something in itself which violently resists it: this is 'creation', the way of making that is art, the sentiment of the absolute. Kant elaborates on the latter in his *Analytic of the Sublime*. I believe we find there a form of recollection (*anamnesis* conducted in 'critical' terms) of the relation of all thought – meditative, literary, pictural, musical – to the unknown thing which inhabits such thought. This relation is necessarily one of a *differend* internal to thought, at once capable and incapable of the absolute – 'sentiment of spirit', not of nature, like the taste of the beautiful. Kant repeats the words: *Widerstreit, Widerstand, Unangemessenheit*, differend, resistance, incommensurability. The same terms used by Van Gogh, Joyce, Schoenberg, Kierkegaard or Beckett (I cite at random) to signify the ordeal undergone by thought when it opens itself to desire for the absolute. One could even say that such thought engenders 'symptoms'. This is so for most of us, for whom the desire is no less pressing than for the writers and artists cited. But the enigma of the 'aesthetic' is that they make of this *angoisse* a work.

RK *Given your readings of Kant, Heidegger, Adorno and Derrida, would you be inclined to the view that the thinker/symptomatologist should take his/her lead more from art and literature than from the more traditional discourses of epistemology and ontology?*

J-FL I think so. But I also believe that if there is an ontology – perhaps negative – it would be found on the side of art and literature. Why? Because on that side, being (or nothing) is not situated or posited on principle as reference to cognitive discourse. It is not projected, or ejected, onto the place assigned to that *about* which one intends to speak, as in the case of the most serious epistemology. On the contrary, it is approached in a 'poetically concrete' fashion, experienced and settled like something immediate to be resolved, something present but not presented. Which word here, which colour there, which sound or melodic form? How can we *know*? It is not a matter of knowledge. Being (or nothing) doesn't wait at the door you identify. It lives in you already waiting for whatever idiom you offer it to reside in momentarily.

RK *When you contrast 'reading' to 'theory' (or interpretation) do you believe this better enables us to engage in aesthetic and ethical judgement? If we abandon 'meaning' out of fidelity to the irreducible singularity of the event, are we not eliminating the very basis of a judgement that could be shared by others in a socially committed way? How is your position compatible with solidarity – or what Hannah Arendt referred to (again in relation to Kant) as 'representative thinking', which she believes is an indispensable tool for ethical judgement?*

J-FL 'Theory' is a system of propositions formulated in explicitly defined terms according to a determined syntax. These propositions are supposed to explain all the phenomena which emerge in the field of reference to which the theory applies. (I am not discussing here the serious objections levelled against this axiomatic model by intuitionism or by the theorem of non-closure of discursive systems.) No aesthetic or ethical judgement could ever satisfy the terms of this system. It is often a 'passionate' business, often 'accomplishing' an unconscious desire, as Freud said. And it is always *dangerous*. The task is to render such judgement 'pure', free of interest, free of ends (conceptualised or not), free of all that subordinates it to something other than the appreciation of the just and the beautiful. It is at the price of such ascesis that judgement of this kind can claim to be shared with others. Everyone tries to argue, for or against, but in truth, one can only rely on the capacity of others to carry out for themselves the same kind of ascesis or 'destitution' ('*dénument*'). Arendt unscrupulously transfers Kant's aesthetic category of *sensus communis* to the order of sociality and interpersonal solidarity, as if it were some kind of 'shared feeling'. But in Kant the *sensus communis* is laboriously deduced, in the name of a transcendental affinity between diverse faculties of thought, on the basis of the 'experience' of a happiness which an 'object' can unexpectedly procure. Moreover, Arendt seems to ignore the case – for me even more significant – where thinking profits not from its affinity but its disaffinity or dissent (*dissentiment*) from itself; this is the case of the sublime, which also demands to be shared by all. As regards *ethical* decisions, if it had to authorise itself by invoking theories of Goodness or Justice, it would forfeit its ethical character forthwith. Why? Because it would lose all responsibility for what it decides submitting itself to the authority of theory. Decisions are ethical precisely when they are not authorised by a system (intelligible or otherwise), when they take upon themselves the responsibility for their 'authority'. An SS torturer is not ignoble because Hitler's 'theory' was false, but because he refuses his own responsibility and believes himself justified by obedience. Arendt refers to this as the 'banality of evil' – the banalisation of responsibility by 'necessity'. Necessity here is poverty, but it is also theory which is the poverty of morality.

RK *If existing politics is defined as a totalitarian model of Grand Narratives, is it ever possible to move from an ethics of the* differend *back to a politics of communal action? Do you think that hermeneutics, structuralism and critical theory are necessarily condemned to totalising paradigms of Grand Narrative? Is there a dialogue possible between these philosophical methods and your own?*

J-FL Such a dialogue is always possible. But the trust one places in dialogue is a hermeneutic prejudice. Can you imagine Antonin Artaud dialoguing with Bill Clinton? Dialogue is an ordinary passion. The true – the rapport with the Real (with the thing) – escapes dialogue. My philosophical colleagues haven't read Freud. If they had, they'd have at least learnt that dialogue is shot through with unconscious demands, fed on unruly transfers and countertransfers. And they would have learned that a controlled transfer, which is the most difficult of all in relation to the other, has nothing to do with 'dialogue'. That said, there is nothing against a politics of common action, and we should lend ourselves to it. As long as we attribute to it a healthy (*salubre*) rather than salvific (*salutaire*) value. It is the minimum commitment to safeguarding elementary rights of humanity as it is.

RK *Do your claims for the 'irrepresentable' and 'incommensurable' not confine you to an endlessly 'deconstructive' practice and thus prevent you from advancing to a rationally coherent model of the just and the good? How would you situate your own thinking here* vis-à-vis *Derrida or Lévinas?*

J-FL I repeat: there is no 'rationally coherent model' of justice and injustice. Such a model is the dream of the system, which someone like Rawls proposes to realise innocently(?). Look at history, at least it has the force of nihilism: abortion, divorce, homosexuality, corporal punishment (guilt itself), child education, old age, death of course, but also birth, hospital care and hospitality, war and murder, the body and competition (the first Olympic Games and Atlanta 1996). The Yes and the No have managed to accommodate each of these situations one by one, and they've always managed to rationalise them. Have my colleagues ever heard that 'rationality' is related to 'rationalisation'? This can lead to scepticism. And to this I would oppose the difficult anamnesis which decision demands: 'in my soul and my unconscious'... As for those who think, along with Spinoza and Hegel, that there is no room for judgement, I don't think they realise that God (including the *Natura naturans*) is dead. This is something Lévinas clearly signals: the risk undertaken in understanding the Other (*l'Autre*) in the other (*autrui*). That isn't an everyday occurrence like the transactions of the Wall Street Stock Exchange which a good Rawlsian reads in his evening newspaper. Finally, as regards 'deconstructive' thought, which I respect and which is also the thought of the undecidable, it has problems of necessity with decision and judgement (*Urteil*). This is as it should be; and I have reason to think it is concerned by this.

RK *Is the politics of the* differend *inevitably a politics of rhetorical dispute without finality – without solution or resolution? Paralogism and paradox as the last word? Anarchism as the last stance? Dissidence as the last cry?*

J-FL There is no 'politics of the differend'. Definitely not. The differend can only give rise to a terrible melancholy, a practice of meditation, a poetics.

RK *Can a postmodern politics do anything more than* problematise *the political as an order of representation (the function of the political in the West since Plato) from the* inside? *Is there any alternative, in your view, to the prevailing system of commodification and exchange other than a defeatist internal critique which exposes our incarceration in the labyrinth but offers no paths leading* beyond *it?*

J-FL I honestly don't think there is anything 'beyond' the system. There is something 'beneath' it, the 'thing' which Freud called infantile. Any work derived from it will itself be made into 'cultural merchandise': mistaken, misappropriated, *méprisé* as of no importance. Its quality as a work – wrestling with the absolute – will perhaps be acknowledged one day by a reader, listener or spectator.

RK *And the charge of 'defeatism'?*

J-FL 'Defeatism', as you understand it, has always been the fact of the serious, *le fait du sérieux*. Every true thought knows itself to be defeated. Aristotle's *episteme* knew itself to be incapable before the *pollakis* that Being opposes to it. The same goes for Platonic idealism before the *chora*. Relieved of doctrinaire ornament, Western thought has always been a resistance. Resistance is the way of the defeated who does not acknowledge defeat. But the claim to triumph – in the Roman sense – is the worst kind of folly. The 'beyond' does not allow itself to be approached without burning you up (*vous foudroyer*). There is nothing 'romantic' in this: it is 'realist' if anything, the relation to the *res*, the thing. That is why it is so severe and so humble to 'learn to philosophise' or to paint, to make music or a film. The apprenticeship is without end and without solution. One can make some progress, but how could one ever be satisfied? There is no defeatism in this recurrent disappointment, except for those who hold to the fantasy of full accomplishment which the system exhibits: you shall be *fulfilled*.

RK *Finally, if the politics of the differend offers no project of* forward *advance, would you claim that your notion of the Immemorial (as that which is irrepresentable to memory yet will not be forgotten) provides us with a critical task of* anamnesis, *as you call it, motivating a resistant reading of our culture? Is there a certain postmodern strategy of* looking back *without representation, a strategy which might offer more effective potential for change than the Enlightenment obsession with* future progress?

J-FL This last question would appear generous. But the alternative *backward/forward* is, in fact, extremely miserly with regard to temporality. It reduces the latter to the opposition of before and after. By the term 'immemorial', I try to express another time, where what is past maintains the presence of the past, where the *forgotten* remains *unforgettable* precisely *because* it is forgotten. This is what I mean by anamnesis as opposed to memory. In the time set out by concept and will, the project is only the 'projection' of present consequences on the future (as in 'futurology'). This kind of projection forbids the event; it prepares, preconceives, controls it in advance. This is the time of the Pentagon, the FBI, Security, the time of Empire. By contrast, what I call anamnesis is the opposite of genealogy, understood as a return to 'origins' (always projected *backward*). Anamnesis works over the remains that are still there, present, hidden near to us. And with regard to what is *not yet* there, the still to come (*l'à-venir*), it is not a matter of the future as such (which shares the Latin root, *fuit*, meaning it *has been*) but that which is still awaited with incertitude: hoped for, feared, surprising, in any case *unexpected*. It will come; but the question is: *what* will come? One can't really talk therefore of a 'postmodern *strategy*'. If there is an enemy (the obscure primitiveness of the thing, indifferent perhaps, a power both threatening and cherished), that enemy is inside each one of us. The labour of 'working through' is to find the idiom that is least inappropriate to it. One is guided here only by an obscure sentiment of *rightness* (*justesse*). But one is never satisfied with the idiom chosen and, more often than not, the other (*autrui*) doesn't understand anything. You only have to read the letters of Van Gogh, Artaud or Kafka, Augustine's *Confessions* or Montaigne's *Essays*, the life of Angelo de Foligno or the studies of Henry James – you see how the 'postmodern' is not confined to a single period – to witness the kind of resistance they encountered. One must not traduce, in the sense of translate (*traduit*), what in itself remains ciphered (*crypté*). Instead of making the ciphered common currency, we must try to do justice to its insignificance. That is what is right. That is *justesse*.

(Atlanta, Georgia, 1994)

Select bibliography in English

The Differend: Phrases in Dispute, trans. G. Van den Abbeele, University of Minnesota Press, Minneapolis, 1983.

Driftworks, trans. R. McKeon *et al.*, Semiotext(e), New York 1984.

The Postmodern Condition: A Report on Knowledge, trans. G. Bennington and B. Massumi, Manchester University Press, Manchester, 1984.
Just Gaming (with Jean-Loup Thébaud), trans. W. Godzich, Manchester University Press, Manchester, 1985.
Peregrinations: Law, Form, Event, Columbia University Press, New York, 1988.
The Inhuman, trans. G. Bennington and R. Bowlby, Stanford University Press, Stanford, 1988.
The Lyotard Reader, ed. A. Benjamin, Blackwell, Oxford, 1989.
Heidegger and the Jews, trans. A. Michel and M. S. Roberts, University of Minnesota Press, Minneapolis, 1990.
Toward the Postmodern, eds. R. Harvey and M. Roberts, Humanities Press, Atlantic Highlands, NJ, 1992.
The Postmodern Explained to Children, trans. J. Pesanis and M. Thomas, Turnaround Press, London, 1992.
Libidinal Economy, trans. I. H. Grant, Athlone Press, London, 1993.
Political Writings of Lyotard, trans. B. Readings and K. Geiman, UCL Press, London, 1993.

APPENDIX
Philosophy as dialogue

For speculation turns not to itself
Till it hath travell'd, and is mirror'd there
Where it may see itself.
Shakespeare, *Troilus and Cressida*, Act III, Scene III

The logical order of clear and distinct ideas presupposes a 'saying' (*Sprechen*) which involves one in a historical community of speakers. Our being-in-the-world is revealed historically in and through language as a dialogical being-in-the-world-with-others.

Hölderlin states this primacy of dialogical saying in the following lines of an unfinished poem:

Viel hat erfahren der Mensch . . .
Seit ein Gespräch wir sind
Und hören können voneinander
(Much has man experienced . . .
Since we are a dialogue
And can listen to one another)

Heidegger offers a gloss on these lines in a passage from his *Commentaries on Hölderlin's Poetry:*

> The being of man is grounded in language; but this really happens only in dialogue (i.e. in speaking and hearing) . . . From the time man places himself in the presence of something enduring, only from then can he expose himself to the changeable, the coming and the going. . . . We have been a dialogue since the time that 'time is'. Since time has arisen and has been brought to standing, since then we have been historical. Both – being-in-dialogue and being-historical – are equally old, belong together, and are the same.[1]

Inheriting and developing this hermeneutic model of dialogue, Gadamer and Ricoeur point out that human consciouness can never know itself in terms of an intuitive immediacy (as Descartes or the early Husserl believed). Consciousness must undergo a hermeneutic detour in which it comes to know itself through the mediation of signs, symbols and texts. In other words, consciousness cannot *intuit* (*anschauen*) its meaning in and from itself, but must *interpret* (*hermeneuein*) itself by entering into dialogue with the texts of a historical community or tradition to which it belongs (*zuhören*).

History, as the communal becoming and preservation of meaning, is a dialogue precisely because I cannot live by my own subjectivity alone. I derive my meaning through my relationship with the other (be it the individual, communal or ontological other). To say, accordingly, that truth is dialogue does not necessitate a return to the Romantic model, advanced by Schleiermacher and others, which construes dialogue in terms of a perfect intersubjective correspondence between one speaker and another. On the contrary, the dialogical model variously developed by Heidegger, Gadamer, Ricoeur and Lévinas insists that meaning always originates in some source *other* than the intuitive immediacies of subjectivity or even intersubjectivity. Meaning always remains irreducible to the immediacy of speaking subjects coexisting in a homogeneous time or space. The Romantic model of dialogue as a mutually intuitive correspondence between two human presences is no more than one possible and derived expression of the more fundamental model of a 'hermeneutic circle' in which meaning always remains *prior* to the contemporaneous co-presence of subjectivities. We do not and cannot miraculously create meaning out of ourselves. We inherit meaning from others who have thought, spoken or written *before* us. And wherever possible, we *recreate* this meaning, according to our own projects and interpretations. But we are always obliged to listen to (*hören*) what has already been spoken, in other times and places, before we can in turn speak for ourselves in the here and now.

This is a crucial distinction, particularly as it pertains to the dialogues contained in this book. We are concerned here with 'dialogue' in the sense of a spoken communication between two subjects recorded and inscribed as a written text. This passage from *speaking* to *writing* is vitally important. For when a discourse passes from speaking to writing, the entire set of coordinates in the dialogue – *subject*, *word* and *world* – undergo a significant change. What is involved is more than a mere external fixation of the spoken words which would preserve them from temporal obliteration. The inscription of a dialogue in writing grants the text an autonomy with respect to the subjective intentions of the authors. Otherwise stated, textual meaning, even in the case of a written conversation, can no longer be deemed to coincide completely with the original intentions of the speakers. While it presupposes and expresses these intentions, it also manages to *exceed* them. Once committed to writing, the meaning of the speakers is distanced or 'distanciated' in some fundamental respect. And in the process, the text transcends the finite intentional horizons of the two interlocutors and opens up new horizons of meaning: the possible worlds of the text which lend themselves to the multiplicity of the reader's own interpretations. We thus discover that the original overlapping of the two speakers' horizons (*Horizontverschmelzung*),[2] is subjected to the additional overlapping of these same horizons with the reader's own infinitely extending horizons. Put in another way, the speakers' original intentions are doubly distanced in the textual process of inscription and reading.

The written dialogue is in itself an open invitation to the reader to fill in the gaps between the original speakers' words. It summons the reader to re-create and reinterpret the authors' original meanings according to his or her own hermeneutic and experiential presuppositions. In this sense, we might say that once the reader has entered the dialogue, it becomes a dialogue that never ends. Laurence Sterne expressed this point succinctly, albeit mischievously, when he addressed his readers in *Tristram Shandy*: 'Writing when properly managed . . . is but a different name for conversation: as no one, who knows what he is about in good company, would venture to talk all; – so no author, who understands the just boundaries of decorum and good breeding, would presume to think all: The truest respect which you can pay your readers' understanding, is to halve this matter amicably, and leave him something to imagine, in his turn, as well as yourself.'[3] Sterne offers a fine blueprint for hermeneutic dialogue; I would only add that the reader will *always* have something to imagine or interpret, whether the author has the good grace to allow for it or not! The imaginative reinterpretation of meaning is not a luxury of literary etiquette but a necessity of textual understanding.

In contrast to the situation of spoken dialogue, limited by the particular *contextualisation* of a synchronic discourse between speaking subjects, the textualisation of dialogue emancipates meaning from the strict intentions of the authors and creates a new audience which extends diachronically to anyone who can read. As Ricoeur observes in *Hermeneutics and the Human Sciences*: 'An essential characteristic of a literary (i.e. written) work . . . is that it transcends its own psycho-sociological conditions of production and thereby opens itself to an unlimited series of readings, themselves situated in different socio-cultural conditions. In short, the text must be able, from the sociological as well as the psychological point of view, to 'decontextualise' itself in such a way that it can be 'recontextualised' in a new situation – as accomplished, precisely, by the act of reading.'[4] Consequently, in the transition from the spoken to the written word, we find that the Romantic model of dialogue as a pre-established harmony of mutual subjectivities is quite inadequate. The 'textualised' dialogue reveals that language is never purely and simply our own (in the sense of a contemporaneous immediacy), but always involves the traces and anticipations of *other* language-users, existing in other places and in other times, past and future.

If the hermeneutic potencies of the *word* undergo such alteration in the transcription of speech into text, what of the *world* about which the authors speak? All discourse, spoken or written, presupposes 'someone saying something to someone about something'.[5] The problem of reference can never be dispensed with altogether. But what happens to reference, we may ask, when spoken discourse becomes a text? In a written dialogue the reference can no longer be limited to the spatio-temporal context of a 'here and now', shared by the interlocutors of a spoken dialogue. All writing, fictional or otherwise, is in some degree a reinscription of an original context of experience; and to that extent it would seem to eliminate the question of reference. But the matter is not so simple. Written discourse certainly abolishes the *first-order reference* to the actual world of experience 'here and now', but this abolition serves in turn to open up a *second-order reference* to the possible worlds proposed by the text. Ricoeur aptly describes this shifting of referential orders as follows:

> The unique referential dimension of the work (as written) . . . raises, in my view, the most fundamental hermeneutical problem. If we can no longer define hermeneutics in terms of the search for the psychological intentions of another person which are concealed *behind* the text, and if we do not want to reduce interpretation to the dismantling of structures, then what remains to be interpreted? I shall say: to interpret is to explicate the type of being-in-the-world unfolded *in front of* the text ... For what must be interpreted in a text is a proposed world which I could inhabit and wherein I could project one of my own-most possibilities ... The world of the text is therefore not the world of everyday language.[6]

We may ask finally: what becomes of the *subject* (i.e. the author or the reader) in the transition of both *word* and *world* from speech to writing? Each reader of these dialogues will be attempting to reappropriate in some dialectical way the authors' words and worlds expropriated by the very process of textual inscription. Because, however, writing is not some reversible process of first-order referential correspondence, the hermeneutic reappropriation (*Aneignung*) of the reader can never claim to achieve an exact correlation (temporal or intellectual) with the intentional reference of the author. In other words, any reader who enters into genuine dialogue with these texts will in principle experience some change in one's own understanding of oneself and one's world.[7]

We might speak accordingly of the reading process as a 'metamorphosis of the ego' which requires a process of 'distanciation' in the relation of the reader's self to itself. The reader's self-understanding must be seen as a *disappropriation* quite as much as an *appropriation*. And this calls for a dialectical realignment of hermeneutics with critical theory:

> A critique of the illusions of the subject, can and must be incorporated into self-understanding . . . We can no longer oppose hermeneutics and the critique of ideology. The critique of ideology is the necessary detour which self-understanding must take, if the latter is to be formed by the matter of the text and not by the prejudices of the reader.[8]

This is the decisive juncture at which Ricoeur's hermeneutic analysis overlaps with the ethical critique of Lévinas, the deconstructive analysis of Derrida and the Marxist-Freudian critique of Marcuse and the Frankfurt school.

While the subject-readers undergo a certain transformation in the reading of these dialogues, so too do the subject-interlocutors who have authored them. For example, my own self-understanding as a dialogical questioner (conditioned by my particular set of cultural, national, religious, philosophical and affective discourses) has had to submit itself to a metamorphosis in the exchange of question-and-answer with the thinkers featured here (each with his/her own specific discourses). And it is probable that these thinkers themselves have undergone a certain transformation of their respective self-understanding – even if this entails no more than an alternative reformulation of their previously formulated *words* and *worlds*. In short, these texts of dialogue bespeak the transmigration of each author into new horizons of *possible* meaning, horizons which remain open in turn to the *possible* reinterpretations of each reader.

Notes

1 Martin Heidegger, *Erläuterungen zu Hölderlins Dichtung*, 4th edn., Klostermann, Frankfurt, 1971, pp. 38–40.

2 Hans-Georg Gadamer, *Wahrheit und Methode*, Paul Siebeck, Tübingen, 1960, pp. 289 *et seq*.

3 Laurence Sterne, *The Life and Opinions of Tristram Shandy*, Penguin, Harmondsworth, 1967, p. 127.

4 Paul Ricoeur, 'The Hermeneutical Function of Distanciation' in *Hermeneutics and the Human Sciences*, ed. and trans. J. B. Thompson, Cambridge University Press, Cambridge, 1981, p. 139.

5 *Ibid.*, p. 138.

6 *Ibid.*, pp. 141–2. In respect of the dialogue in this book, we might even speak of a *third-order reference*, in so far as these dialogues involve authors producing dialogical texts *about* their own second-order philosophical texts, which are themselves in some sense *about* a first-order reference to lived experience. (And one might even argue, as Derrida does, that this first-order reference is itself already a text: a pattern of infinitely self-erasing traces or *archi-écriture*.) We may conclude, therefore, that the dialogues contained between these covers are not in fact attempts to retrace the texts of these thinkers back to some 'original' discourse of everyday language or experience. They are texts about texts about texts. This self-confessed parasitism is not, however, intended in the negative sense of alienating or obscuring the meaning of the philosophies at issue. It is not meant in the mimetic sense of being a copy of a copy, invoked by Plato in the *Republic* to denounce literary artefacts as 'poor children of poor parents' (i.e. the text as a mere imitation of natural experience itself construed as a mere imitation of some otherworldly, transcendental

truth). Our aim is to deploy the textual reordering of reference as a means of communicating the interpretative horizons of the author's world to the interpretative horizons of the reader's world. Such, at any rate, is our intention. The ultimate proof of the hermeneutic pudding is, of course, in the eating – the response of the reader.

7 Once again, I can do no better than recite Ricoeur's own concise account of the reader's dialectic of self-understanding in front of the text:

> (The reader's) appropriation is quite the contrary of contemporaneousness and congeniality: it is understanding at and through distance . . . In contrast to the tradition of the *cogito* and to the pretension of the subject to know itself by immediate intuition, it must be said that we understand ourselves only by the long detour of signs of humanity deposited in cultural works. . . . Thus what seems most contrary to subjectivity, and what structural analysis discloses as the texture of the text, is the very medium within which we understand ourselves. . . . Ultimately what I appropriate (qua reader) is a proposed world. The latter is not *behind* the text, as a hidden intention would be, but *in front* of it, as that which the work unfolds, discloses, reveals. Henceforth to understand is to *understand oneself in front of the text*. It is not a question of imposing upon the text our finite capacity of understanding, but of exposing ourselves to the text and receiving from it an enlarged self, which would be the proposed existence corresponding in the most suitable way to the world proposed. *Ibid.*, p. 144.

8 *Ibid.*, p. 144.